Brazil in the Making

Brazil in the Making

Facets of National Identity

Edited by

Carmen Nava and Ludwig Lauerhass, Jr.

ROWMAN & LITTLEFIELD PUBLISHERS, INC.
Lanham • Boulder • New York • Toronto • Oxford

ROWMAN & LITTLEFIELD PUBLISHERS, INC.

Published in the United States of America
by Rowman & Littlefield Publishers, Inc.
A wholly owned subsidiary of The Rowman & Littlefield Publishing Group, Inc.
4501 Forbes Boulevard, Suite 200, Lanham, Maryland 20706
www.rowmanlittlefield.com

P.O. Box 317, Oxford OX2 9RU, UK

British Library Cataloguing in Publication Information Available

Library of Congress Cataloging-in-Publication Data

Brazil in the making : facets of national identity / edited by Carmen Nava
and Ludwig Lauerhass, Jr.
p. cm.
Includes bibliographical references and index.
ISBN-13: 978-0-7425-3756-9 (cloth : alk. paper)
ISBN-10: 0-7425-3756-0 (cloth : alk. paper)
ISBN-13: 978-0-7425-3757-6 (pbk. : alk. paper)
ISBN-10: 0-7425-3757-9 (pbk. : alk. paper)
1. Brazil—Civilization. 2. Identity (Psychology)—Brazil.
3. Nationalism—Brazil. 4. Ethnicity—Brazil.
I. Nava, Carmen, 1964– II. Lauerhass, Ludwig.
F2510.B726 2006
981—dc22

2005022648

Printed in the United States of America

♾™ The paper used in this publication meets the minimum requirements of
American National Standard for Information Sciences—Permanence of Paper for
Printed Library Materials, ANSI/NISO Z39.48-1992.

Contents

Introduction

❧

A Four-Part Canon for the Analysis of Brazilian National Identity

Ludwig Lauerhass, Jr.

The singularity of Brazil has intrigued travelers, scholars, and other observers since the early years of European colonization in the sixteenth century.[1] But only following Brazil's declaration of independence in 1822 did the question of national identity assume any prolonged vitality; even then, it had to await the founding of the republic in 1889 before it gained a prominent and permanent place on the country's intellectual and political agendas. Thereafter, the quest for national identity has been increasingly pursued until it has come to form the core of what is now called Brazilian Studies. Generation after generation, fresh variations have been added to the accumulating corpus of writings on the theme. Nineteenth-century *pensadores* (intellectuals) through present-day social scientists and cultural theorists have explored and reexplored the question of Brazil's distinctiveness—the national experience, *brasilidade*, the national character or reality, the collective memory, and the "national problem"—against a constantly changing social, political, economic, and intellectual background and in the light of new academic theories and methodologies. Brazil's cultural identity in its broad anthropological sense, then, is like that of other nations: it is perpetually evolving and is ever in need of reappraisal.[2] To grasp its meaning at any point in time we must understand its constants as well as its novelties and the variations resulting from their interplay.

This collection is designed to explore anew the lasting yet changing singularity of Brazil with the aim of explaining how the national culture, through its remarkable richness and cohesion, has developed into its present configuration. In particular, the chapters ask, what do Brazilians

1

collectively identify with that gives them their sense of being Brazilian? What memories bind them, and how are these repeatedly manifested with variations over the passage of time? What patterns of metaphors and stereotypes of identity have emerged over time? These questions do not imply that all, or even most, Brazilians are attracted by exactly the same sets of cultural identifiers, let alone that they all share a sense of national identity with the same intensity. But a sufficient majority of Brazilians adhere to a sufficient number of national ties to make for the viability of a strong and unified nation-state despite the inherent problems brought on by the country's vast size and heterogeneous social, racial, and ethnic composition.

In searching for the cultural manifestations that have gone into forging this Brazilian identity, we can delimit four distinct yet interrelated categories: texts, facts, sights, and sounds. Taken together, they form a four-part canon for the analysis of Brazilian national identity. These cultural expressions carry messages of identity to which Brazilians have been and are repeatedly exposed. These mechanisms instill in Brazilians their common sense of who they are and who they ought to be. Together they form facets of national identity that embody the views, ideas, and values of the Brazilian people, distinguishing them from the Argentines, the Americans, the French, and other national groups. As a focus for cultural analysis, the canon conveys three distinct yet interrelated and overlapping meanings: authority, as embodied in religion (e.g., canon law); standards, as used in literature (e.g., the canon of Brazilian literature); and repetition, as in music (e.g., repetition of themes). Thus, the search is for commonalties imposed by authority, selected or agreed upon as standards, and experienced by repetition. The concept of canon is also related to the concept of cultural literacy.[3] Thus, culturally literate Brazilians identify with certain sets of texts, facts, sights, and sounds and share a similar sense of identity with the other culturally literate members of their national society.

While there is no single immutable cultural canon for the Brazilians or anyone else, a canon of national identity has been in ascendancy over the course of the past century. Many cultural canons have, however, coexisted and overlapped: geographical variations, regional and local as well as cosmopolitan and national; other, often conflicting focuses of identity determined by race, ethnicity, religion, occupation, educational level, class and social background, and gender; and, finally, expressions of popular culture and high culture and their interplay. These chapters explore the emergence, strengthening, and growing dominance of the national canon and the catalytic forces promoting it. The educational system and the media have become increasingly national in their outlook and standards. The national government has increased its position of power relative to the local and state levels and has greatly expanded its role in the promotion of a cohesive national culture. The scope of the economy has also become more truly national while becoming evermore diversified. Thus, formal agencies and informal mechanisms have worked in tandem with such generally modernizing tendencies as urbanization and improved communications to homogenize and enhance identity with the national culture.

At no time has the problem of national identity seemed more compelling than it is now, in both its global and its Brazilian context. For more than a decade the repercussions of nationalism have been strongly manifested in the realms of practical politics and theoretical expression. Such international cataclysms as the fragmentation of the multiethnic and multicultural Soviet and Yugoslav states with the rapid reunification of the two ideologically opposed Germanies have once again brought questions of national identity to the center of the world's stage. In Brazil, however, the accelerating process of redemocratization following two decades of political dominance by the military brought under scrutiny the long-accepted nationalist agendas, which had been operative since the regimes of Getúlio Vargas in the 1930s and 1940s. Under president Fernando Henrique Cardoso (1995–2002)—politician and academic sociologist—older tenets of nationalist faith, such as protectionism and large-scale state ownership, gave way to fundamentals of freer trade and private ownership. In the same years, Brazilian intellectuals have reflected the worldwide retreat from the historical materialism of Marxist ideologies and are expressing a renewed interest in the dynamics of culture as a force in national development. As elsewhere around the globe, the quest for national identity that now holds sway is in the form of a more personalized and often more democratic concept away from earlier more abstract and organic formulations of national character.

QUESTIONS OF IDENTITY

Questions such as Who are we? and Who should we be? are age-old, going back to at least the Greeks, for whom it was important to be culturally distinct from the barbarians (i.e., those who could not speak or understand the Greek language—in short, non-Greeks). At Delphi every Greek was admonished to "know thyself" as a person in a cultural setting. This concept of identity was not tied to politics, to a particular state, or even to a form of state. In the eighteenth and early nineteenth centuries these questions were repeated and expanded in pursuit of cultural distinctions within a growing, "enlightened," secular, and universal order, as exemplified by the couplet of Alexander Pope:

> Know then thyself, presume not God to scan
> The proper study of mankind is man.

Still later, the romantic movement in belles lettres and the arts further emphasized the exotic, the culturally distinct, and the ideal of the "national past" as being grounded in cultural heritage. This wave accompanied the growth of literary history, folklore, and national history as popular fields of writing. Another legacy of this era that came with republicanism and evermore secular worldviews was the perceived need to fuse the nation and the state. Revolutionary France became the new model for the nation-state in which political legitimacy was based on the people and the nation rather than on loyalty to a monarch. Ultimate political loyalties then increasingly became culturally rather than dynastically or religiously based.

During the independence period of Latin America (1810–1830), the need arose to distinguish between "Brazilians," "Argentines," "Chileans," "Peruvians," and others in cultural terms in order to legitimize their claims for political separation from each other as well as from their former royal colonial masters in Portugal and Spain. In most cases doing so also meant a shift of allegiance to a new, republican form of government, but not in Brazil. There, under a local form of imperial monarchy, Brazilians prolonged their loyalty to a branch of the Bragança family until the belated triumph of republicanism in 1889. Thus, while the political imperative to replace dynastic with national identification only later affected Brazil, intellectuals there throughout the nineteenth century, like their Spanish American counterparts, were nonetheless concerned with the identification and construction of their own culture.

Modern history since the American and French revolutions, then, has largely been concerned with the reconciling of new and older cultures within the structure of the national state. Concepts of nationalism, nations, and nation-states, however, are relatively new historically. Many traditional political units, especially the large ones from the Roman Empire to imperial Russia, were multicultural. The Hapsburg Empire, for example, included at one time or another Spain, Portugal, Flanders, Austria, Slavic and Italian realms, the Americas, and the Philippine Islands. Even France, often looked upon as the prototype of the modern nation-state, was largely the creation of the postrevolutionary, post-Napoleonic nineteenth century. It was then that the demands of a more modern form of urbanized, industrial society in league with a secular, national state worked in concert to turn peasants into Frenchmen and Frenchwomen through such agencies as the school system, the army, improved transportation networks, new communications media, and the bureaucracy. Even language presented a problem. French, German, Italian, Breton, langue d'oc, and other languages were widely spoken in 1789, and only 50 percent spoke French at all with perhaps 13 percent speaking it correctly.[4] Other states or would-be nation-states had far less to build on—Germany and Italy even lacked territorial unification. As late as 1870 with the success of the Risorgimento, Massimo d'Azeglio commented, "We have made Italy, now we have to make Italians."[5] The processes of nation building and strengthening of national cultural identity were ongoing in the nineteenth and twentieth centuries in Europe, the United States, and Latin America, especially after World War II in Asia, the Near East, and Africa.

An even broader concern with different types of identity developed over the course of the same centuries, running the gamut from the self, emphasized by Sigmund Freud, to the universal. Several years ago the anthropologist Clyde Kluckhohn described three logical possibilities for humanity:

1. Each man is unique.
2. All men are alike.
3. Some men are more alike than others.[6]

The concept of national cultural identity is clearly based on the third possibility, but so is any other form of collective identity—family, clan, regional, class, caste, religious, racial, educational, occupational, generational, and gender. These points of identity clearly overlap and vary in their relative importance from one individual or culture to another. The primacy given to national cultural identity stems from the political realities of the times. The national state is and has been the preeminent form of social organization within our modern economic, political, social, and intellectual lives. Moreover, most states actively protect and promote the well-being of their national cultures above all others, and a variety of formal and informal mechanisms are at work to achieve these ends. Despite predictions for New World economic orders, the end of history, and the emergence of a global cosmopolitan culture, it is most likely that national states and hence national cultures in one form or another will prevail as the primary form of social organization into the foreseeable future.

Before refocusing on Brazil, let us consider the working definitions of some key terms.

> *Culture*: an integrated social group grounded in shared patterns of knowledge; common values or beliefs; social structures; material traits; and ways of behaving, communicating, and thinking. While constantly adjusting to dynamic historical contexts, significant components are transmitted from generation to generation through formal and informal educational processes.
>
> *Nation*: a people sharing a common cultural identity, usually grounded in the same language, geographic territory, and historical experience. If these bonds do not exist or are weakly developed, they must be strengthened, revived, or created as a basis for the nation. While

perhaps thousands of nations or potential nations exist, only a fraction
are fully realized.

Nation-state: the state is the agency within society that holds the ultimate
political power, "a monopoly of legitimate violence" and coercion (to
use the terms of Max Weber). The nation-state exists when the state is
congruent with the nation.

National identity: a collective form of identity in which individuals feel a
sense of belonging to a nation or national group. Various formal and
informal mechanisms, processes, and agencies function to encourage
this sense of belonging.

Nationalism: the political principle and value system that assume that the
state and the nation should be congruent and that the nation-state is
the primary focus of loyalty, the highest group in the social order. Nationalism calls for the organization of human groups into large, commonly educated, culturally homogeneous units. The major thrusts of
nationalism are a quest for and an instilling of national identity, protection against foreign threat, internal integration, the establishment
and preservation of political legitimacy and morality, a striving for
economic development, and a concern for social improvement.

Nationalist ideology: written statements, manifestos, and critiques of existing societies offering plans for national renovation, rediscovery, or re-
creation; national self-realization; and self-determination. If a nation-
state does not exist or exists only in rudimentary form, nationalist
ideologies present blueprints for nation building. Nationalism creates
nations, not the reverse.[7]

Note that several of the contributors to this volume consider questions
about the historical debate on these concepts. Their perspectives enrich an
interdisciplinary discussion of Brazilian national identity.

Despite the primacy of national cultures, they have been anything but
rigidly fixed or static. New World cultures, like that of Brazil, have been
especially flexible and open to change. Not only was Brazil a Creole vari-
ant of a European (Portuguese) culture, but its early colonial development involved the large-scale admixture of, first, American Indians and,
then, African Negro populations. From its inception, Brazil has been multicultural and multiracial, grounded in the interplay of cultures and racial
miscegenation. From the late nineteenth century onward Brazil was spo-
radically open to renewed cultural infusions from abroad—European and
Japanese immigrants; Jewish refugees; and successive waves of Arabs,
Spanish Americans, and Koreans. The Brazil of today is hardly the Brazil
of the 1960s, let alone that of the 1930s or 1890s. Sixty years ago Brazil was
75 percent rural and 25 percent urban. Today the proportions are reversed.
Sixty years ago Brazil was emerging from a period of internal political strife

and regional conflict. Today it is one of the world's most successful and cohesive megastates, comparable in this sense to the United States and in contrast to Canada or the former Soviet Union. It is the fifth largest in land area, the sixth in population, and ninth in size of economy. It is the largest Catholic country in the world and has more people of African heritage than any country aside from Nigeria.

THE DEVELOPMENT OF BRAZILIAN IDENTITY

The formation and analysis of Brazil's national cultural identity have continued apace over the past two centuries. In the early periods of development, contributions were mainly by intellectuals working independently, and the levels of institutionalization remained low. As time wore on following the establishment of the republic in 1889 and especially after 1930, the concern for national identity and nationalism took on a greater sense of importance within political and governmental circles. Successive regimes and the factions opposed to them developed nationalist ideologies and tried to encourage popular identification with the nation. Nationalism was never the monopoly of one type of political regime but combined with a variety of parties, movements, and administrations—right, center, and left; democratic and authoritarian.[8] As the historian Eric Hobsbawm aptly puts it, "nationalism has been part of a political cocktail" and as such has become an essential ingredient of modern political life—in Brazil and throughout the world. A brief chronology and description of the major periods of the development of Brazil's national cultural identity follow.

Before and After Independence (1808–1830s)

The transfer of the Portuguese court to Brazil in 1808 sparked royal efforts to assess Brazilian realities. In turn, this shift prompted a series of scientific and cultural missions and expeditions as well as a great influx of foreign observers, including the scientists George Heinrich von Langsdorf, Maximillian zu Wied-Neuwied, Johann Baptist von Spix, Karl F. P. von Martius, and Auguste de Saint-Hilaire; travelers such as Maria Graham and Henry Koster; artists Johann Moritz Rugendas, Jean Baptiste Debret, Hercules Florence, and Zeferino Ferrez; and writers such as Ferdinand Denis. These visitors produced many of the Ur-sources of verbal and visual description and interpretation of Brazil, its landscape, cities, people, resources, and culture. A foreigner, Robert Southey, who never visited the country, wrote the first great history of Brazil. This period witnessed the beginnings of a continuing interplay of foreign and local writings on the theme of national identity. The Royal Library and later National Library provided the first major institutional depository for research materials on Brazil.

The Romantic Generation in Brazil (1838–1880)

Brazilian poets, novelists, playwrights, artists, photographers, and other intellectuals turned to the Ur-sources, produced mainly by foreigners, and continued the patterns set in the previous period. Antônio Gonçalves Dias (poetry), José de Alencar (novel, *O Guarani*), and Francisco Adolfo de Varnhagen (history) were members of the generation born in the 1820s and writing in the 1840s through the 1870s, many of whom stressed the vastness and exotic nature of Brazil, especially with respect to the Indian. Their work was supplemented by that of a new wave of foreign scientists: Charles Darwin, Alfred Russel Wallace, Henry Walter Bates, and Louis Agassiz. Institutional development for the study of Brazil was advanced by the founding of the Instituto Histórico e Geográfico Brasileiro and the publication of its *Revista* in 1838. This first journal of Brazilian studies included an important article by Martius on how Brazilian history should be approached as a fusion of races.

Turn-of-the-Century Critiques of Brazilian Society (1880s–1920s)

Contemporary currents of thought included the abolitionist movement, republicanism, positivism, Spencer's evolutionism, after 1900 the Bergsonian attack on positivism, and finally the Brazilian modernist movement in the 1920s. Among the important nineteenth-century contributors to the more widely emergent sense of national identity were Sílvio Romero, a provincial who sought to explain Brazil through folklore and literature, and Joaquim Maria Machado de Assis, a *Carioca* (person from Rio de Janeiro) poet, novelist, and short-story writer, who analyzed the distinctiveness of Brazil's new urban society in fiction. Euclides de Cunha stood out among the social critics early in the next century, and Oliveira Viana provided an interpretive historical introduction for the census of 1922. Institutional development included the founding of the National Museum and the Brazilian Academy of Letters and the flourishing of national publishers, such as Laemert, Garnier, and later Monteiro Lobato.

The Generation of 1930 (1920s–1940s)

There was an outpouring of culturally introspective studies in this period, including Paulo Prado, *Retrato do Brasil* (1929); Gilberto Freyre, *Casa-Grande e Senzala* (1933); Caio Prado Jr., *Evolução histórica do Brasil* (1934), a Marxist interpretation; Sérgio Buarque de Holanda, *Raízes do Brasil* (1936); and

Fernando de Azevedo, *A cultura brasileira* (1942; *Brazilian Culture*, [1950]), an introduction to the census of 1940. The broader ideological currents of the day—communism, fascism, Christian corporatism, anti-Semitism, and welfare statism—were also reflected in Brazil. Institutionalization for Brazilian studies reached a significantly higher stage of development. The University of São Paulo was founded, and it became more highly professionalized with the help of foreign visiting faculty; publishing houses began to issue series with a national encyclopedic focus, such as Brasiliana and Documentos Brasileiros, which included original studies and new editions of Ur-sources. This tradition has persisted to the present day with series such as Reconquista, published jointly by the university and Itatiaia. Furthermore, intellectuals in growing numbers were hired by the government to produce propaganda and other works of national identity for the Ministry of Education, the Department of Press and Propaganda, the journal *Cultura Política*, and other agencies.

Developmental Nationalism (1950s–1964)

In this period national identity was viewed in conjunction with problems of underdevelopment. If Brazil was to progress, it would need greater economic independence and a series of basic internal reforms that would allow for a revolution of modernization. The quest for identity also focused on the need to define *o povo brasileiro* (the common people of Brazil). Within the Instituto Superior de Estudos Brasileiros, intellectuals such as Cândido Mendes, Roland Corbisier, Nelson Werneck Sodré, and Guerreiro Ramos sought the development of an authentic national sociology and social sciences that would help to solve national problems. Because of its political activism and concern for practical matters, the institute was called by Renato Ortiz the "factory of ideology" for the Juscelino Kubitschek government.[9] Other series, such as Os Cadernos do Povo, followed a similar approach. By the early 1960s a new wave of foreign scholars, "Brazilianists," joined the local intellectuals in their socioeconomic analysis.

The Authoritarian Regimes (1964–1984)

There was throughout this period not only a heightened concern for both high and popular culture but also an increased level of institutionalization with respect to film, the arts, and the national patrimony. Certain nationalist intellectuals, such as Gilberto Freyre, who accepted military control over the government, continued to play a public role. The further development of cultural policy and the active promotion of national identity accompanied a growing interest in popular and mass cultures. The government cooperated with the private sector, especially with the television, film, and publishing industries, in this effort. Within the educational system courses in civic culture—*problemas nacionais*—were required curricula. Intellectuals in opposition to the military continued to publish their visions of national identity either in exile or through channels that remained open to them at home. Major nationalist critiques of the regimes were also added by Brazilianists abroad.

Redemocratizing Brazil (1984–)

The freeing of Brazil from military control has allowed for a new flurry of writings on national identity by Brazilians across the political spectrum as well as by Brazilianists in the United States and Europe. Among the more active contributors have been Roberto da Matta, Carlos Guilherme Mota, Sérgio Miceli, José Murilo de Carvalho, Renato Ortiz, Flora Sussekind, Alfredo Bossi, Simon Schwartzman, Roberto Schwartz, and Vilmar Faria. Intellectuals have continued to play their traditional roles as symbolic mediators in the constructing and reconstructing of national identity. Sociologist Fernando Henrique Cardoso, Brazil's former president, has remained an active participant in this process, working to redirect Brazil's intellectual vision and nationalist agenda along new lines of a more open economy with a greater role for the private sector as a stimulus for accelerated national development.

REPRESENTATIONS OF THE FOUR-PART CANON

The chapters in this collection are set within the theoretical and periodic framework briefly outlined here.[10] The first part of the canon, or category of cultural manifestation, comprises texts, taken from sources such as literature, scripture, slogans and sayings, folklore, laws, and fundamental political documents. With texts, the exact wording—not just the meaning and the content—is important. Excerpts of texts are often memorized and quoted. Familiar non-Brazilian examples include the plays of Shakespeare, a poem of Camões, the Declaration of Independence, the Gettysburg Address, the Psalms, the Lord's Prayer, the salute to the flag, or the Star-Spangled Banner. In general, literary texts and laws fall into this category.

The first three chapters assess the ongoing contribution to the development of national identity by the texts of three canonical writers and interpreters of Brazilian culture. Each has generally been recognized as a leading spokesman of his generation, and each one's work has inspired continued reevaluation from its inception to the present day. In "Machado de Assis and the Question of Brazilian National Identity" Efraín Kristal and José Luis Passos show how Machado was Latin America's first major author to depict the newly forming urban society in the latter half of the nineteenth century. In a brilliant series of portrayals he captures the transformation of imperial society as it turns away from its colonial rural traditions to embrace a new, cosmopolitan style of progress with all of the ironies and pretensions that involved. From then on the realities of national identity became increasingly urban even with the heavy overlay of nostalgia for what was becoming a fading rural past. In "Euclides de Cunha's View of Brazil's Fractured Identity," Dain Borges questions the cleavage of identity between the city and the *sertão* (backlands). As part of Euclides's national vision the civilized urban sectors of the country had the responsibility to share education and the benefits of progress with the illiterate rural rustics who in the 1890s still formed the bedrock of Brazilian nationality in the interior. The Canudos campaign was a metaphor for the failure of Brazil to bring these unfortunate rebels into the national fold. The third text is analyzed by José Luis Passos and Valéria Costa e Silva, in "Gilberto Freyre's Concept of Culture in *The Masters and the Slaves*." A dominant figure of his generation of 1930, Freyre represented a hybrid approach to social analysis, combining methodologies of the modern social scientist with those of the traditional literary *pensador* (intellectual). For him the core of Brazilian cultural reality has its roots in the patriarchal plantation system of the colonial northeast, which was gradually extended to the rest of Brazil and transfigured into an urbanized form during the nineteenth and twentieth centuries.

The next two chapters address the second part of the canon: facts. Culturally literate Brazilians are expected to have a general grasp of their nation's history, geography, government, society, economy, and culture. They can gain this knowledge from any number of specific sources, such as schoolbooks, college texts, general books and magazines, and, more recently, movies and television. The category comprises information derived from facts, as well as interpretation and presentation of facts. The authors of *"Brasiliana:* Published Works and Collections" are José Mindlin and Cristina Antunes. Prior to 1808 the production of printed materials on Brazil was carried on abroad. Since then, government, commercial publishers, and public institutions in Brazil and abroad have shared responsibility for book, document, and journal production as important sources in the formation of national identity. So, too, have the great public and private library collections from the National Library through Mindlin's own. Mindlin and Antunes provide valuable insights into many of the increasingly rich depositories of both the textual and the factual canonical materials that convey a sense of Brazilian culture. As the power of the national government has increased, especially since 1930, the state has evermore actively sought to expand and strengthen national unity among its citizenry. In "Forging Future Citizens in Brazilian Public Schools, 1937–1945," Carmen Nava examines how the Estado Novo carried out an ambitious campaign to create support for the centralization of power while increasing the primacy of nationalism at the expense of regional, class, racial, or other competing group identities. The authoritarian state inculcated public school children with an increasingly standardized education that used officially approved "civics" instruction to instill patriotism. Nava argues that this curriculum established a framework for state intervention in the cultivation of Brazilian national identity that would be fundamental to later twentieth-century administrations.

The next three chapters address the canon's third part: sights. These are the recognizable visual images of places, people, and events—past and present. The sources here include prints, book and magazine illustrations, photographs, works of art (including monuments), television, films, and personal viewing of people and urban and rural landscapes. Brazilians would, for example, commonly identify with Sugar Loaf, Dom Pedro II, the national flag, Brasília, Xuxa, Maracanã, the Amazon River, President Luiz Inácio Lula Da Silva, palm tress, and *capoeira*. My own chapter, "The Visual Imaging of Brazilian Identity," traces the visual imaging of Brazil by means of reproducible still images—engravings, lithographs, photographs, and book and magazine illustrations—from the early nineteenth century to the present day. This period witnessed an explosion in the spread of visual imagery from materials that were expensive and in limited distribution to the mass circulation of periodicals and newspapers today. In "Cinematic Images of the Brazilian Indian," Robert Stam analyzes the similar explosion of visual imagery in Brazilian film, using the treatment of the Indians, beginning with their "discovery" by Cabral in 1500, as an illustration. He shows how the Indian has been an enduring symbol of Brazilian identity yet one that is constantly subjected to nuanced reinterpretation. In "The Emperor and His Pedestal: Pedro I and Disputed Views of the Brazilian Nation, 1860–1900," James Green turns our attention to the visual realm of sculpture, focusing on a fascinating example of contested historical memory. Green documents the contentious debates about a statue commemorating emperor Dom Pedro I as the founder of the Brazilian nation and explores reinterpretations of the monument's significance in subsequent political-social moments.

The fourth part of the canon of identity comprises sounds. These are mainly in the realm of music, from both the high cultural and the popular cultural level, although some other sounds, such as the cries of street vendors, also convey cultural identity. The sound or music input to Brazilian identity ranges from *choros*, samba, *forro*, and bossa nova to the operas of Carlos Gomes and the *bachianas brasileiras* of Heitor Villa-Lobos. In "Two Musical Representations of Brazil: Carlos Gomes and Villa Lobos," Cristina

Magaldi contrasts the nationalist contributions of Gomes and Villa Lobos, including their impact on the level of popular culture. The chapters in this collection focus on selected representations of the four-part canon of Brazilian national identity. While these particular manifestations are unique to Brazil, they illustrate broad, ongoing processes that have been shared to varying degrees by all countries achieving a sense of national identity. It is important to remember that such identities are always adapting to new conditions and challenges. Brazil, like other nations, is still in the making.

NOTES

1. While the exotic distinctiveness of Brazil was commonly extolled by European visitors from the earliest days of discovery, the term *singularity* was first applied to the area by André Thevet in his *Les Singularités de la France Antarctique*, originally published in Paris in 1557–1558.

2. On the anthropological sense of culture as an integrated social group and the totality of its product, see Clifford Geertz, *The Interpretation of Cultures* (New York: Basic, 1973).

3. See E. D. Hirsch Jr., *Cultural Literacy: What Every American Needs to Know* (Boston: Houghton Mifflin, 1987).

4. Eugene Weber's *Peasants into Frenchmen: The Modernization of Rural France, 1870–1914* (Stanford, Calif.: Stanford University Press, 1976) offers a cogent case study of the problems and process of nation building.

5. Quoted in Eric Hobsbawm, *Nations and Nationalism Since 1780: Programme, Myth, Reality* (Cambridge: Cambridge University Press, 1990), 44. This slender volume is a useful recent account on the development of nationalism.

6. Clyde Kluckhohn and Henry Murray, quoted in Jacques Maquet, *The Aesthetic Experience: An Anthropologist Looks at the Visual Arts* (New Haven, Conn.: Yale University Press, 1986), 169.

7. The definitions and theoretical analysis of *nation* and its derivative terms or concepts have long stimulated academic discussion. Nationalism as a primary focus of research and publication, however, has gone in and out of favor. From the late 1920s into the mid-1960s there was a rising interest in the subject based in the United States. Among its most notable expressions are works by Carlton J. H. Hayes, *Essays on Nationalism* (New York: Macmillan, 1926) and *The Historical Evolution of Modern Nationalism* (New York: Macmillan, 1931); Hans Kohn, *The Idea of Nationalism* (New York: Macmillan, 1944); Louis Snyder, *The Meaning of Nationalism* (New Brunswick, N.J.: Rutgers University Press, 1954); Karl W. Deutsch, *Nationalism and Social Communication* (Cambridge, Mass.: MIT Press, 1953); Kalman H. Silvert, ed., *Expectant Peoples: Nationalism and Development* (New York: Random House, 1963). Following a waning of this focus into the late 1970s, a resurgence of interest by scholars in England then refined approaches to nationalism with a special emphasis on national identity. Major works include those of Eric Hobsbawm, *Nations and Nationalism since*

1780; Terence Ranger, *The Invention of Tradition* (Cambridge: Cambridge University Press, 1983); Ernest Gellner, *Nations and Nationalism* (Ithaca, N.Y.: Cornell University Press, 1983); Anthony D. Smith, *Theories of Nationalism* (London: Duckworth, 1971) and *Nationalist Movements in the Twentieth Century* (New York: New York University Press, 1979); Benedict Anderson, *Imagined Communities* (London: Verso, 1983); Peter Boerner, *Concepts of National Identity: An Interdisciplinary Dialogue* (Baden-Baden, Germany: Nomos, 1986); David Miller, *On Nationality* (Oxford: Clarendon Press, 1995); John H. Hall, ed., *The State of the Nation: Ernest Gellner and the Theory of Nationalism* (Cambridge: Cambridge University Press, 1998). See also the journal *Nation and Nationalism* (Cambridge University Press, 1995–) and Louis L. Snyder, *Encyclopedia of Nationalism* (New York: Paragon House, 1990). Of special interest on the United States is Seymour Martin Lipset, *The First New Nation: The United States in Historical and Comparative Perspective* (New York: Basic, 1963).

8. On the various types of Brazilian nationalism from the founding of the republic in 1889 through the end of World War II in 1945, see Ludwig Lauerhass Jr., "Getúlio Vargas and the Triumph of Brazilian Nationalism," PhD. diss., University of California, Los Angeles (Ann Arbor, Mich.: University Microfilms, 1972). The writing on Brazilian nationalism is extensive—much of it polemical. Many of the academic studies have approached the theme from a cultural perspective and recently have concentrated on the idea of national identity. See, for example, Gilberto Freyre, *Brazil, an Interpretation* (New York: Knopf, 1945); José Honorario Rodrigues, *Aspirações nacionais*, 4th ed. (Rio de Janeiro: Civilização Brasileira, 1970); Dante Moreira Leite, *O carácter nacional brasileiro*, 2d ed. (São Paulo: Pionera, 1969); Carlos Gilherme Mota, *Ideologia da cultura brasileira* (São Paulo: Atica, 1977); Hélio Jaguaribe, *O nacional na atualidade brasileira* (Rio de Janeiro: ISEB, 1958); Cândido Mendes, *Nacionalismo e desenvolvimento* (Rio de Janeiro: IBEAA, 1963); Renato Ortiz, *Cultura brasileira e identidade nacional* (São Paulo: Brasiliense, 1985); Reginaldo Moraes, Ricardo Antunes, and Vera B. Ferrante, eds., *Inteligencia brasileira* (São Paulo: Brasiliense, 1986); Roberto Schwartz, *Misplaced Ideas: Essays on Brazilian Culture* (London: Verso, 1992); Darcy Ribeiro, *O povo brasileiro: A formação e o sentido do Brasil* (São Paulo: Letras, 1995).

9. Ortiz, *Cultura brasileira*, 46.

10. For the most part, these chapters are outgrowths of presentations prepared for the interdisciplinary graduate seminar "Brazil's National Cultural Identity," offered annually between 1991 and 1997 by the UCLA Program on Brazil for the Latin American Center and the History Department (University of California, Los Angeles).

I

TEXTS

1

Machado de Assis and the Question of Brazilian National Identity

Efraín Kristal and José Luiz Passos

In Brazilian literary history, Joaquim Maria Machado de Assis has a reputation that has been uncontested for over a century,[1] and many critics have argued that his narrative fiction signaled the literary coming of age of the Brazilian novel from an artistic point of view.[2] But when Brazilians first read Machado's novels, they found that his approach went against the grain of most other nineteenth-century Brazilian novelists, whose literary works appealed to the national elite or emerging bourgeoisie as being representative of their nation.[3] Machado's novels lacked the images, characters, and symbols of national identity that had informed the most representative Brazilian novels of the nineteenth century, such as the *indianista* novels of the romantic period.[4] In this chapter we explore the reception of Machado's novels in connection to discussions of Brazilian national identity from the late nineteenth century to the present day.

BACKGROUND

Machado was born in Rio de Janeiro. His mother was a Portuguese immigrant and his father a housepainter descended from freed slaves. One year after his birth Brazil entered the Second Empire (1840–1889) under the tutored leadership of then fourteen-year-old emperor Dom Pedro II, who henceforth would rule the largest Latin nation in the New World and, at that time, the only autonomous slaveholding monarchy of the Americas. During the five decades of the Second Empire, Brazil experienced a rapid process of economic and social modernization. Machado was born at a time when coffee was displacing sugar as the primary Brazilian export commodity, definitively shifting the economic balance of power from the traditional northeastern agrarian elites toward the cities of Rio de Janeiro and São Paulo.[5]

Machado began publishing his first literary works a few years after the 1850 prohibition of transatlantic slave trade, which liberated a considerable amount of capital—previously reserved for the purchase of slaves—toward the expansion of domestic trade, the enhancement of the urban landscape, and the development of infrastructure (the establishment of new banks, small businesses and industries, etc.). This transformation would inform many aspects of Machado's narrative fiction, but Machado himself was somewhat skeptical about literature's role in documenting social realities.

Machado's contemporaries debated his relationship with issues of national identity. Critics such as José Veríssimo argued that Machado's contributions to literature were universal rather than local. Others, such as Sílvio Romero, disagreed, insisting that Machado's works be evaluated strictly in the context of national concerns.[6] Does Machado's writing address Brazilian reality and the question of its national identity, or does the value of his literature reside elsewhere? This question, reformulated according to shifting criteria of literary analysis over the last hundred years, continues to inform many discussions on Machado: contemporary critics are no longer as interested in issues involving the representation of a "universal human nature" in literature as they might have been in the past, but they continue to debate whether Machado's stories and novels address national issues or more general concerns akin, for example, to the claims of postmodernism.[7] In short, the unresolved question of Machado and national circumstances has been long-standing in the history of Brazilian literary criticism and is worth our review with respect to some of its vicissitudes, but first we need to discuss the context in which Machado made his mark as a seminal writer of Brazilian literature.

BRAZILIAN LITERARY NATIONALISM

In the 1840s Brazilian novelists began to explore local themes while taking cues from early nineteenth-century French feuilletons and the like.[8] In *The Guarani* (*O Guarani*, 1856), the first Brazilian bestseller, José de Alencar draws on French literary models to address Brazilian nationalism. Alencar's novel exemplifies the tendency in the Brazilian novel to depict characters whose physical and psychic traits are drawn directly from descriptions of the geographical regions and social milieus of the nation. After Alencar many Brazilian novels were written, and read, as allegories of national history, often informed by views on the racial configuration of the nation. The impulse toward historical allegories carried on from romanticism to naturalism and set the tone for a critical reception of the Brazilian novel based on the ability of a writer to depict the predicaments of characters representative of national types. By the second half of the nineteenth century, lighthearted entertainment had given way to a more complex, critical exploration of Brazilian society. As examples of this shift, one can point to José de Alencar's indictment of hypocritical love, prostitution, and sublimated shame in *Lucíola: Portrait of a Woman* (*Lucíola: Perfil de mulher*, 1862) or to Machado's *Dom Casmurro*, a sophisticated critique of aristocratic idleness. As opposed to Alencar, however, Machado's nationalistic statements are neither on the surface of the novel nor expressly discussed by his characters. In *Dom Casmurro* Machado's critique of the nostalgia for an irretrievable aristocratic past is filtered through the disguised motives of a disarming, unreliable narrator, the likes of which had never been previously attempted in Brazilian literature. Notwithstanding his will to be conciliatory with his contemporaries, Machado's own writings clearly indicate that he was looking for a literary mode of expression that would transcend simplistic nationalistic pronouncements.

NATION AND MORAL CHARACTER

In a letter sent from New York on September 22, 1872, José Carlos Rodrigues, a freelance journalist and editor of *Novo Mundo* (a periodical edited by Brazilians living in the United States, printed and distributed in New York between 1870 and 1877) invited Machado to reflect on the state of Brazilian literature: "[Our journal] needs a good study on the state of contemporary Brazilian literature, identifying its positive and negative tendencies, its literary and moral characteristics. We need to provide our readers with an accurate picture of our literary production and its trends. . . . Would you, my friend, be willing to write that study?"[9]

Machado accepted the invitation and published his "A Report on Contemporary Brazilian Literature: An Instinct of Nationality" in March 24, 1873. In this well-known essay, Machado argues that "whoever examines contemporary Brazilian literature will identify a certain instinct of nationality. Poetry, the novel, and the other genres seek to dress up in the country's colors."[10] Machado did not object to the depiction of distinctive national episodes, representations of indigenous cultures, or other regional elements in Brazilian literature, but he argued that the portrayal of national types and symbols should not be the main criterion with which to determine the originality of a literary work. Two years after writing this essay Machado contributed to the *indianista* tendency within Brazilian romanticism with a collection of thirteen poems entitled *Americanas* (1875), which dealt directly with indigenous Brazilian culture while celebrating a New World sensibility attuned to the peculiarities of its people and geography.

Notwithstanding his belated *indianista* contribution to Brazilian poetry, Machado remained skeptical with respect to the strong claim that national literature must always address national themes. The 1873 essay is clearly informed by his ardent view that the main purpose of the novel is not the depiction of national types but the empathetic understanding of human motives and feelings. He therefore criticizes what he considers to be an excess of "local color" in the Brazilian novel, even in its style, themes, and vocabulary. Machado openly regretted that Brazilian literature lacked significant novels of moral insight and scrutiny: "The examples of Brazilian novels that offer persuasive analysis of passions and character are few and far between. This kind of literary exploration ranks among the most difficult achievements of a novelist, but it also marks the superiority of the genre."[11]

It goes without saying that Machado attempted to fill what he considered to be a gap in Brazilian literature by writing novels of moral complexity. He says as much in his writings about his own works. In each of the introductions to his first two novels, *Resurrection* and *The Hand and the Glove* (*A mão e a luva*, 1874), Machado underscores his desire to address the singularities of his characters' moral world with sophistication. Machado knew that in so doing, he was writing against the current of his Brazilian antecedents. His first novels lack the colorful descriptions and fanciful plots of redemptive love in local settings characteristic of Brazilian romantic narratives. Machado shuns the melodramatic plot devices or representative character types of writers such as José de Alencar and Joaquim Manuel de Macedo. Against all that, Machado's first four novels are built on a fairly sparing lexicon and on frugal plots, avoiding the dramatic strokes of luck and twists of fate that inform most novels by his contemporaries. Machado's views with respect to the significance of moral insight informed his creative process in every one of his nine novels, published between 1872 and 1908. He clearly aimed to offer a nuanced, complex psychological portrait of his protagonists that would eschew simplifications. A tension has always resided between Machado's forceful attempts to avoid types and stereotypes and one's will to find, in Machado's plots and characters, straightforward allegories of Brazilian nationalism. Abel Barros Baptista has pointed out that many Brazilian literary critics have attempted to force Machado into interpretative frameworks of various types, into simplistic representations of the nation, like a square peg into a circular hole. Notwithstanding his own exaggerations, Baptista has a valid point. He correctly deduces that Machado's approach no longer involves fashioning a national literature based on preconceptions about Brazilian reality but rather on fashioning a national literature according to literary imperatives: "[Machado's main concern] is not the production of Brazilian literature by taking into account the reality of Brazil, but the production of Brazilian literature by taking into account what literature is all about."[12]

If national identity is to be meaningfully addressed in Machado's novels, it is not in the overt depiction of distinctive social groups, regional settings, racial composition, or sociocultural diversity but in nuanced allusions, subtleties of literary form, or touches of character development. How can we identify unambiguous signs of Brazilian identity from his early protagonists' quests for social stability, self-knowledge, and ultimate deliverance from the feelings of shame that abound in his oeuvre? How can we read his late unreliable narrators as enigmas of the nineteenth-century Brazilian elite? These intriguing questions have no uncontroversial answers. Some critics, in fact, consider Machado an unrepresentative Brazilian author.

MACHADO AS A BRAZILIAN WRITER

In his own lifetime, Machado's status as a representative Brazilian author was claimed by some critics but challenged severely by others. In a study published in 1897, Sílvio Romero dismisses Machado's mature fiction—today considered to be his best—on the basis that he fails to capture the ethos of his Brazilian world. According to Romero, a writer's style ought to conform to one's personality, offering a seamless continuum between physical and cultural traits. Machado was of mixed race, but his writings, Romero would argue, do not capture this fundamental aspect of his Brazilian self. Romero insists that Machado's novels are failures because his skepticism, pessimistic humor, and irony are incompatible with the natural features of a true mestizo soul.[13] Romero read Machado's novels as sterile, artificial attempts to emulate the humor of the eighteenth-century English novel, and he condemns them because Machado's protagonists are not appropriate expressions of the national ethos. Romero's general criteria with respect to literature and national identity, and his specific assessment of Machado, had profound repercussions in the history of Brazilian literary criticism.

Mário de Andrade, José Lins do Rego, and Gilberto Freyre were unwilling to dismiss the significance of Machado outright, but one feels traces of Romero's disapproval in their assessments. Andrade expresses his admiration for Machado's literary prowess but argues that it is impossible to love an author who holds such a merciless view of human nature and lacks any true manifestation of Brazilian optimism or cheerfulness.[14] José Lins do Rego thought that every novel written in Brazil after Machado owes an artistic debt to Machado, and yet he also thought that Machado's narrative fiction was seriously flawed from a social point of view. Lins do Rego points out that Machado does not offer any solution to the most urgent problems of Brazil or a feeling of commiseration for human suffering in the national setting.[15] Gilberto Freyre summarizes the Brazilian uneasiness with respect to Machado when he insists that José de Alencar's status as the true father of Brazilian letters is secure, notwithstanding Machado's unparalleled mastery of European literary forms.[16]

The legacy of Machado has clearly been a burden of sorts to many Brazilian writers, from Lima Barreto to Milton Hatoum. Responding to Machado's purported shortcomings with respect to his depiction of Brazilian reality, a number of Brazilian authors made important and unambiguous attempts to rewrite Machado's literary conceits in novels addressing social issues germane to the Brazilian situation. For example, Graciliano Ramos's *São Bernardo* (1936) is arguably a rewriting of *Dom Casmurro* in which guilt is no longer the province of a complex and equivocal individual, as is the case in Machado, but of a social class.[17]

If some critics and writers had dismissed Machado as an unrepresentative Brazilian author, others saw him as a puzzle with a Brazilian solution. In 1936 Lúcia Miguel Pereira argued that Machado, the self-taught mulatto and epileptic civil servant, was torn between his humble origins and his reverence for aristocratic values. To understand his fiction, one must appreciate the ways in which Machado overcame the obstacles and stigmas associated to his racial constitution and social milieu. Miguel Pereira agreed with Romero's view that a writer's style must be commensurate with his or her national being, but she disagreed with Romero's contention that Machado obfuscates Brazilian reality with his irony and skepticism.[18] She regarded Machado's later novels as masterpieces that shed light on profound personal as well as national dilemmas because they are cunning sublimations of racial and social stigmas Machado had struggled with in his own life.

Lúcia Miguel Pereira opened the door to many influential interpretations of Machado, including Marxist ones. In 1939 Astrojildo Pereira published an essay entitled "Machado de Assis: Novelist of the Second Reign" in which he argues that "there is an intimate and profound consonance between Machado de Assis's literary labor, and the meaning of Brazilian political and social development."[19] Astrojildo Pereira praises Machado for carefully and convincingly representing Brazilian bourgeois life. He was one of the first critics to contend that Machado's literary themes, such as the resistance of archaic institutions to modernization, were informed by the most relevant sociohistorical tensions in Brazil.

MACHADO AND BRAZILIAN SOCIETY

Antonio Candido draws on the three aforementioned critics as well as Barreto Filho to arrive at his own, influential views on Machado.[20] He understands Machado as the culmination of a progressive effort in Brazilian literature to assert itself as an autonomous system. For Candido, social imperatives and biographical variables can transform into persuasive works of art insofar as these variables are rigorously conditioned by artistic principles of composition. The critic's task is to understand how the objective data—the writer's social context, knowledge, sources, beliefs, and intentions—convert into an aesthetic form and how they create a relatively autonomous symbolic structure.

Candido argues that the aesthetic autonomy of Machado's most engaging novels derives from his ability to address fundamental aspects of national life in a relatively autonomous literary system. Candido seems to imply that the national element of a literary work involves a "structural reduction of external data," that is to say, the aesthetic mimesis of real-life social processes.[21] Candido's view of Machado is at once reverential and laconic. In Candido's major work, *The Formation of Brazilian Literature*, Machado takes pride of place as the culmination of a long process of literary emancipation from external models, but Candido does not discuss a single novel by Machado in any detail. In his only article exclusively devoted to Machado, a seventeen-page essay written 1968, Candido sums up what most attracts him to Machado—namely, his ability to offer a sense, rather than a document, of class tensions in Brazil:

> Throughout his entire body of work there is a profound sense, nothing documentary, of *status*, of the duel of salons, of the movement of social strata, of the power of money. Gain, profit, prestige, the sovereignty of interest—these are the springs of action of his character.... And the most disagreeable, the most terrible, of his characters are men of an impeccable bourgeois cut, perfectly geared into the *mores* of their class.[22]

Since the 1970s we have come to accept that Machado's literary realism may offer us many insights into class relations in nineteenth-century imperial Brazil. But this thesis, first suggested by Candido, was not worked out in detail until the influential writings of Roberto Schwarz. Following Candido, and drawing on contemporary Marxist literary theory, Schwarz has argued that Machado's novels apprehend the subtlest nuances of Brazilian social structures, transforming them into effective narrative forms. For Schwarz, the social world depicted in Machado's novels is characterized by a penchant for a perverse imbalance of power: asymmetrical ties of dependence—patronage and favor—mediate human interactions in Machado's fictional world. Schwarz argues that these power relations of imbalance express and define the uneasy situation of the landless individual in a slave-owning society who assumes a liberal ideology to rationalize his or her own reality.[23] This account of Brazilian literary realism is dependent on our willingness to accept that novels are able to capture, even against their authors' stated intentions, the deep structures of social life and transfigure them into narrative topoi and literary techniques.[24]

Schwarz believes, for example, that a satisfactory interpretation of *The Posthumous Memoirs of Brás Cubas* depends on the critic's ability to articulate the parallels between aesthetic form and the structure of nineteenth-century Brazilian society with its characteristic impasses. A homology of structures between literary form and mode of production is at the core of Schwarz's conception of literary value. Schwarz argues that the innovative Brazilianness of Machado's novels rests on the assimilation of Brazilian social relations into the structure of his narrative conceits. The shifting nature of the narrative perspective in *The Posthumous Memoirs of Brás Cubas*, for example, is taken as a fictional mirroring of the Brazilian elite's characteristic fickleness: "The literary device captures and dramatizes the structure of the country, transforming it into a rule of composition."[25] Schwarz takes the narrator, Brás Cubas, as the aesthetic embodiment of a specific historical configuration: he is as unreliable, vain, and opinionated as the social class he represents. In short, his malicious intrusiveness and fickleness are historically rooted; they represent, for Schwarz, the fundamental underlying principle of composition in *The Posthumous Memoirs of Brás Cubas*.[26]

The elliptical, fragmentary, and intrusive nature of Machado's late narrators is, according to Schwarz, commensurate with a writing strategy that emulates the historical impasses of Brazilian nineteenth-century society. Machado's narrators erect elegant and unpredictable schemes to convey the absurdity of their messages, akin to the contradictions of paternalism in Brazilian society. The homology between literary and social structures is grounded in Schwarz's belief that the development of Brazilian modernity was shaped by its dependence on backwardness as a necessary condition for social reproduction. In this sense, liberalism, the ideology of the late Brazilian Empire, could only match slavery as a "misplaced idea." Machado's seemingly frivolous heroes and narrators are poignant mirrors of the very historical clashes that shape and inform his narrative structures.

CONCLUSION

Roberto Schwarz's analysis is arguably the most sophisticated response to Sílvio Romero's dismissal of Machado as an unrepresentative Brazilian novelist. But even among penetrating critics such as Dain Borges, who

admire Schwarz's insights, is it possible to detect José Veríssimo's linger-
ing suggestion that Machado's fiction may at some level transcend national concerns? Borges argues that Machado "is the only Latin American
writer of the nineteenth century and early twentieth century who created
characters with both believably complex motivations, and believably Latin
American ones. Surely there is more to be found in his work than an analysis of paternalism."[27] Borges acknowledges the significance of Schwarz's
influential argument but writes,

> Is Machado only speaking about the soul of Brazilians, after all? One risk of the
> virtuoso analyses of Machado's critique of social institutions of the empire is
> that the brilliant reflections will wind up implying, as Roberto Schwarz does,
> that Machado's ultimate aim was to analyze the *Brazilian* upper class. Surely
> Machado was doing that. But as surely, he was also aiming at many other
> things. . . . The contemporary Brazilian deciphering of Machado's imaginings
> of human motivation has revealed a Machado whose insights can speak to
> people and situations beyond Brazil.[28]

Even John Gledson, the most authoritative critic on Machado in the
English-speaking world and an eloquent practitioner of historical interpretation of Brazilian literature, has expressed the view that much more
critical work needs to be done to fully come to terms with Machado's contributions to literature: "when we compare the state of studies on Machado
to those of a great contemporary like Henry James, with whom one can
draw such interesting parallels, I cannot help but conclude that there is a
great deal of—fascinating, revealing—spade-work to be done before we
have the materials fully to understand him and his own peculiar kind of
greatness."[29] The most recent literary criticism on Machado has not resolved the question of whether his "peculiar kind of greatness" involves
his ability to represent Brazilian reality or some other imperatives or a combination of both; but after some one hundred years of literary discussion,
the question has become much more sophisticated and nuanced, enriching
the study of Brazilian literature.

NOTES

1. Machado de Assis (1839–1908) founded the Brazilian Academy of Letters
in 1897 and was the author of nine novels, four books of poetry, eight plays, and
over two hundred short stories. He also wrote many nonfictional writings, and
his collected works number over thirty volumes. For a detailed bibliography of
Machado's work, see José Galante de Sousa, *Bibliografia de Machado de Assis* (Rio de
Janeiro: Ministério da Educacão e Cultura, 1955).

2. Alfredo Pujol, *Machado de Assis: Curso literário em sete conferências*, 2nd ed. (Rio
de Janeiro: Editora José Olympio, 1934), vii; José Veríssimo, "Machado de Assis," in

Estudos de literatura brasileira, ed. Melânia Silva Aguiar (São Paulo: Editora Itatiaia, 1977), 6:103; José Guilherme Merquior, "Machado de Assis e a prosa impressionista," in *De Anchieta a Euclides: Breve história da literatura brasileira*, 3rd ed. (Rio de Janeiro: Livraria J. Olympio Editora, 1977), 150; Lúcia Miguel Pereira, *Machado de Assis: Estudo crítico e biográfico*, 6th ed. (São Paulo: Editora da Universidade de São Paulo, 1988), 288–95; Antonio Candido, *Formação da literatura brasileira; momentos decisivos*, 7th ed., 2 vols. (São Paulo: Editora Itatiaia, 1993), 2:104–5; Alfredo Bosi, *História concisa da literatura brasileira*, 35th ed. (São Paulo: Editora Cultrix, 1994), 174–83.

3. Candido, *Formação*, 2:97–105; Bosi, *Historia*, 97–103, 26–47.

4. Renata R. Mautner Wasserman, *Exotic Nations: Literature and Cultural Identity in the United States and Brazil, 1830–1930* (Ithaca, N.Y.: Cornell University Press, 1994), 186–219; Luiz Roncari, *Literatura brasileira: Dos primeiros cronistas aos últimos românticos* (São Paulo: Edusp; Fundação para o Desenvolvimento da Educação, 1995), 275–300, 477–88.

5. In the decade that followed Brazilian independence, between 1821 and 1830, coffee and sugar cane represented, respectively, 18.4 percent and 30.1 percent of total Brazilian exports; by the time of Machado's birth, the proportion inverts to 43.8 percent (coffee) and 24 percent (sugar); at the beginning of the Republic (1889), during the 1880s, the figures had drastically reached 61.5 percent and 9.9 percent, respectively, indicating a clear restructuring of Brazilian economy that slowly left behind the traditional northeast and its sugar cane plantations in favor of the coffee produced by southeastern states of Rio de Janeiro and São Paulo. See Hélio Schlittler Silva, "Tendências e características gerais do comércio exterior no século XIX,"*Revista de História da Economia Brasileira* 1 (1953).

6. Veríssimo, "Estudos 6," 103–8; Sílvio Romero, *Evolução da literatura brasileira (vista synthetica)* (Campanha, 1905), 361–64.

7. Some of the most penetrating postmodern studies on Machado do not take Brazilian identity as a relevant criterion of literary accomplishment. Earl Fitz, for instance, argues that *Dom Casmurro* (1899) "is Machado's most nearly perfect single novel and one of the greatest of its time.... *Dom Casmurro* epitomizes what Derrida, Culler, Paul de Man, J. Hillis Miller, and others consider to be the essential feature of deconstructive criticism, that a text necessarily undercuts itself, that because of the unstable, arbitrary, and mutually creative relationship between signifier and signified a text is inescapably in the process of 'deconstructing itself' at the same time that thematically, structurally, and every other way it is trying to 'construct itself' into an organically cohesive artistic whole." Fitz, *Machado de Assis* (Boston: Twayne, 1989), 53–55. A similar point is made by Abel Barros Baptista, see note 12.

8. In most cases, Brazilian literary historiography has taken *The Little Brunette* (*A moreninha*, 1844) as the starting point for the romantic novel in Brazil. However, a case can also be made in favor of the less-structured feuilleton *The Fisherman's Son* (*O filho do pescador*, 1843). In both novels the depiction of national settings brings forth idealized elements of Brazilian geography and social relations that would soon become a norm of composition attuned to the audience's expectations. See Candido, *Formação*, 2:126–45.

9. Machado writes, "Dou-lhe parabéns pelo brilhante sucesso da sua *Ressurreição*, que li há dias e de que hei de dizer por extenso o que penso nalgum dos

próximos números do *Novo Mundo*. Este jornal . . . precisa de um bom estudo sobre o caráter geral da Literatura Brasileira contemporânea, criticando as suas boas ou más tendências, no aspecto literário e moral; um estudo que sendo traduzido e publicado aqui em inglês, dê uma boa idéia da fazenda literária que lá fabricamos, e da escola ou escolas do processo de fabricação. . . . Quererá o amigo escrever sobre isso?" R. Magalhães Júnior, *Vida e obra de Machado de Assis*, 4 vols. (Rio de Janeiro: Civilização Brasileira; Instituto Nacional do Livro, 1981), 128. Unless otherwise indicated, all translations are ours.

10. In the original, "quem examina a atual literatura brasileira reconhece-lhe logo, como primeiro traço, certo instinto de nacionalidade. Poesia, romance, to-das as formas literárias do pensamento buscam vestir-se com as cores do país." Joaquim Maria Machado de Assis, "Notícia da atual literatura brasileira: Instinto de nacionalidade," in *Obra completa*, ed. Afrânio Coutinho, 2nd ed., vol. 3 (Rio de Janeiro: J. Aguilar, 1962), 815.

11. The English quote is a paraphrase of the following text: "Do romance pu-ramente de análise, raríssimo exemplar temos. . . . Pelo que respeita à análise de paixões e caracteres são muito menos comuns os exemplos que podem satis-fazer à crítica. . . . Esta é, na verdade, uma das partes mais difíceis do romance, e ao mesmo tempo das mais superiores." Machado de Assis, *Obra completa*, 818.

12. "Não já o problema de saber como construir uma literatura brasileira tendo em conta o que é o Brasil, mas o problema de como entender e como construir uma literatura brasileira tendo em conta a questão da literatura. . . . Machado não retira da tradição européia qualquer princípio que impeça a literatura brasileira de ser brasileira, mas também não extrai do Brasil qualquer critério ou garantia de nacionalidade." Abel Barros Baptista, *Em nome do apelo do nome: Duas interrogações sobre Machado de Assis* (Lisboa: Litoral Edições, 1991), 99, 110–11.

13. See Sílvio Romero, *Machado de Assis: Estudo comparativo de literatura brasileira* (Campinas: Editora da Unicamp, 1992). For a modern account of race relations in Brazil, see David T. Haberly, *Three Sad Races: Racial Identity and National Consciousness in Brazilian Literature* (Cambridge: Cambridge University Press, 1983). On the debate between Machado and Romero, see José Luiz Passos, "Crítica en-gajada e texto engasgado: Machado de Assis e Sílvio Romero na autonomização do campo literário brasileiro," *Chasqui: Revista de literatura latinoamericana* 26, no. 1 (1997); Roberto Ventura, *Estilo tropical: História cultural e polêmicas literárias no Brasil, 1870–1914* (São Paulo: Companhia das Letras, 1991).

14. See "Machado de Assis" in Mário de Andrade, *Aspectos da literatura brasileira*, 5th ed. (São Paulo: Martins, 1974).

15. See the chapter on Machado de Assis in José Lins do Rego, *Conferências no Prata: Tendências do romance brasileiro* (Rio de Janeiro: Casa do Estudante do Brasil, 1946).

16. Gilberto Freyre, *Reinterpretando José de Alencar* (Rio de Janeiro: Ministério da Educação e Cultura, 1955).

17. Graciliano Ramos, *São Bernardo*, 19th ed. (São Paulo: Martins, 1973).

18. Pereira, *Machado de Assis*.

19. Astrojildo writes, "existe uma consonância íntima e profunda entre o labor literário de Machado de Assis e o sentido da evolução política e social do Brasil."

Astrojildo Pereira, *Interpretações* (Rio de Janeiro: Casa do Estudante do Brasil, 1944), 15–16.

20. Barreto Filho, *Introdução a Machado de Assis* (Rio de Janeiro: Livraria AGIR, 1947).

21. See, for instance, Antonio Candido, "Dialética da malandragem: Caracterização das Memórias de um sargento de milícias," *Revista do Instituto de Estudos Brasileiros* 8 (1970): 67–89.

22. Antonio Candido, "An Outline of Machado de Assis," trans. Howard Becker, in *On Literature and Society* (Princeton, N.J.: Princeton University Press, 1995), 117.

23. Roberto Schwarz, *Ao vencedor as batatas: Forma literária e processo social nos inícios do romance brasileiro* (São Paulo: Livraria Duas Cidades, 1977), 13–25.

24. Under this rather daring set of assumptions, the critic's task is to shed light on the resemblance between literature structure and the actual patterns of social organization. This homology of structures, according to Schwarz, allows a successful work to represent reality with a sense of unity and totality. For a recent criticism of this view, see Harry E. Shaw, *Narrating Reality: Austen, Scott, Eliot* (Ithaca, N.Y.: Cornell University Press, 1999), chaps. 1 and 2.

25. Roberto Schwarz, *Um mestre na periferia do capitalismo: Machado de Assis* (São Paulo: Livraria Duas Cidades, 1990), 11.

26. Schwarz, *Mestre*, 31.

27. Dain Borges, "Machado de Assis and the Historians," unpublished essay presented to the History Department-Oliveira Lima Library colloquium, September 27, 2000, 9.

28. Dain Borges, "The Relevance of Machado de Assis," in *Imagining Brazil*, ed. Jessé Souza and Valter Sinder (Lanham, Md.: Lexington Books, 2005), 14. Borges provides the most comprehensive assessment of the contributions of historians and critics, such as Raymundo Faoro, John Gledson, Roberto Schwarz, and Sidney Chalhoub. See Raymundo Faoro, *Machado de Assis: A pirâmide e o trapézio* (São Paulo: Companhia Editora Nacional, 1974); John Gledson, *The Deceptive Realism of Machado de Assis: A Dissenting Interpretation of Dom Casmurro* (Liverpool, England: F. Cairns, 1984); Sidney Chalhoub, "Dependents Play Chess: Political Dialogues in Machado de Assis," in *Machado de Assis: Reflections on a Brazilian Master Writer*, ed. Richard Graham (Austin: University of Texas Press, 1999).

29. John Gledson, "Dom Casmurro: Realism and Intentionalism Revisited," in *Machado de Assis: Reflections on a Brazilian Master Writer*, ed. Richard Graham (Austin: University of Texas Press, 1999), 18.

2

❧

Euclides da Cunha's View of Brazil's Fractured Identity

Dain Borges

If a wounded national consciousness—wounded by defeat and collective humiliation—is the strongest goad of nationalisms, then it took real effort for Brazil to feel its wound at the turn of the century.[1] Elsewhere in Latin America, the United States victory in the War of 1898 provoked anxious reflections about identity and inferiority, Ariel and Caliban.[2] In Brazil it inspired little overt reaction. Compared to Germany, or Russia, or any of the Spanish American nations, Brazil could smugly claim to be an undefeated nation with a "clean and glorious history."[3] Brazil had won the Paraguayan War in 1870, abolished slavery without civil war in 1888, and carried out an almost bloodless republican revolution in 1889. In the 1870s, Brazil's intellectual elite began to dissent from that complacent sense of self-satisfaction, and social criticism grew stronger in the abolitionist campaign of the 1880s but was still relatively marginal at the turn of the century. Euclides da Cunha's *Rebellion in the Backlands* (*Os sertões*, 1902) is in a sense the foundation of critical and passionate inquiries into Brazilian national identity because it invites readers to recognize an apparent military victory—the annihilation of the Canudos millenarian rebellion in 1897—as a tragic self-defeat.[4] It establishes themes that have become constants in Brazilian social thought and Brazilian reflections on national identity.[5]

DA CUNHA'S PERSPECTIVE ON THE CANUDOS REBELLION

In 1896, Bahian state police set out to arrest Antonio Conselheiro, "Antonio the Counselor," the leader of the Canudos religious community. Their pretext, which we now know had been schemed up by local bosses jealous of the Counselor's political influence, was refusal to pay sales taxes. People from Canudos resisted the police with sticks and gunshots. When they fought off a second army detachment, the city was considered in rebellion. A third expedition was organized with patriotic fanfare in Rio de Janeiro and led by Colonel Moreira Cesar, a cutthroat with political ambitions, but was ultimately routed. News of Cesar's death and of officers' bodies strung from trees shook the young Brazilian republic. The new government had just survived a much broader civil war in southern states and a rebellion by its navy in Rio's harbor. Carefully now, the army mobilized a fourth expedition in a slow buildup from Salvador to inland railheads, eventually concentrating almost half of the Brazilian army in the Bahian backlands. In late 1897, it began an artillery bombardment with Krupps howitzers, besieged and encircled Canudos, burned down five thousand huts with kerosene and dynamite, and slaughtered every man remaining.[6] As most saw it, fanatical religion and monarchism had been halted by modern military science, by anticlerical republican military officers (though as it turned out, these officers would face another rural millenarian uprising fifteen years later). But because of Euclides da Cunha's *Rebellion in the Backlands*, the fall of the city of Canudos became an enduring symbol of anguishing schisms in the Brazilian nation.

Euclides da Cunha (1866–1909) arrived at the dusty frontline trenches toward the end of the buildup, only a few weeks before the final massacre. He had been hired by the *Estado de São Paulo* to cover the war because he had written a patriotic editorial that compared Canudos to the counterrevolutionary Vendée and its uprising during the French Revolution. The best of his dispatches portrayed a boy taken prisoner as an unrepentant fanatic and a calloused criminal—and this incident may be the closest that he ever came to talking with a man from Canudos. His private ambition was more literary and scientific than journalistic; he spent less time at the front than in the libraries of Salvador, reading maps of the backlands and treatises on the skull shape and brain mass of "born" criminals. The most prominent psychiatrist in Bahia, Raimundo Nina Rodrigues, had just diagnosed the people of Canudos as racial primitives whose mentality was capable only of revering chiefs and kings, not respecting an abstract republic. But Da Cunha seemed skeptical, and he later jettisoned most of the anthropological notes he had taken.[7] He retained analysis of races—but races understood primarily by their geography and milieu.

Da Cunha was not a professional journalist but rather an engineer trained at Rio de Janeiro's military academy. His troubled career in the decade before Canudos epitomizes the way in which members of the small urban middle class of an agrarian empire could mix their personal identity crisis with questions of national identity. His cohort of cadets idolized their mathematics professor, who taught them Auguste Comte's cult of science and progress (for a few, Comte's new-age Positivist Church of love and science was to replace the Roman Catholic Church). They earnestly debated the idea that nations and individuals rise from a primitive and fetishistic stage, through a medieval theocratic stage, through a metaphysical stage of philosophy and the horrible turbulence of the French Revolution, to arrive at a "positive" scientific stage with both order and progress.[8] They were a generation with a modernizing mission who believed themselves energetic, scientific, and self-sacrificing in contrast with the effete, lawyerly, and corrupt civilian politicians who ran the empire. Da Cunha was expelled from the military academy in 1888—at the height of a week of insubordination among the cadets—for a republican protest on the parade ground.[9]

The 1890s, the first decade of the republic, were not orderly but rather highly divisive for politically active Brazilians such as Da Cunha.[10] Shortly after the army overthrew the empire in 1889, Da Cunha was reinstated at the military academy as a minor republican hero. He married a prominent officer's daughter. But soon he was out of favor again because he declined a post with the so-called Jacobin followers of Field Marshal Floriano Peixoto, the second military dictator of the republic. When Peixoto cracked down on dissidents, Da Cunha left Rio, resigned from the army, and looked for civilian work as an engineer. In a sense, the war-correspondent assignment to Canudos rehabilitated him by bringing him back among his classmates. Politics in the 1890s were a contest among radical Jacobins, many of them junior officers in the army; the army's senior officers, who did not have the stomach or a mission to stay in power; holdout monarchist politicians of the empire and pragmatic local machine politicians in each state; and the rising business-political elite of São Paulo state, business republicans such as the owners of the newspaper that sent Da Cunha to the front. By the time of the Canudos war, São Paulo civilian politicians had taken control of the national government and had begun to impose a program of conservative modernization that lasted for a generation.

Da Cunha was able to condense this crisis into *Rebellion in the Backlands* because he took five years after Canudos to write it while he supervised the reconstruction of a rural iron bridge. Thus, the book was much more than timely journalism. In fact, it seemed untimely, and his publisher was skeptical of its prospects because by 1902 the Brazilian market had already been saturated with instant books about the Canudos rebellion: a novel, a denunciation of atrocities by a medical student, military memoirs, and editorials. Some of these books had borrowed heavily from Da Cunha's newspaper dispatches, and in turn Da Cunha lifted passages from them, even from the novel.[11] Yet *Rebellion in the Backlands* became the best-seller about Canudos. It was immediately recognized as a challenging statement about Brazilian national identity. Provincial intellectuals who had written regionalist novels on the theme of the noble *sertanejo* backlanders championed it as a realistic, scientific version of their own novels of rural life and landscapes. The urban public felt that it met their need to answer the question Who are we? to explain Brazilian national identity. Da Cunha was quickly elected to the Brazilian Academy of Letters by its hard-headed, "sociological" faction, who thought Brazil needed scientific social criticism and a literature informed by science.[12] On the strength of this acclaim, the literary engineer was invited to join the Brazilian diplomatic service, not in European embassies but on Amazonian border commissions. He published two more books, one on national affairs and one on the plight of the Amazon rubber tappers, leaving hints that his political ideology was moving in the direction of socialism. In a sense, his development is irrelevant because his career was cut short when he died in a shootout with his wife's lover in 1909. Only *Rebellion in the Backlands* has captured the imagination of Brazilian readers.

THE NATIONAL REALITY

Rebellion in the Backlands impressed readers at the time more as a scientific text on national reality than as one on national identity.[13] At the time, reviewers corrected Da Cunha on botanical names or quibbled over fine points of race classification. Today, its deterministic sociology—particularly its race science—is discounted by any serious reader as a causal explanation of Brazilian society and culture. In the 1930s, race sociology came under direct attack by Gilberto Freyre and others; in the 1950s, Dante Moreira Leite published a dismissive critique of the whole genre as an "ideology of national character." By the 1970s, some progressive intellectuals rejected any characterization of national culture as obfuscating class interests and class conflict.[14] But the ambition to find a science that can capture and explain the nation is still strong among Brazilian social thinkers. Da Cunha's argument that analysis of Brazil should begin from a duality between city and country remained influential until the last two decades (Brazil today is 80 percent urban; then it was 80 percent rural). The idea that Brazil's national identity can be understood as a dialectic of splits and fractures is perhaps as strong today as it ever was.[15]

Today, *Rebellion in the Backlands* is read most often for the rhetorical and literary qualities of its "portrait of the people" and for its poetic insights into Brazilian national identity, much as Sarmiento's *Facundo* is still read as a portrait of Argentina. It is seen as being more than half a novel or essay and less than half a scientific treatise. Historical research on Canudos has abandoned most of Da Cunha's deterministic explanation of causes of the rebellion, and revisionist research has seriously questioned whether

Antonio Conselheiro intended any rebellion at all.[16] When *Rebellion in the Backlands* is revisited as a living text, it is done so to rework it as fiction, in films such as Glauber Rocha's *Deus e o Diabo na terra do sol* (*Black God, White Devil*, 1964) or in novels such as Mario Vargas Llosa's *War of the End of the World* (1981). Yet I argue that Euclides da Cunha constructed *Rebellion in the Backlands* so that its scientific argument would be inextricable from its literary style and the development of his narrative. To analyze or reconstruct Da Cunha's argument, we must follow the sequence of his argument.

The first part of *Rebellion in the Backlands* is a description of "The Land," the dry *sertão* around Canudos that sets the themes and tone of the analysis. The terrain is fractured and unbalanced; the climate oscillates between rains and drought. Struggle is immanent in the land, as plants and animals exist on a wavering borderline between life and death. Twenty pages into this description of geography comes the first hint of the Canudos war and of an eerie strangeness that pervades the book: the dryness of the climate may be measured by the cadavers of a horse and rider, perfectly mummified upright along a slope, giving an illusion of life because the horse's mane waves in the wind. The shock effect of these "unusual hygrometers" is the first warning to readers that this is a book about war and the first hint that there will be something magical mixed in with the science.

The second part of *Rebellion in the Backlands* moves from the land to a study of "Man" in Brazil, emphasizing the contrast among social types of Brazilian regions, particularly the antitheses between people of the coast and those of the northern *sertão*. Da Cunha's explanation of national identity is partly geographical: the unbalanced climate of the drought-stricken backlands unsettles persons. It is a historical account of the formation of populations by settlement and of the institutional neglect of the rural backlands. And it is also a racial analysis, dwelling on nineteenth-century racism's typical preoccupations with intelligence, energy, and beauty. In terms of their mentalities and civilization, the *sertanejos* of Canudos stand roughly at the level of medieval Portuguese religion or perhaps at the level of Mediterranean peoples during the encounter between early Christianity and pagan religion. Da Cunha argues that race mixture and regional circumstances explain that backwardness. On the Brazilian coast, race mixture between Portuguese and Africans produced the hybrid mulatto, weak, ugly, and neurasthenically inadequate for the stresses of urban civilization, one's two disparate ancestries carrying on a self-destructive "civil war" within one's own body. This passage troubles virtually all readers today and makes it impossible to wholeheartedly embrace Da Cunha.[17] Da Cunha himself seems to have felt ambivalence; he titled this section on race "An Irritating Parenthesis." In the Brazilian interior, Da Cunha argues, race mixture primarily between Portuguese and Indians produced the hybrid mestizo, strong and ugly, adapted to context but still backward. There were at least two types of mestizo in Brazil: the southern *gaucho* and the northern *sertanejo*, a cowherd with a different, more fatalistic temperament.[18] This argument was fairly conventional in nineteenth-century race sociology: brown or mixed-race people were not adaptable to competition in a white-collar or industrial setting but were perhaps acceptable and, if Indians, even noble in "their place"—in the tropics, the jungle, or the backlands.[19]

Even in Da Cunha's racism, however, there is patriotic hope for Brazil. The Brazilian land is at present populated by unbalanced, divided people, but over time, the strong mestizo backlanders might have been civilized into a strong, racially unified nation. The physical "family resemblances" among *sertanejos* are a promising sign of a future unification.[20] Among all the race sociologies available in 1900, Da Cunha chose to cite Ludwig Gumplowicz's *The Struggle of Races* (1883).[21] Gumplowicz was an extreme polygenist who argued that human races had radically separate origins. Da Cunha took from Gumplowicz (and perhaps from Herbert Spencer) an emphasis on the convergence and unification of humankind into larger social units. Gumplowicz argues that human societies form by a process of struggles that amalgamate and fuse originally separate bands into larger groups with wider solidarities. And in *Rebellion in the Backlands*, Da Cunha is desperately concerned to prove that, although Brazil is currently frac-tured and divided, at some point in the future it will become "fused." It will have one unitary identity of race. If not, Da Cunha believes, it will be destroyed in the imperialist struggle among nations.

Most critics have missed this key to his political psychology of Brazil. Although Da Cunha believes that there are inferior and superior races, the Brazilian identity problem is not that Brazilians have inferior race but that they have no race at all. They lack common heritage and disposi-tions. This point is crucial to the next step in his reasoning. Following Gustave Le Bon and the new French social psychology of the 1890s, Da Cunha argues that lack of race inclines people to a particular sort of polit-ical volatility. A national population that has fused into a race is naturally conservative in politics because of its homogeneous dispositions and tra-ditions. Heterogeneous people are much more likely to be hypnotized by a dangerous magnetic leader into a crowd, a kind of superorganism whose separate minds merge hypnotically into a more primitive and more vio-lent collective mind.[22] Thus Canudos's fanaticism: Antonio Conselheiro was a charismatic crowd leader, a hypnotizer. His sermons merged the raceless backlands people into a degenerate mob. Conselheiro's city of Canudos became a degenerating milieu, a "sinister urbs," an anticity, a "mud-hut Jerusalem" that transformed good-hearted country people, *ser-tanejos*, into fanatical bandits, *jagunços*. Hypnotized people are capable of drawing upon subliminal powers of mind and body and becoming either greater or more dangerous. As an explanation of the political action of poor Brazilians, *Rebellion in the Backlands* shows affinities with conservative European social psychology's explaining the political barbarism of the Paris mob, anarchist bomb throwers, or violent strikers. In this sociology, any radical political opposition is reduced to criminal mental imbalance, and democracy is often devalued as a phenomenon of irrational mob rule.[23]

The third and longest part of *Rebellion in the Backlands* is a narrative of "The Struggle" at Canudos. Da Cunha views the war as a struggle of races but also one of brothers. He is less interested in what it tells about barbaric country people than in what it reveals about "civilized" urban Brazil. In his analysis, not just the *sertanejos* are "retrograde"; urban populations are degenerate, and the army—Da Cunha's own corporation—even more so. Its soldiers are a mixed-race grab bag, a crowd held together not by trained discipline but by the personal magnetism of their officers. The campaign exposes a deficiency in the officers' mentalities, too. The officers are "geometrically" minded. They cannot shift from the field maneuvers of their European textbooks to the guerrilla tactics demanded by the backlands' labyrinthine terrain. Their strongest leader, Colonel Moreira Cesar, is an epileptic, a sort of mad genius. Indeed, Da Cunha describes the crazed monarchist prophet Antonio Conselheiro and the violent republican demagogue Moreira Cesar in virtually the same words, as doubles of one another.[24]

Canudos is even a "dark mirror" of the city of Rio de Janeiro. The riots in Rio after the third expedition's defeat are a crucial revealing symptom of the newborn degeneracy of the Brazilian republic and the thuggish ultranationalist Jacobins: during the riots, Rio's most fashionable street, the Rua do Ouvidor, was "worth about as much as some path through the thornbush." In the mirror of the Canudos war, the face of Brazilian national identity is split and monstrous.

A NATIONALIST TEXT

If *Rebellion in the Backlands* is so pessimistic about Brazilian society and culture, why did it become a classic on Brazilian national identity? Neither its science nor its stock of literary themes and imagery is much different from that found in other narratives of imperialist expeditions written at the same time (none of which, as far as we know, Da Cunha read).[25] Joseph Conrad's novel *Heart of Darkness* (1899), for example, imagines punitive expeditions and a strange journey from coast to backlands to rescue Kurtz, the colonial agent whose civilized savagery in the Congo unmasks the civilized pretense of Europe.[26] Heriberto Frías's novel *Tomóchic* (1892) gives a fictionalized account of the Mexican army's massacre of millennial rebels in 1892.[27] It offers similar criticisms of the army and of national policies, symbolizing the essential brotherhood between Mexican rebels and soldiers through a love affair between a "fanatic" girl and a troubled young officer. James Mooney's investigative report *The Ghost Dance Religion and the Sioux Outbreak of 1892* (1896) examines the causes of the Wounded Knee massacre.[28] Like *Rebellion in the Backlands*, it uses the social psychology of mass hypnosis to explain the Ghost Dance religion of the Sioux rebels. All of these texts criticize imperialist civilization and modernity; all draw on contemporary sciences of mind; and all of them take note of the unexpected energies that emerge in the resistance of oppressed people. They are even better than *Rebellion in the Backlands* at recognizing the humanity of the Other. Frías symbolizes national reconciliation through a marriage between the army and the people of Tomóchic, and Mooney actually interviewed the Ghost Dance religion's founder, Wowoka. *Rebellion in the Backlands* lacks the dialogue between opposed characters that gives life to so many novels.[29] But none of these other texts has become fundamental to a nationalist canon. Perhaps what *Rebellion in the Backlands* has that makes it a foundational classic in the ideology of Brazilian national identity is a special resonance with the worldview of the Canudos rebels: the resonance is oblique, but it is a crucial part of Da Cunha's recognition of Brazil's national tragedy.

Toward the end of his narrative of the campaign, Da Cunha's sympathies turn, and his tragic vision changes. The campaign is not only a homicide, as in the army's massacre of the *sertanejos* in atrocious war crimes, but also a suicide, as in the Brazilian race's destroying itself. As he describes the inexorable bombardment and siege of Canudos by the fourth expedition, he portrays the last stand of the rebels as admirable and inexplicable courage. He speaks again and again of the *sertanejos* as the essence, the "living bedrock," and the "heartwood" of the Brazilian nation.

The most powerful epiphany is his anecdote about soldiers' leading a prisoner to execution with their officers' connivance. The prisoner was "from the lowest rung of the scale of our race"; that is, he was black. He was not just black but hideously ugly: emaciated with a jutting jaw, a flat nose, small eyes, and bent legs. "An orangutan . . . an animal. It wasn't worth while interrogating him." But when led out to slaughter, he put the noose on his own neck. "And they saw the wretch transmute, once he had taken the first steps toward execution. From that blackened and repugnant frame, barely supported on long, withered legs, there suddenly burst forth admirable lines—terribly sculptural—of a splendid physique. A masterpiece of sculpture modeled in mud." The prisoner took on a noble bearing and became "an old statue of a Titan, buried for four centuries and now flowering, blackened and mutilated, in that immense ruins of Canudos. It was an inversion of roles. A shameful antinomy."[30] It is something like a recognition scene in tragedy: Da Cunha, at least, is able to see something of the *sertanejo* faith.[31] Such glimpses of critical self-recognition are what makes the national-identity essays of Latin America something more than complacent clichés about national character.

Through its narrative of the final days of the campaign, *Rebellion in the Backlands* becomes a nationalist text as well as a clinical diagnosis of the birth defects in national identity. The Brazilian people are backward because of powerful, determining natural forces, but their backwardness is reversible or redeemable. A prospective optimism lurks inside Da Cunha's pessimism. When the book is reread in light of this passage, the transfiguration of the *jagunço* echoes other transformations, such as Da Cunha's earlier sketch of the *sertanejo* social type that depicts him squatting and apparently idle, then abruptly leaping onto his horse to chase a runaway steer. There are "complete transmutations . . . unchaining sleeping energies. . . . The man transfigures himself." Da Cunha sums up the *sertanejo* as a paired antithesis, a "Hercules-Quasimodo."[32] These transformations are sometimes more than movement from apathy to energy. Some are even shifts across the borderline between death and life, as when the mummified horse and rider appear to resurrect. Da Cunha's theme of transfigured identity is both scientific and animistic, magical.[33]

The theme of transformation inheres deeply in the rhetoric, structure, and images of the text. The most powerful stylistic feature of *Rebellion in the Backlands* is its rhetorical figures of opposition, paradox, and antithesis. These, of course, are constitutive ideological elements of Da Cunha's explicit central argument about the ruptures and divisions in national society. But another feature, images from and allusions to Christian and Greek myth, reinforces the nationalist theme of redemptive transformation that grows out of the main theme of inevitable defeat and destruction.[34]

Some of the allusions to Greek myth in *Rebellion in the Backlands* seem to be merely redundant Gongoresque games. For example, the landscape of the *sertão* is a labyrinth (literally "um dédalo," a Daedal), and the soldiers become lost in it like minotaurs. It is likely that Da Cunha meant to titillate erudite readers with the suggestion that Brazilian soldiers are minotaurs because they are the freakish children of miscegenation, just as the literary Minotaur was the monstrous offspring of queen Pasiphäe's perverse mating with the white bull. If so, he was simply underlining his scientific diagnosis of racial degeneration and national doom.

But Da Cunha adds a countercurrent to his argument about the nature of national defeat through another set of allusions to the Greek origin myths of the Titanomachy, the struggle between the Titans and the Olympians that ended with Zeus's banishment of the defeated Titans to the underworld of Tartarus.[35] In *Rebellion in the Backlands*, the *sertanejos* are repeatedly described as "titans." By itself this could be just a dead metaphor sedimented into idiom. But the allusions move beyond idiom to simile, describing the *sertanejos* as being rooted in the earth like the giant Antaeus. Ultimately, the many allusions to the myth of the replacement of the old gods of the land by the new generation of Olympian gods amount to a grand organizing metaphor that sacralizes the struggle between Brazil's races at Canudos. The analogy between the *sertanejos* and the Titans becomes more frequent toward the end of the siege, as Da Cunha writes more and more sympathetically of their heroism. Throughout the book, geological strata are metaphorically overlaid historical stages and stratified racial groups. For example, Antonio Conselheiro is described as an "anticline," a geological fault who brings to the surface—to progressive, civilized coastal Brazil—social layers that ought to have remained buried in the archaic countryside. Toward the end of the book, the final stages of the siege are described as the nation's blasting its own bedrock: "Shaken by the cataclysm of war, the surface layers of a nationality shattered and split open, laying bare its deepest elements in those resigned and stoical Titans."[36] Titanic virtues are not limited to the *sertanejos*. Da Cunha consistently reverses and exchanges antinomic qualities between victors and vanquished, accumulating paradoxes.[37] The issue, as Da Cunha poses it at the end of the text, is that the soldiers and the *sertanejos* are of the same people, yet a handful of brave snipers from the nationality's archaic stratum are able to rout well-armed battalions from its modern stratum.[38] Only reconciliation (and pragmatically speaking, uplifting education) will solve this problem. Canudos is a ruins of death and shards, but from its fragments a new national unity and national race can be forged.

Key Christian references also change Da Cunha's argument about the nature of the defeat. Of course, Canudos is a Christian sect, and Da Cunha offers an explicit discussion of the mistaken doctrines of Antonio Conselheiro and the mistaken beliefs of the *sertanejos*.[39] He describes the visit by missionary priests in 1895 that tried to bring Conselheiro and the Canudos movement back into line with the church. To analyze *sertanejo* religiosity (and to dismiss it as a legitimate challenge to modern republican rationality), Da Cunha displaces it temporally onto the late Middle Ages or onto Roman antiquity. He cites Ernest Renan's *Marcus Aurelius* (1882) for its description of the excesses of the millenarian Montanist sect in early Christianity, and he seems to borrow other pieces of Renan's vision of taming early Christianity into a Roman state religion.[40] Specifically, he argues that Brazil's Catholic church failed the *sertanejos* by not catechizing them in an orthodox Christianity that would have inoculated them against the apocalyptic preaching of Antonio Conselheiro, and he implies that Catholic missions in combination with primary schools would have been the state's appropriate, elevating, and nonmilitary response to the condition of its people.

The key Christian theme in *Rebellion in the Backlands*, however, is the Transfiguration of Christ, and it comes from Da Cunha, not from the sermons of Antonio Conselheiro or the words of the *sertanejos*. In the New Testament, the Transfiguration is the moment when Christ reveals clearly to his disciples that he is the Son of God, a hiatus between his preaching in Galilee and his entrance into Jerusalem. He takes them up to a mountain and lets them see him as he truly is, transfigured, whiter than the sun. His physical, carnal body transforms into divine presence; his ministry will give way to the messianic sacrifice and resurrection of the Crucifixion.[41] Da Cunha made transfiguration, along with its synonyms *metamorphosis*, *transformation*, and *transmutation*, one of the most frequently used words in *Rebellion in the Backlands*.[42] Parched land is transfigured by rain; irrigation can transfigure a desert into farmland; an inert cowboy can be transfigured by his rush to rescue a calf; the certainty of drought can transfigure a feckless *sertanejo* into a resolute fatalist; true faith can transfigure the *sertanejo* soul perverted by fanaticism; good missionary preaching can transfigure souls; divine inspiration can transfigure Antonio Conselheiro as a prophet; the addition of towers to a half-built church can transfigure it into a crude Gothic cathedral; and flags and banners can transfigure a small town into a patriotic celebration.

The Christian theme of transfiguration in *Rebellion in the Backlands*, then, suggests a different sort of recognition than the tragic Greek recognition of fate. To recognize the *sertanejos* is not to see the inevitability of their destruction but to see them transfigured, in their true light. Many recent defenders of Da Cunha have wanted to dismiss his scientific vision as being flawed and reactionary but his sympathetic sentiments as being accurate and progressive.[43] But through the theme of transfiguration Da Cunha arrives at his second sight, a vision of the people's bodies and of national identity that is much less deterministic than his sociology and perhaps more attuned to the *sertanejo* worldview.[44] This vision is typically nationalist because most nationalisms at some level sacralize the nation and its people as God's chosen people. It is typically *criollo* Latin American in seeing the people as deficient citizens today but potentially glorious citizens in the future. And it is both quasi religious and secular. It certainly could be secularized. Whether or not Da Cunha's concept of transfiguration was a direct influence on the formation of ideas such as Paulo Freire's *concientização* (political consciousness-raising through the teaching of literacy) in the 1950s, something resembling his theme of redemptive transformation has been part of Brazilian nationalisms ever since 1902. If themes of national identity and special mission develop as intellectuals brood on wounds and defeats, then because of Euclides Da Cunha's interpretation, the Canudos campaign was a shameful, self-inflicted defeat but one from which Brazil can have its revenge by redeeming and transfiguring itself.

But can this twist of a critical inquiry about national identity into a quasi-millennial nationalist enthusiasm provide an imaginary foundation for politics? Like most Latin American literature and social science—including the Boom novels of the 1960s, such as *One Hundred Years of Solitude*—*Rebellion in the Backlands* fails to create characters that take responsibility for their own actions.[45] Da Cunha's central actors are vivid, but they are inanimate manifestations of social forces, such as Antonio Conselheiro: "a puppet, passive as a shadow, an automaton." No one at Canudos can be entirely accountable for his criminal actions or omissions—not Antonio Conselheiro, not Moreira Cesar, not any commanding officer. Da Cunha acknowledges and openly criticizes the attitude among the army that "the backlands meant impunity" for war crimes. But he hesitates to locate responsibility: symptomatically, civilian president Prudente de Morais, who took sick leave during most of the war, goes almost unmentioned throughout the essay. As long as Latin American literature and the national-identity essay dwell on fantasies of the people's making a new start and then meeting their inevitable destruction—whether at Canudos or Macondo—it is hard to imagine that they will provide anything but a higher fatalism of alibis for postponing democracy.

NOTES

1. Isaiah Berlin, "The Bent Twig: On the Rise of Nationalism," in *The Crooked Timber of Humanity: Chapters in the History of Ideas* (London: John Murray, 1990), 238–62.

2. Emir Rodriguez Monegal, "The Metamorphoses of Caliban," *Diacritics* (September 1977): 78–83; and Rodriguez Monegal, "La utopia modernista: El mito del nuevo y el viejo mundo en Darío y Rodó," *Revista Iberoamericana* 46, nos. 112–113 (July–December 1980): 427–42.

3. José Vasconcelos, *La raza cósmica: Misión de la raza iberoamericana, Argentina y Brasil*, 17th ed. (1st ed., 1925; Mexico City: Espasa-Calpe Mexicana, 1994), 115.

4. Euclides da Cunha, *Os sertões: Campanha de Canudos*, 35th ed. (1st ed., 1902; Rio de Janeiro: Francisco Alves, 1991). All citations are to this edition; the English translations are my own, consulting the Samuel Putnam translation: Euclides da Cunha, *Rebellion in the Backlands* (Chicago: University of Chicago Press, 1944).

5. On the meaning of "national identity" and particularly for a useful distinction between studies of cultural *identidad* and environmental-circumstantial *realidad*, see Richard M. Morse, "The Multiverse of Latin American Identity, c. 1920–c. 1970," in *The Cambridge History of Latin America*, vol. 10, *Latin American since 1930: Idea, Culture, and Society*, ed. Leslie Bethell (Cambridge: Cambridge University Press, 1995), 1–127, esp. 1–8.

6. Robert M. Levine, "Mud Hut Jerusalem: Canudos Revisited," *Hispanic American Historical Review* 68, no. 3 (August 1988): 525–72; and Levine, *Vale of Tears:*

Revisiting the Canudos Massacre in Northeastern Brazil, 1893–1897 (Berkeley: University of California Press, 1992).

7. Raimundo Nina Rodrigues, "A loucura epidêmica de Canudos: Antonio Conselheiro e os jagunços," in *As collectividades anormaes*, ed. Arthur Ramos (Rio de Janeiro: Companhia Editora Nacional, 1939), 50–77; and Nina Rodrigues, "A loucura das multidões: Nova contribuição ao estudo das loucuras epidêmicas no Brasil," in Ramos, *As collectividades anormaes*, 78–153. Euclides da Cunha, *Caderneta de campo*, ed. Olímpio Sousa de Andrade (São Paulo: Cultrix, 1975), 13–25, 40–47, 146–47, 154–57; Leopoldo M. Bernucci, *A imitação dos sentidos: Prógonos, contemporâneos e epígonos de Euclides da Cunha* (São Paulo: Editora da Universidade de São Paulo, 1995); Walnice Nogueira Galvão, "De sertões e jagunços," *Saco de gatos: Ensaios críticos* (São Paulo: Livraria Duas Cidades, 1976), 65–85.

8. Da Cunha was briefly a Comtean but was much more influenced by Herbert Spencer's theories of social forces. Frederic Amory, "Euclides Da Cunha and Brazilian Positivism," *Luso-Brazilian Review* 36, no. 1 (1999): 87–94; and Amory, "Historical Source and Biographical Context in the Interpretation of Euclides da Cunha's *Os Sertões*," *Journal of Latin American Studies* 28, no. 3 (October 1996): 667–85.

9. Celso Castro, *Os militares e a República: Um estudo sobre cultura e ação política* (Rio de Janeiro: Jorge Zahar Editor, 1995), 146–49.

10. The novelist Machado de Assis represented these confused times through the allegory of a girl in love with identical twin brothers, one a monarchist and the other a republican. Machado de Assis, *Esau and Jacob*, trans. Elizabeth Lowe, ed. Dain Borges (1st. ed., 1904; Oxford: Oxford University Press, 2000). On the crisis of ideology, legitimacy, and symbolism in the early republic, see José Murilo de Carvalho, *Formação das almas: O imaginário da República* (São Paulo: Companhia das Letras, 1990).

11. Galvão, "De sertões"; Bernucci, *Imitação*.

12. Regina de Abreu, *O enigma de Os Sertões* (Rio de Janeiro: Rocco and Funarte, 1998).

13. See Morse, "Multiverse of Latin American Identity."

14. See chapter 3 in this volume, on Gilberto Freyre, and Carlos Guilherme Mota, *Ideologia da cultura brasileira, 1933–1974* (São Paulo: Ática, 1977); Thomas Skidmore, *Black into White: Race and Nationality in Brazilian Thought* (New York: Oxford University Press, 1970).

15. Nísia Trindade Lima, *Um sertão chamado Brasil: Intelectuais e representação geográfica da identidade nacional* (Rio de Janeiro: IUPERJ, UCAM and Editora Revan, 1999); Paulo Eduardo Arantes, *Sentimento da dialética na experiência intelectual brasileira: Dialética e dualidade segundo Antonio Candido e Roberto Schwarz* (São Paulo: Paz e Terra, 1992).

16. Levine, *Vale of Tears*.

17. One can only imagine what Machado de Assis, president of the Academy of Brazilian Letters and a mulatto who suffered from epilepsy, thought of this passage. Machado manifested neither opposition nor enthusiasm regarding Da Cunha's election to the academy.

18. Roberto González Echevarría, "A Lost World Re-discovered: Sarmiento's *Facundo* and Euclides da Cunha's *Os Sertões*," in *Myth and Archive: A Theory of Latin American Narrative* (Cambridge: Cambridge University Press, 1990).

19. There is nothing in *Rebellion in the Backlands*'s race analysis that Theodore Roosevelt wouldn't have found familiar and plausible—in fact, in his introduction Da Cunha drops an oblique reference to the Spanish-American War as a struggle between races.

20. Luiz Fernando Valente, "Brazilian Literature and Citizenship: From Euclides da Cunha to Marcos Dias," *Luso-Brazilian Review* 38, no. 2 (Winter 2001): 11–27, argues that recognition of a "family resemblance" is the sign of Da Cunha's tentative acceptance of the *sertanejos* as citizens within a hierarchical Brazilian "family" of races.

21. Presumably Da Cunha read the French translation of *Der Rassenkampf*, Louis (*sic*) Gumplowicz, *La lutte des races: Recherches sociologiques*, trans. Charles Baye (Paris: Librairie Guillaumin, 1893), esp. 192, 227–29. Compare with Maria Alzira Brum Lemos, *O doutor e o jagunço: Ciência, mestiçagem e cultura em Os Sertões* (São Paulo: Arte & Ciência, 2000).

22. Gustave Le Bon, *Psychologie des foules*, 29th ed. (1st ed., 1895; Paris: Librairie Félix Alcan, 1921); Luiz Costa Lima, *Terra ignota: A construção de Os sertões* (Rio de Janeiro: Civilização Brasileira, 1997), 70, also detects the unacknowledged influence of Le Bon.

23. Susanna Barrows, *Distorting Mirrors: Visions of the Crowd in Late Nineteenth-Century France* (New Haven, Conn.: Yale University Press, 1981); Jaap van Ginneken, *Crowds, Psychology, and Politics, 1871–1899* (Cambridge: Cambridge University Press, 1992); Dain Borges, "'Puffy, Ugly, Slothful and Inert': Degeneration in Brazilian Social Thought, 1880–1940," *Journal of Latin American Studies* 25, no. 2 (1993): 235–56.

24. González Echevarría, *Myth*, points out the similarities between Antonio Conselheiro and the Argentine caudillo Facundo but neglects Moreira Cesar as a villainous political counterpart to Antonio Conselheiro.

25. Patrick Brantlinger, *Rule of Darkness: British Literature and Imperialism, 1830–1914* (Ithaca, N.Y.: Cornell University Press, 1988); Martin Green, *Dreams of Adventure, Deeds of Empire* (New York: Basic, 1979).

26. Joseph Conrad, *Heart of Darkness*, 3rd ed. (1st ed., 1899; New York: W. W. Norton, 1988).

27. Heriberto Frías, *Tomóchic: Novela histórica mexicana*, 5th ed. (Mexico: Editora Nacional, 1973); see Antonio Saborit, *Los doblados de Tomóchic: Un episodio de historia y literatura* (Mexico: Cal y Arena, 1994).

28. James Mooney, *The Ghost-Dance Religion and Wounded Knee* (New York: Dover, 1973), reprint of "The Ghost-Dance Religion and the Sioux Outbreak of 1890," in Smithsonian Institution, *Fourteenth Annual Report of the Bureau of Ethnology to the Smithsonian Institution, 1892–93*, part 2 (Washington, D.C.: Government Printing Office, 1896), 641–1136.

29. Antonio Conselheiro and Moreira Cesar may be world-historical doubles, twin Ahabs, but *Rebellion in the Backlands* has no Ishmael.

30. "Alguns se aprumavam, con altaneria incrível, no degrau inferior e último da nossa raça.... um orango...Era um animal. Não valia a pena interrogá-lo.... E viram transmudar-se o infeliz, apenas dados os primeiros passos para o suplício. Daquele arcabouço denegrido e repugnante, mal soerguidos nas longas pernas murchas, despontaram, repentinamente, linhas admiráveis—terrivelmente

esculturais—de uma plástica estupenda. Um primor de estatuária modelado em lama.... uma velha estátua de titã, soterrada havia quatro séculos e aflorando, denegrida e mutilada, naquela imensa ruinaria de Canudos. Era uma inversão de papéis. Uma antinomia vergonhosa." Da Cunha, *Os sertões*, 380.

31. In so describing the transformation, Da Cunha is not explaining it as an effect of crowd hypnotism, since Antonio Conselheiro dies before the end of the siege. However, his description is consistent with observations in the nineteenth-century sciences of mesmerism and hypnotism, which often stress the emergence of unimagined talents from hypnotized subjects. See Deborah Silberman, *Art Nouveau in Fin-de-Siècle France: Politics, Psychology, and Style* (Berkeley: University of California Press, 1989); Alan Gauld, *A History of Hypnotism* (Cambridge: Cambridge University Press, 1992); and John Cerullo, *The Secularization of the Soul: Psychical Research in Modern Britain* (Philadelphia: ISHI, 1982), on F. W. H. Meyers and "subliminal consciousness."

32. "Transmutações completas... desencadear das energias adormidas. O homem transfigura-se." Da Cunha, *Os sertões*, 81.

33. Morse, "Multiverse of Latin American Identity," argues that the emphasis on deterministic "forces" in naturalistic literature of the 1880s moved, through a series of dialectical steps, into the world of magical realism of the 1960s.

34. Antonio Candido may have been the first to observe this, but Nicolau Sevcenko, *Literatura como missão: Tensões sociais e criação cultural na Primeira República* (São Paulo: Brasiliense 1983), 201, makes the most of the difference between the weight of destiny in tragedy and the weight of determinist natural laws in *Rebellion in the Backlands* and notes the heavy load of Greek allusions in Da Cunha's journalism, 156n19, including a claim that he wrote by Thucydides's method, 221n51.

35. Presumably Da Cunha's source for allusions to the Titanomachy or Gigantomachy was Hesiod's *Theogony*, but it might also have included Ovid's *Metamorphoses* and compendia of mythology.

36. "Abaladas pelo cataclismo da guerra, as camadas superficiais de uma nacionalidade cindiam-se, pondo à luz os seus elementos profundos naqueles titãs resignados e estóicos." Da Cunha, *Os sertões*, 324.

37. The only unambiguous comparison of a soldier to a Titan is the heroic cavalry officer Wanderley, killed in a charge. Da Cunha, *Os sertões*, 310, compare with 24–25. There is an ambiguous title, *titãs contra moribundos*, in which "titan" appears at first to refer to the army but then turns out to refer to the apparently moribund *sertanejos*, who fight like titans. The third section of the book repeatedly counterpoises two terms—*fanatical* and *panic*—in order to discredit the army by comparing it to the *sertanejos*.

38. Da Cunha, *Os sertões*, 324.

39. Recent revisionist historians, examining writings from Canudos that were not available to Da Cunha, argue that Da Cunha misinterpreted the theology of Conselheiro, which was not exceptionally millenarian before the war began. Alexandre Otten, *Só Deus é grande: A mensagem religiosa de Antônio Conselheiro* (São Paulo: Edições Loyola, 1990).

40. Ernest Renan, *Marc-Aurèle et la fin du monde antique* (Paris: Calmann-Lévy, 1882), 345–46, argues that it was a miscalculation for the Roman state to try to fight

the Christians directly; rational education in primary schools, "un enseignement d'Etat rationaliste," would have been the better method.

41. The Transfiguration is mentioned in Matthew 17:1–6, Mark 9:1–8, Luke 9:28–36, II Peter 1:16–18, and John 1:14. The Greek gospels use a cognate of *metamorphosis*, the Latin Vulgate a cognate of *transfiguration*; see "Transfiguration," in *The Catholic Encyclopedia* (New York: Encyclopedia Press, 1913). See also Thomas Aquinas, *Summa Theologica*, part III, chap. 45, "Of Christ's Transfiguration."

42. Variants of *transfiguration, transformation, transmutation,* and *metamorphosis* appear dozens of times in *Os sertões*. In later works, Da Cunha continues to use the term *transfiguration*—with reference to irrigation works transfiguring the desert, in descriptions of statues and effigies transfiguring and coming to life, and in descriptions of the political transfiguration of a polity. González Echevarría, *Myth,* 135, correctly points out the strong presence of monstrous mutation in *Os sertões*—"the sertão is the blank page, without brilliance . . . in which all mutations are possible"— but does not take into consideration the uplifting mutations.

43. Both Mario Vargas Llosa, in *War of the End of the World,* and Robert M. Levine, in *Vale of Tears,* use metaphors of optical distortion to criticize Da Cunha's "science."

44. Obviously this recognition could be little more than a starting point in a Brazilian dialogue that would face all the dilemmas raised in Charles Taylor et al., *Multiculturalism: Examining the Politics of Recognition,* ed. Amy Gutmann (Princeton, N.J.: Princeton University Press, 1994).

45. Efraín Kristal, *Temptation of the Word: The Novels of Mario Vargas Llosa* (Nashville, Tenn.: Vanderbilt University Press, 1998), drawing on E. R. Dodds, *The Greeks and the Irrational* (Berkeley: University of California Press, 1951); compare with Sevcenko, *Literatura,* on free will and determinism in *Os sertões*.

3

࿎

Gilberto Freyre's Concept of Culture in *The Masters and the Slaves*

José Luiz Passos and Valéria Costa e Silva

Gilberto de Mello Freyre (1900–1987) was one of the most influential Brazilian sociologists of the first half of the twentieth century, largely because of his masterwork *The Masters and the Slaves* (*Casa-grande & senzala*, 1933). Freyre's retelling of Brazilian social history has shed light on the singularity of Brazilian culture and has shaped the way that Brazilian culture has been defined and redefined for the past seven decades.[1] In *The Masters and the Slaves*, Freyre distinguishes between purely racial and cultural relativist approaches to Brazilian social history and presents his own hypothesis about the meaning of Brazilian culture. However, the predominant way of assessing Freyre's contribution to an understanding of Brazilian culture is essentially misleading. This chapter argues for a theoretical reconsideration of Freyre's concept of culture. We intend to reveal some of the basic assumptions made in most debates connecting national identity to the interpretation of a particular culture and reassess Freyre's definition of *culture* in *The Masters and the Slaves*. Contrary to most contemporary reappraisals of his work, which predominantly follow biographical, ideological, or rhetorical criticism, this chapter follows a strictly analytical approach to the subject.

Some of the most important Brazilian paradigms for interpreting the development of Brazilian colonial society and national identity emerged between the 1920s and 1940s. In spite of the differences in perspectives and goals among Gilberto Freyre, Sérgio Buarque de Holanda, Caio Prado Júnior, and *modernistas* such as Mário and Oswald de Andrade, they all shared a tendency for displacing the nineteenth-century deterministic notion of race as the key concept for social analysis and aesthetic production.[2]

Much of today's cultural criticism and history of Brazilian social thought have been devoted to the reconsideration of that shift.[3] A common view among critics is that, within classical social theories, the concepts of culture and class have unjustly displaced that of race. This is a curious inversion of what took place at the beginning of the twentieth century, when social scientists started to realize that the notion of race had subsumed the notion of culture. It was precisely with Gilberto Freyre that the concept of race lost the central place that it had held for Brazilian social theorists of the late nineteenth and the early twentieth century, such as Sílvio Romero and Oliveira Vianna.[4]

At the end of the nineteenth century a period of debate in Brazil revolved around the ideas of nation and nationality. The modernization process, the abolition of slavery (1888), and the proclamation of the republic (1889) stimulated the discussion of the challenges involved in the construction of a "modern" and "civilized" national identity. Before Gilberto Freyre, these discussions focused on questions of race and environment and were characterized by a fundamental pessimism due to the influences of thinkers such as Gobineau, Agassiz, and Buffon upon Brazilian intellectuals. Social Darwinism and Spencerian theories of evolution were also firmly established presuppositions, which almost unquestionably had an influence on any reflections about Brazil. Discussed in this context were the supposedly dangerous and deleterious effects of a tropical environment and miscegenation on Brazilian society and, more specifically, the effects of the African influx on Brazilian blood. The question that presented itself was, How does a nation manage these liabilities to create a reasonably modern and civilized society? The most optimistic perspectives on the future of Brazil aligned themselves with the "theory of whitening" and hoped that time would dilute the harmful effects of miscegenation.[5] In 1922 the modernists proposed the first consistent criticism of the deterministic paradigm, but it was in 1933 that Freyre's *The Masters and the Slaves* modified the terms of discussion on a systematic and scientific level. His essay offered a new conceptual, theoretical, and methodological context in which the issues of national identity could be reconsidered and new answers elaborated. To elucidate how Brazilian culture came into being, Freyre adopted Franz Boas's sharper distinction between race and culture.

RACE AND CULTURE

The traditional understanding of culture as the totality of material and symbolic products of human interaction has long lost its pertinence among social scientists, though it continues to influence nonspecialized uses of the word.[6] "Culture" is an unsettling concept. If a given culture is defined in terms of its collective symbolic and material products, an encyclopedic dictionary of its language should be enough to account for what such a culture is. However, this is clearly not the case. The definition of a culture is not equivalent to the mere description of its products and the way they relate to each other, for the concept of culture cannot be made clear through ostensive definition.[7] In other words, if we point to an object and say, "This is Brazilian and so are things like it," we have not yet said anything meaningful about what "Brazilian culture" is, for "an ostensive definition can be variously interpreted in *every* case."[8] For many years the explanation of cultural facts and identity was given in terms of what one could call an essentialist argument; the reason given to explain what was distinctive about a specific human fact—including bodily traits, objects, symbols, values, beliefs, and so forth—was the biological concept of race.

In *Anthropology and Modern Life*, originally published in 1929, Franz Boas raises a logical challenge to the then widely accepted definition of race as an immanently descriptive concept. Boas contends that race cannot be inferred from the biophysical description of an individual nor, once known, can it account for the individual's anthropological identity. For instance, if we consider two racially distinct populations, say southern Brazilians and midwestern North Americans—then it is likely that we can find two individuals, one taken from each group, who share almost identical physiological traits, such as stature, color of skin, type of hair, and so forth. Consequently, if race is taken as the result of phenotypic descriptions, then both the Brazilian and the American can identify as members of the same race. Boas concludes that even near-identical similarity of biophysical characteristics is not an adequate criterion for racial identification and that race is a typical concept that can be applied successfully only to groups as an abstraction of certain empirical and genealogical traits of a given community. For Boas, the anthropological study of individuals is relevant insofar as the individual is a "member of a racial or a social group."[9] Thus the individual represents the group when acting out, and acting upon, a set of specific biophysical dispositions, social functions, and a body of knowledge and beliefs shared with other members of the group. In this sense, Boasian anthropology takes the human being to be the convergence of ancestry and external social and biological conditions, and the individual is seen solely as an empirical instance of the primary object of anthropology: the group. This perspective is the most important underlying assumption of Gilberto Freyre's *The Masters and the Slaves*.[10]

The extent of Freyre's personal contact with Boas is debatable. During his studies in Texas and New York, Freyre certainly had contact with the new Anglo-American school of ethnography, from which he acquired some of the most significant theoretical tools of his career. More specifically, what Freyre took seriously from Boas were his conclusions of 1929: that "race" is a type-concept, an abstraction of phenotypic traits, which does not scientifically support any notion of purity or superiority;[11] that the notion of "racial heredity" is meaningless and should be substituted for "heredity in family lines," which emphasizes the social aspect of the transmission of traits within a given stable community;[12] that general mental and bodily dispositions are affected by social occupations—that is, by the group's interaction with its environment—and that these traits are transmissible from one generation into the next;[13] that the formation of racial groups and race consciousness is the product of political and social interaction and not the necessary consequence of racial descent;[14] that the idea of nationality does not derive from blood ties or linguistic unity but rather as a result of cultural cooperation;[15] and, finally, that "the specific *forms* of our actions are culturally determined."[16]

Although Boas explicitly draws these conclusions in only *Anthropology and Modern Life*, they represent the culmination of his efforts to displace the notion of racial heredity and to rule out a purely biological hypothesis for explaining human behavior. In its place, culture becomes the only concept that can ground a more realistic and humanistic interpretation of the motives behind the diverse manifestations of social interaction. Boas understood culture as the specific way through which a group of people meets the challenge of its environment by means of collective agency. Hence, the study of a given culture was the attempt to understand how tools, behaviors, and values emerge from the community's cooperative action and evolve into stabilized habits or, rather, into a particular culture. This conclusion seems to have been Freyre's aim in *The Masters and the Slaves*.

FREYRE'S HYPOTHESES

What Freyre puts forth in *The Masters and the Slaves* is not a theory of Brazilian national or cultural identity but a hypothesis about the origins and the development of the northeast Brazilian patriarchal family. His book is a study in historical sociology. Freyre's aim is to show how a specific type of family organization with a system of producing economic and domestic goods and values can partially account for the basic disposition of Brazilian culture. In other words, *The Masters and the Slaves* is an attempt to construct a cultural genealogy, from the initial encounter and subsequent fusion of the three main sociohistorical groups to their shaping of what Freyre calls modern Brazilian civilization.

Had *The Masters and the Slaves* been published in the United States or in England, it would most certainly have been criticized for precisely what earned it praise in Brazil: the novelty of its style, which combined lexical and syntactical informality with a strong sense of authorial presence, and a voluminous set of unorthodox research sources. In this respect, Freyre cannot be regarded as a typical cultural relativist; his methods are too unconventional and eclectic when compared, for instance, to the logical precision of Boas's argumentation.

The introduction to the first edition offers a detailed overview of what is to come: an idiosyncratic account of the Brazilian colonial past presented from Freyre's new perspective on miscegenation. Though *The Masters and the Slaves* is a strongly confessional work and worthy of examination based solely on this merit, exclusive attention to this aspect would overshadow its broader aim: a revision of Brazilian social history. What such a project owes to Boas is presented explicitly from the start:

> The scholarly figure of Professor Boas is the one that to this day makes the deepest impression upon me. I became acquainted with him when I first went to Columbia. . . . It was as if everything was dependent upon me and those of my generation, upon the manner in which we succeeded in solving ageold questions. And of all the problems confronting Brazil there was none that gave me so much anxiety as that of miscegenation. Once upon a time, after three straight years of absence from my country, I caught sight of a group of Brazilian seaman—mulattoes and *cafusos*—crossing Brooklyn Bridge. I no longer remember whether they were from São Paulo or from Minas, but I know that they impressed me as being the caricatures of men, and there came to mind a phrase from a book on Brazil written by an American traveler: "the fearfully mongrel aspect of the population." That was the sort of thing to which miscegenation led. I ought to have had someone to tell me then what Roquette Pinto had told the Aryanizers of the Brazilian Eugenics Congress in 1929: that these individuals whom I looked upon as representative of Brazil were not simply mulattoes or *cafusos* but *sickly* ones.
>
> It was my studies in anthropology under the direction of Professor Boas that first revealed to me the Negro and the mulatto for what they are—with the effects of environment or cultural experience separated from racial characteristics. I learned to regard as fundamental the difference between *race* and *culture*, to discriminate between the effects of purely genetic relationships and those resulting from social influences, the cultural heritage and the milieu. It is upon this criterion of the basic differentiation between race and culture that the entire plan of this essay rests, as well as upon the distinction to be made between racial and family heredity.[17]

Freyre has masterfully dramatized the presentation of his main motivation (the issue of miscegenation) and his method (the anthropological distinction between race and culture) by means of a personal anecdote. A recurrent strategy in *The Masters and the Slaves* is Freyre's resorting to a self-referential mode in order to legitimize data, themes, and perspectives. In the passage, the move encompassed by Freyre's narrative is to present the author as possibly resembling the reader's own position with regard to the eugenic view of miscegenation; to suggest the limitation of the author's former stance as a misapprehension of the phenomena; and, finally, to offer a method through which both author and reader can properly overcome their mistakes. In other words, what had appealed to the senses of the young Freyre in his vision of the Brazilian sailors as being representative of Brazil is the fact that they embodied the consequences of racial degeneration. However, as the author of *The Masters and the Slaves*, Freyre argues precisely that the reader should take those sailors only as representatives of the specific social conditions of their racial groups. Thus, Boas is present between the episode and the 1933 preface, and with his aid Freyre has learned to distinguish the causes for potential degeneration among organically determined dispositions, environmental influences, and the "heredity in family lines." It is clear from the start that Freyre's arguments work through a complex set of interwoven hypotheses.

The first hypothesis to stand out is that of the interpenetration of cultures and ethnicities—the central characteristic of Brazilian social organization—whose occurrence in Brazil was due in part to the scarcity of white women as well as to the Portuguese colonists' ethnic and cultural disposition toward miscegenation.[18] With this assertion, Freyre uses the Portuguese colonists' past to develop the argument—actually a subhypothesis of the first hypothesis—that the Portuguese as a people are characterized by hybridity and plasticity as a result of their "vague, indefinite" position between Europe and Africa.[19] This indefinition, according to the author, derives from the cultural and racial composition of the Portuguese people, whose dispositions toward mobility, interbreeding, and acclimation guaranteed the success of their colonizing the tropics. Throughout his discussion of hybridity, Freyre articulates its historical, racial, and cultural dimensions. Although cognizant of the phenomenon of mixed races, he insists on distinguishing it from cultural miscegenation and eventually attributes much more explicatory importance to culture than to race in the formation of the Portuguese character. Consider his dramatic description of the African influence over European culture: "the hot and oleous air of Africa mitigating the Germanic harshness of institutions and cultural forms, corrupting the doctrinal and moral rigidity of the medieval Church, drawing the bones from Christianity, feudalism, Gothic architecture, canonic discipline, Visigoth law, the Latin tongue, and the very character of the people."[20]

However, his argument strays onto dangerous ground when he refers to the Portuguese character, even speculating about certain psychological traits belonging to the Portuguese, to Jews, and to Moors. We know that Freyre undeniably associates races with specific psychological traits, but how can we explain his using this notion of character? Certainly not in an essentialist way. When he speaks of character, he is not referring to essential qualities inherent to specific races but rather to psychological, physical, and cultural standards and characteristics that are all historically bound. Through the specific relationships established between people, physical environments, and modes of production, these standards develop and become associated with certain populations, becoming fixed hereditary traits that are maintained through the passage of time and are transmitted from generation to generation by what Boas himself had called heredity along family lines. In other words, Freyre is apparently speaking of psychic dispositions resulting from certain social conditions repeated over the passage of time and how such dispositions can become characteristics acquired by the group and, in that sense, be deemed transmissible. It appears to be the same argument, of neo-Lamarckian basis, as that identified by Ricardo Benzaquen de Araújo as one central in *The Masters and the Slaves*.[21] This flexible notion of character allows Freyre to claim that the "rigid" Portuguese are transformed; they are "softened" into something different after coming into contact with Moors, with Jews, and then are transformed again in the Brazilian colony into something still different after interpenetration with Africans and indigenous people. Moreover, at the moment of Brazilian colonization, the Portuguese character was plastic. Freyre understood this indefinition as a sociohistorical tendency toward the incorporation of varied ethnic elements. This indefinition of the Portuguese character—vague and imprecise—is important insofar as it allows the reunion of contrasts. In this sense, racial and cultural miscegenation would have made the colonization of a tropical environment quite successful. With this argument, Freyre directly opposes geographic determinism, which would condemn any mixed tropical civilization to backwardness. For him, Portuguese plasticity allowed rapid incorporation and adaptation of African and indigenous cultures, which resulted in new and efficient modes of relating to the tropical environment. Here we arrive at a second central hypothesis of *The Masters and the Slaves*: that the successful adaptation of the Portuguese to the Brazilian environment, through miscegenation, produced the most stable tropical civilization in modern history.

In this interpretive scheme, where plasticity is a trait of Portuguese character, we should consider that the aforementioned scarcity of white women at the beginning of colonization was partially responsible for the formation of the early racially and culturally hybrid Brazilian populations. This process was further developed with the introduction of African slaves to Brazil. For Freyre, the profound and ample process of miscegenation would become the fundamental marker and the potentiality of Brazilian society and culture. This point brings us to the third of the central hypotheses of *The Masters and the Slaves*. Freyre appears to conclude that miscegenation favored the process of social democratization in Brazil in the sense that it rendered more flexible what could have been a society of rigidly polarized social extremes:

> The scarcity of white women created zones of fraternization between conquerors and conquered, between masters and slaves. While these relations between white men and colored women did not cease to be those of "superiors" with "inferiors," and the majority of cases those of disillusioned and sadistic gentlemen with passive slave girls, they were mitigated by the need that was felt by many colonists of founding a family under such circumstances and upon such a basis as this.[22]

It is important to note that in using the expression "social democratization," Freyre does not refer to the modern political idea of democracy but to democracy in cultural terms. This perspective sets him in direct opposition to Sérgio Buarque de Holanda, as discussed later. For now we should keep in mind that when Freyre speaks of social democratization (as a synonym for cultural contribution), he is conscious that unbalanced power relations are part of Brazilian social reality. If Freyre speaks of "social effects of miscegenation," he also insists on the fact that, from the beginning, the relationships between Portuguese, indigenous people, and Africans were conditioned by the violent system of economic production.[23] Here we find his fourth hypothesis: the formation and the importance of patriarchy as a social system based on a landholding monoculture slavocracy, which constitutes the very structure of colonial Brazilian society.

Freyre analyzes Brazilian patriarchy as a system of social relationships based on the sugarcane monoculture. He is concerned with the relationships of production in and of themselves—conveyed through forms of interaction and through man's acting upon his environment—and with the forms of sociability associated with this productive system. The complex of the Big House (*casa-grande*) and its slave quarters (*senzalas*), in his interpretation, corresponds to an entire social, economic, and political system characteristic of the patriarchy in Brazil. Considering the effects of such a system of production on Brazilian social formation, Freyre incorporates Marxist theory as yet another analytic tool among the many in his varied and eclectic repertoire.[24] In a manner unusual for Brazilian thought at that time, Freyre transfers from race to systems of production the explanation for a series of phenomena thought at that time to be ills inherent to people of mixed race and to the supposedly racially inferior. In his opinion, the problems associated with Africans should be associated with the social condition of slavery; here, he deepens the idea put forth by Joaquim Nabuco in *Abolitionism* (1883), applying it to social analysis. Freyre makes it clear that the slave-owning, landowning, single-crop culture is not only sterilizing but corrupting for masters and slaves and is responsible for the chronic malnutrition and diseased appearance of many Brazilian populations.

Freyre contends that unfavorable social and economic conditions have harmful effects on population and that such conditions are capable of provoking changes in the biological constitution of these populations, which can become transmissible characteristics if the adverse conditions persist over time. Again, it is the same neo-Lamarckian principle pointed out by Araújo and to which Freyre refers textually. In a direct dialogue with the most recent studies on the subject—especially those by Boas involving immigrant populations who suffered phenotypic changes related to their new, material lives—Freyre seeks out arguments destined to limit or minimize racialist assertions:

> Studies in eugenics and cacogenics are still in a state of flux, and much of what is supposed to be the result of hereditary characteristics or tares ought rather to be ascribed to the persistence for generations of economic and social conditions favorable or unfavorable to human development.[25]

Note how Freyre alludes to Marxist theory and how the argument operates analytically in *The Masters and the Slaves* to restrict the explicative capacity of the concept of race. Having proved the organically deleterious consequences of the landowning, single-crop slavocracy, Freyre returns to its negative social and economic effects, pointing out the asymmetries of power that mark Brazilian social organization as well as effects such as the extreme eroticization of Brazilian society (as a social perversion of sexual nature) or the authoritarianism and tyranny that masters and plantation overseers had over slaves, women, and children.

Despite the assertions of some critics, Freyre neither ignores nor denies the existence of conflict or the extreme social differences in Brazil. Quite to the contrary, as different revisionists of Freyre's contribution have recently pointed out, *The Masters and the Slaves* at many points makes explicit the extremes of cruelty produced by the patriarchal Brazilian system.[26] What it does not do, as suggested here, is extend its criticism to the perverse implications of the system, with its essential antidemocratic effects to Brazilian political organization. In fact, this aspect can be elaborated as a consistent critique of *The Masters and the Slaves*, which would set it and Freyre in direct opposition to some of his contemporaries, notably, Sérgio Buarque de Holanda.

Freyre directs his attention to other consequences of the phenomenon studied by Holanda—for example, the association between miscegenation and patriarchy in Brazil. His emphasis on this last aspect is what permits Freyre to frame social democratization in cultural terms: as processes of cultural interpenetration that counteracted the social, political, and economic distances. However, immediately following the publication of Holanda's study, *The Roots of Brazil* (1936), the Freyrean interpretation ages sociologically, and its concept of cultural democracy becomes problematic. Despite identifying patriarchy as a fundamental phenomenon in the development of Brazilian social life, Freyre does not appear to concern himself with the problem of the political rationalization of agency within this social system; for Freyre a politically universal concept of the individual is not an issue as it is for Holanda. The relationship between history and political agents dissolves in *The Masters and the Slaves* into the question of cultural fusion. Because Freyre underestimates the treatment of the individual as a political actor, he can then construct an optimistic interpretation of Brazil. In this sense, the impossibility of an all-inclusive and accomplished democracy in the Brazilian public sphere is substituted in *The Masters and the Slaves* for an analysis of the historical and cultural function of the patriarchal family in the configuration of Brazilian nationality. For Freyre, the important fact is that, in the patriarchal formation of Brazil, the whites had to settle for native Brazilians and Africans, albeit violently, as a strategy of colonization, which caused a specific historical result whose consequences can be felt in the organization of Brazilian culture today. Thus, according to Freyre, Brazil had an agrarian, slave-owning society but one hybrid from inception—as opposed to North America, which had a pattern of racial and cultural mixture.

Considering the pros and cons, one can say that the important contribution made by the Freyrean interpretive scheme is to point out that, despite the enormous gap between the extremes of Brazilian society, the profound ethnic and cultural miscegenation guaranteed that the formation of Brazil was not merely a transposition of a European civilization to the tropics. Quite the opposite. According to Freyre's view, Brazil, in a way similar to the social formation of Portugal, was characterized by an often violent equilibrium of antagonistic forces in which many elements acted to create conditions of fraternization between distinct cultures: ethnic miscegenation, lyrical Christianity, a relatively tolerant morality, and so forth. Even the very geographical space, he argues, did not create any serious obstacle to territorial unity. Brazilian society, then, would be marked by an interpenetration of tendencies that created a new, hybrid phenomenon, in opposition to the idea of synthesis. Freyre's analysis of the Portuguese language in Brazil, quoting from João Ribeiro in regard to pronoun usage, is an interesting example of his overoptimistic argument:

> Brazilian Portuguese, linking the Big Houses to the slave quarters, the slaves to their masters, the slave girls to the young masters, became enriched with a variety of antagonisms that is lacking to the language as spoken in Europe. One example, and one of the most expressive, that occurs to me is in connection with pronouns. We have in Brazil two ways of placing them, where the Portuguese admits only one—the "stern and imperative mode": *diga-me,*

faça-me, espere-me. Without condemning the Portuguese usage, we have created a new one, entirely new and characteristically Brazilian: *me diga, me faça, me espere*. A mild and pleasing way of phrasing a request. And we make use of both ways.... The strength or, better, the potentiality of Brazilian culture appears to me to lie wholly in a wealth of balanced antagonisms: and the case of pronouns may well serve as an example.... We are two fraternizing halves that are mutually enriched with diverse values and experiences; and when we round ourselves out into a whole, it will not be with the sacrifice of one element to the other.[27]

Here we close the circuit of the main interrelated elements that, according to Élide Rugai Bastos, are utilized by Freyre to interpret Brazilian society: the patriarchy, the interpenetration of ethnicities and cultures, and the tropical environment.[28] These elements are articulated in the interrelated hypotheses that we have attempted to explore here, and they can be summarized as follows: the hybrid Portuguese past guarantees a plastic character, which allows the success of colonization in the tropics; this disposition toward plasticity, along with the scarcity of white women, caused a widespread racial and cultural miscegenation among Europeans, Africans, and indigenous people, which would become the fundamental characteristic of Brazilian society; this process of miscegenation caused a specific kind of "social democratization," bringing extremes closer together and forming a hybrid culture; miscegenation was the principal mechanism of this patriarchal, land-owning, slave-owning, single-crop system, as well as the source of its most typical problems and detriments (malnutrition, authoritarianism, sadomasochistic eroticization, etc.); and finally, a flexible Catholicism functioned as a national cement, contributing to the process of hybridization of Brazilian culture.

The Masters and the Slaves reaches the end of its more than six hundred pages without presenting a single substantive definition of Brazilian character, as discussed later; and even when Freyre does refer to the formation of nationality, he does so as an essentially historical phenomenon: nationality as military, political, economic, social, and cultural processes, to which certain psychological traits, dispositions, and potentialities are associated.

CRITICISMS OF FREYRE

Although enthusiastically received upon publication, *The Masters and the Slaves* was vilified in the 1960s for its idyllic vision of slavery and the colonial past, which supposedly culminated in the idea of racial democracy.[29] Recently in Brazil, there has been a widespread reconsideration of Freyre's contribution to Brazilian social thought. However, texts that became classics of Freyrean criticism after the 1960s, such as *The Brazilian National Character* (1969) by Dante Moreira Leite, *Ideology of Brazilian Culture* (1977) by Carlos Guilherme Mota, and *Brazilian Culture and National Identity* (1985) by Renato Ortiz, are examples of the most lasting and penetrating—if often unfair—criticisms of Freyre's canon. The discrediting of Freyrean interpretation in these cases generally presents the following arguments. First, *The Masters and the Slaves* has great historical value because it helped to undermine the geographic and racial determinisms that were dominant at the time, although it never succeeded in completely overcoming racial determinism; in this sense, Freyre's book misues Boas, especially when it establishes connections between race and psychological traits.[30] Second, the book is imprecise and impressionistic, which makes its status as a scientific work questionable; therefore, it is essentially an essay that has survived because of its stylistic or literary value rather than its interpretative importance.[31] Third, the ideological perspective of *The Masters and the Slaves* is set from the porch of the Big House because, through the valorization of miscegenation, it constructs a discourse on national identity without space for social contradictions or racial conflict, creating the idea that Brazil lives a serene racial democracy.[32] Such arguments, pertinent in some cases but often based on a biased reading of the work, focus on rhetorical or political assessments of Freyre's position in an attempt to undermine the importance of *The Masters and the Slaves* to the development of Brazilian social thought.

The first argument is of particular interest to us in that it concerns the inappropriate or partial appropriation of Boas's cultural relativism. The thesis is that Freyre cannot free himself from the concept of race as Boas does. In this sense, Leite points out that "Gilberto Freyre speaks of qualities 'conditioned' by race, or says that race can confer 'dispositions'—expressions that would probably not be employed by Boas."[33] Furthermore, Mota puts forth that, whereas Boas privileges the social environment as a basic fact for the study of social behavior and "merely does not dismiss the possibility of the existence of psychological differences between the races," Freyre bases his studies from this latter perspective.[34]

Works such as those by Leite, Mota, and Ortiz are recurrent references in the criticism of Freyre. More recently, a text by Luiz Costa Lima restructures this type of reading, drawing on a much more sophisticated analysis than the preceding ones.[35] A counterpoint to this line of criticism, predominant in Brazilian social sciences until recently, is that of Ricardo Benzaquen de Araújo.[36] In this section, we briefly examine the confrontation between what we understand to be the two most accurate and exhaustive criticisms of Freyre's work.

Lima's central argument is that Freyre causes a rift between Brazilian social thought and Enlightenment's rationalism, connecting Brazilian social thought to German historicism through Franz Boas. According to Lima, however, Boas subordinates race and environment to culture, whereas Freyre does not succeed in overcoming them; rather, he only succeeds in distinguishing the effects of race from those of culture. In brief, pointing out the "extreme limitation of his reception of Boas," Lima contends that "in Freyre, the cultural element cannot substitute the old prejudice that had privileged race without providing it with a way of becoming more visible."[37] The weight that Freyre attributes to the concept of race distances him from Boas's truly cultural relativist approach. Lima criticizes the Freyrean indefinition of the range of race, environment, and culture. He concludes that, in a parallel way, Freyre's emphasis on culture conceals the socioeconomic conditioning in Brazilian social development when, in fact, "the plasticity present in our formation does not correct the asymmetry of power."[38]

In another recently published essay, Lima reiterates and extends his criticism to Freyre's *The Mansion and the Shanties* (1936), suggesting that the author's contribution was merely to combat the monocausalism attributed to race, placing it as a factor in competition with the notion of culture.[39] He argues that Freyre could have reached the same interpretation as did Sérgio Buarque de Holanda—who took Brazilian personalism as a remnant from the patriarchal system—if "in a line opposite from that of his alleged master Boas, [Freyre] hadn't chosen to maintain the usage of a biological concept of race." In conclusion, according to Lima, Freyre ambiguously rejects racial determinism while keeping "a biological conceptualization of the races."[40]

Araújo's book is the first systematic formulation of a counterpoint to the criticism outlined here. He acknowledges that raciological vocabulary permeates Freyre's argument, but he characterizes *The Masters and the Slaves* as an interpretation attentive to the singular and hybrid articulation of distinct traditions that Freyre encountered in Brazilian culture. Araújo admits that Freyre's use of the terms *race* and *culture* in *The Masters and the Slaves* is imprecise, but he argues that the concept of environment resolves such imprecision as an analytical problem by functioning as an intermediary between the concepts of race and culture, relativizing them, modifying their more frequent meanings, and making them relatively compatible with each other. This resolution is possible only because

Gilberto [Freyre] works with a neo-Lamarckian definition of race, that is, a definition that, basing itself on the demonstrated aptitude of human beings to adapt to the most varied environmental conditions, emphasizes above all else their capacity to incorporate, transmit and inherit the characteristics acquired in their—varied, discrete and localized—interactions with the physical environment.[41]

Araújo emphasizes Freyre's choice of syncretism, rather than synthesis, in his interpretation of Brazilian culture—in the specific sense that something from each original element is maintained in the hybrid forms. He reminds us that hybridism, which comes from *hybris*, conveys the idea of excess, which implies a necessarily unstable result. Freyrean miscegenation corresponds to this hybridization, this interpenetration of differences, while being characterized by ambiguity and indefinition. Finally, Araújo emphasizes that Freyre does not operate with an ordinary concept of culture that merely implies order and identity. His concept of culture "tolerates an almost surprising degree of differentiation and disorder, or better, of anarchy, in the very matrix of social life."[42] A stable whole cannot exist, because the model presupposes a break in the relationship between the parts and the whole. The whole "ends up being viewed much more as an eventual possibility than as a pre-existing and obligatory form of the idea of society." The important fact is that culture tends toward plasticity, hybridization, and the balance of antagonistic forces.[43]

Araújo concludes that the discomfort that many feel about Freyre's indefinition lies in its great richness and complexity, for it corresponds to a refusal to compromise with the idea of totality. In the following section, we examine the arguments set forth by Araújo, returning to the discussion of Freyre's notion of culture and his connection with the tradition of the German thought via Franz Boas and Georg Simmel.

THE LOGIC OF CULTURE

Perhaps the mistaken criticism that considers Freyre a bad disciple of Boas is due less to a biased reading of Freyre than to an inattentive reading of Boas himself and to the lack of perspective about the development of anthropological theory. A careful reading of Boas reveals that he did not definitively discard the idea of race but only restricted it to the spectrum of phenomena that could be explained exclusively by the race factor—always emphasizing its interdependence with environment, culture, production technique, and so on—to such an extent that the concept of race, initially quite ample, became progressively limited as the concept of culture gradually gained its modern anthropological meaning.

According to George W. Stocking Jr., Boas is a transition thinker, and it is a mistake to suppose that his shift from racial to cultural explanation happened at once or that it went unchallenged. Boas made a gradual transition—making advances and retreats—from a singular, absolutist conception of culture to a plural, relativist one as he restricted the analytic capacity of the concept of race.[44] He eventually stopped referring to the singular *culture* as a synonym for civilization in favor of the plural *cultures*. In fact, Stocking's research shows that, before 1900, the term *culture* referred solely to the accumulation of manifestations of human creativity, which allowed researchers of human societies to make distinctions between degrees of culture in the same way that they distinguished between degrees of civilization, frequently exchanging one for the other. *Culture* in its pluralistic and open sense appears systematically in only the first generation of Boas's students, around 1910, as part of the perspective that regarded all human beings as being cultivated or cultured in some way.[45]

This commentary on Boas is intended to elucidate certain aspects of Freyre's work. Once the genealogy of Boas's thought and the possibilities and limits within which his concept of culture operates are understood, it seems clear that Freyre does not distance himself very much from his master. A good part of Boas's efforts vis-à-vis the heritage of German Romanticism consists of defining *"the genius of a people* in other terms than racial heredity. [Boas's] answer, ultimately, was the anthropological idea of culture."[46] Although Boas does not empirically explore the concept of nature, this notion is always on the horizon as he works, and what we want to suggest here is that Freyre operates with this same perspective when he uses the concept of Brazilian culture. Similarly, Freyre may also be taken as a transition thinker in the context of Brazilian social thought, and in this sense he is marked by a sense of ambivalence analogous to that which characterized Boas.

Thus, the work's most problematic aspect is not in the permanence of the concept of race—whose analytic power is extremely relativized and constrained by the cultural, economic, and historical components—but rather in Freyre's ambivalence toward the evolutionist paradigm. In fact, *The Masters and the Slaves* imprecisely uses the terms *race* and *culture* in that Freyre exchanges one for the other in many passages; nevertheless, the conflation of terms does not imply a conflation of concepts, and it does not compromise the book's interpretive scheme. In other words, the interchangeability of the terms does not eliminate the fact that Freyre always distinguishes between genetic and cultural phenomena, using the latter as the central analytic concept, albeit directly articulated to genetic, historical, and economic conditionings. The various modes of cooperative interaction that human beings establish with their environments are found and explained in terms of these conditionings. Freyre maintains race as an important factor, as a sort of substrate with specific yet malleable and adaptable potentialities such that in themselves they explain almost no social phenomenon. However, his argument becomes seriously problematic in his use of an evolutionist method, which allows him to awkwardly refer to "advanced" and "backward" cultures and, more significant, to use this differentiation to interpret the development of Brazilian culture. For example, it is this scheme that makes the chapter on the indigenous contributions quite misleading. In it, Freyre makes extensive reference to the contributions of material indigenous culture, but he is clearly using an evolutionist perspective of the relationship between Portuguese and native Brazilian cultures, with the latter characterized as a "green" culture, yet to be developed. Interestingly, Freyre argues exhaustively against a differentiation between superior and inferior races, resorting to the most recent sources and studies of the time all the while taking the concept of cultural evolutionism as a fact and as an analytical tool. Significantly, when Freyre mentions that the backward race was degraded by contact with the advanced one, he is referring to the notion of culture. Such is a clear example of his imprecise terminology.

Freyre oscillates between the singular and plural concept of culture. At one point, he speaks of indigenous culture as being backward and contends that the African came from a "stage of culture" that was more advanced than that of the native Brazilian because it was already agricultural. He goes on to refer to areas and complexes (systems) of culture—those of the tortoise, cassava, cashew, hammock—in another attempt to bring cultural phenomena together through diffusionism. Finally, he speaks of cultures in the most modern sense of the word, showing a sharp perception for the implications of unequal power relations on the cultural dynamic. For example, Freyre argues that the Jesuit missionaries were the great destroyers of non-European cultures, referring to the unequal clash between antagonistic cultures and to the "cultural earthquakes...on the part of oppressed cultures bursting forth in order not to die of suffocation."[47] Only a complex notion of culture would allow Freyre to conclude that "primitive culture," as a component of Brazilian culture, is not restricted to "indigestible lumps," that it is not a collection of "archaisms" or "ethnographic curiosities" but that it "makes itself felt in the living, useful, active, and not merely, picturesque presence of elements that have a creative effect upon the national development."[48] It is precisely this plural concept of culture that makes Freyre's interpretation interesting and useful because it is capable of dealing with the subtleties and complexities of Brazilian culture that would otherwise become crystallized and fixed in essentialist concepts, such as those put forth by the racially based concepts of identity still present when his book was published.

To conclude our analysis of Gilberto Freyre's concept of culture, we propose an approximation between Georg Simmel and Freyre or, rather, a possible genealogy of the influence of Simmel's thought on *The Masters and the Slaves*. As Sebastião Vila Nova suggests, Simmel may not ever be textually cited in *The Masters and the Slaves*, but the German sociologist permeates the entire book.[49] Furthermore, if we return to the diary kept by the young Freyre and other texts that allow the reconstruction of his intellectual path leading to *The Masters and the Slaves*, we see what an impression Simmel made on Freyre as a young scholar and how much he wished he could have read Simmel in the original German.[50] The connection between Freyre and Simmel deserves detailed examination, and in the following we suggest a new reading of Freyre that takes these influences into consideration.

When Freyre speaks of Brazilian culture, he never speaks of a substance, a specific, unified, or permanent essence, as if one could discover such a thing and reveal it to the world in a book. Freyre seems to be adopting the concept of culture in Simmel's terms, which incidentally is a conception similar to Boas's, thereby revealing a connection between the three and the German romantic tradition. Culture is understood simultaneously as a subjective and an objective reality, as a collection of existing facts that orient or condition social forms and behaviors but which always need to be updated and cultivated—and through this very process, culture incorporates new elements that transform those already present. The image of a coral reef suggests this double process in that crystallized and objectified cultural forms feed other emerging cultural phenomena and behaviors, which are processed through social life while adhering to their preexisting forms—all in accordance with Simmel's distinction between objective and subjective culture.

Also of interest is Simmel's influence on Freyre from a methodological perspective, which brings us to Freyre's emphasis on day-to-day interactions where social reality is continuously negotiated. One of Simmel's basic presuppositions is that social life takes place through the interactions between individuals, that society exists when individuals cooperate as a group to realize their expectations. Therefore, according to Simmel, the object of sociology should be these interactions, these forms of sociability. They should be examined in relation to the specific times and places where they occur, as well as in relation to the historical development of specific groups. Simmel also considers relevant the understanding of sociability as a psychological phenomenon. In other words, Simmel may have heavily influenced Freyre's "sociology of the everyday," and the connection between the Brazilian author and the American school of sociology, as widely noted, clearly reveals its roots in the German thought.

Finally, remember that Simmel's important and suggestive text on conflict as a fundamental part of social reality was translated and published in the United States as early as 1908. Perhaps the parallel readings of this text and *The Masters and the Slaves* can help us to reexamine the relationships between masters and slaves. One of the central arguments in the criticisms of *The Masters and the Slaves* is that the author masks or ignores racial conflict. Even Élide Rugai Bastos, after enumerating a series of Freyre's analytical and methodological innovations, concludes that he is an "organic intellectual from the dominant sectors of the agro-industrial block," directly alluding to what she understands to be a convenience of Freyrean discourse in the context of a new arrangement of political and social forces in Brazil at the time immediately following the 1930 revolution. Bastos criticizes the fact that Freyre constructs the idea of a racial democracy by making a direct connection between miscegenation and democratization (a supposedly automatic passage between a biological fact and a political fact). According to Bastos, there is in *The Masters and the Slaves* a vision of social conflict marked by balance where the antagonisms disappear in the everyday life of the patriarchal family: "to analyze the national ethos as the sum of races, regions, cultures, and social groups, is to destroy the possibility of perceiving the social as contradictory, where domination reinforces itself exactly because it is exercised over diversity."[51]

Bastos is correct in her perception of conflict's place in *The Masters and the Slaves*. She is exactly right in her assertion that conflict functions as a sort of balance that the day-to-day resolves, serving to eliminate tensions that would, at their maximum, cause the social system to collapse. The problem is that she extends this observation to the contention that Freyre eliminates "the possibility of imagining the real as contradictory." In fact, it is not that conflict does not exist or disappear in Freyre's interpretation. Rather, conflict is always present, but it appears to resolve itself in the everyday life, in the range of a social system where the predominant disposition is toward a fragile balance between antagonisms that are not resolved in a definitive and mutually exclusive synthesis. Freyre does not eliminate conflict, but he does deal with it in a conceptually different way—as opposed, for example, to a Marxist analysis. He seems to deal with conflict in the terms proposed by Simmel: "Conflict is thus designed to resolve divergent dualisms; it is a way of achieving some kind of unity, even if it be through the annihilation of one of the conflicting parties."[52]

In other words, what makes *The Masters and the Slaves* out of date as an interpretive scheme is not that it puts forth some idyllic vision of Brazilian reality where there is no space for conflict. Neither does it make a connection between a biological fact and a political one, since Freyre does not even concern himself with the political organization of the Brazilian public sphere—such is his fascination with the cultural dimension and the capacity that it has to deal with and resolve conflicts. Certainly, Freyre's lack of interest in the modern construction of the formal political sphere of Brazilian society is one of the major impasses of *The Masters and the Slaves*. That said, we propose the following question: what exactly is in *The Masters and the Slaves* that can help us understand Brazilian reality?

GILBERTO FREYRE TODAY

This chapter has focused on the meaning of Gilberto Freyre's concept of culture in *The Masters and the Slaves*, with its genealogy, limitations, and potentialities. We hope, above all else, to have contributed to a discussion of Freyre's work in terms more analytical than those of other critics. However, before concluding, we wish to highlight the many contributions that recent criticism on Freyre has emphasized as being innovative in *The Masters and the Slaves*. Élide Rugai Bastos details some of the methodological innovations that allowed Freyre to elaborate the first interpretation of the Brazilian agro-industrial society's everyday life. This elaboration would place him at the forefront of movements with analogous methodological perspectives, such as the one represented by the *École des Annales*. Bastos also strongly emphasizes Freyre's important contribution to the systemization of sociology in Brazil: "From Gilberto Freyre, sociology received a definitive systemization and a discourse of its own, and would occupy a special place in the explanation of the peculiarities of Brazilian society."[53] In this sense, it is important to note that Freyre's training and legitimization as a social scientist preceded the very institutionalization of sociology in Brazil.

Evaldo Cabral de Melo Neto notes, among the methodological and thematic innovations of *The Masters and the Slaves*, the emphasis on modern themes such as ecology and the conditions of oppression of women and children. In turn, Peter Burke points out Freyre's surprising interest in material culture: nutrition habits, clothing, furniture, and so on. Roberto Ventura asserts that Freyre innovated in object, method, and style, elaborating the first history of Brazilian private life as well as having irreverently incorporated spoken language into a scientific text. Finally, Enrique Larreta compliments Freyre's anthropological sensibility toward the pronounced presence of eroticism in Brazilian society, incorporating it as part of his analysis.[54]

Recent critics have highlighted various aspects of Freyre's heterodoxy and eclecticism as important elements in his work: the refusal to cast himself as an adherent to any perspective or approach in particular; the strong influence of literature on his thought and intellectual production; the innovative use of informal language in combination with a voluminous body of scientific sources; empathy with his object of study; and the very concept of research as a sort of introspection, all articulated with keen literary sensibility and style. Recognizing the thematic, aesthetic, and methodological merits of Freyre's work is important because it allows one to reassess his intellectual production in a way that is more detached than the enthusiastic reception received in the 1930s and less biased than the later sheer ideological readings, which attempt to undermine a work whose complexity embraces obvious contradictions and ambiguities.

Here we return to the initial question of this chapter: How can a rereading of *The Masters and the Slaves* help us in the contemporary debate around culture and identity? The answer may be in the book's perception of Brazilian culture as a system whose basic disposition is *plasticity*, which results in a fragile—and often violent—balance between antagonisms. Gilberto Freyre's concepts of social patterns and dispositions find their origins at the intersection of sociology and history, and the concepts that he uses to describe the tendencies that govern Brazilian society are historically bound descriptions of social practices derived from the way that groups face the challenges and conditions imposed by their environment. Such social practices lead to the development of a common code that, in turn, conditions the group members' behavior as well as orients the incorporation of new elements and values in the process of resignifying established elements. In Brazil, for Freyre, this process is marked by plasticity.

However, Freyre seems to have mistrusted this flexibility of Brazilian culture, when in *The Mansions and the Shanties* he points out the risks of a re-Europeanization of Brazil. In light of the evidence presented by Brazilian modernization since the beginning of the nineteenth century, with which Freyre did not sympathize, he seems to have doubted the disposition of Brazilian culture toward the incorporation of the new and the antagonistic.[55] Here resides yet another of the limits and contradictions of his thought. As to the rest, Freyre's interpretation, even with its problems and ambiguities, can still offer valid perspectives as well as an essential vocabulary from which to speak of Brazilian reality in the present and with which to think of the ways that Brazilian culture has responded and can respond to the problems and challenges presented by globalization.

Last, we find it interesting that Freyre, a seemingly politically conservative sociologist, proposed and systemized a daringly modern and flexible concept of Brazilian culture at the same time that he was imprisoned within his disguised sympathies for an evolutionist concept of culture. Furthermore, one can clearly distinguish as a major drawback in *The Masters and the Slaves* an aristocratic exclusion of reflections on the problems of social structure and the constitution of political agents in Brazil. Nevertheless, we hope that we have made it clear that Gilberto Freyre's work continues to be rich in possibilities and perspectives on the phenomena that we call Brazilian culture. This notion refers to the sharing of values among community members, which founds the basis for historical forms of sociability, which in turn link to shared visions of the world and the constitution of collective identities. As the anthropologist Gilberto Velho insists, the insertion of the subject into national life—as a phenomenon of cultural belonging—is one among various affiliations that constitute the identities of contemporary subjects.[56] A careful and critical reading of Gilberto Freyre can certainly help us to understand better this dimension of Brazilian social life in the twenty-first century.

NOTES

1. The first English-language edition was published in 1946; we quote from the second revised edition: Gilberto Freyre, *The Masters and the Slaves: A Study in the Development of Brazilian Civilization*, trans. Samuel Putnam, 2nd ed. (New York: Knopf, 1963).

2. See Mário de Andrade, *Macunaíma; o herói sem nenhum caráter* (São Paulo: Estabelecimento Graphico Eugenio Cupolo, 1928); Gilberto Freyre, *Casa-grande & senzala: Formação da família brasileira sob o regime de economia patriarcal* (Rio de Janeiro: Maia & Schmidt, 1933); Sérgio Buarque de Holanda, *Raízes do Brasil* (Rio de Janeiro: José Olympio, 1936); Caio Prado Júnior, *Evolução política do Brasil: Ensaio de interpretação materialista da história brasileira* (São Paulo: Revista dos tribunais, 1933); Caio Prado Júnior, *Formação do Brasil contemporâneo* (São Paulo: Livraria Martins Editora, 1942).

3. Lourdes Martínez-Echazábel, "O culturalismo dos anos 30 no Brasil e na América Latina: Deslocamento retórico ou mudança conceitual?" in *Raça, ciência e sociedade*, ed. Marcos Chor Maio and Ricardo Ventura Santos (Rio de Janeiro: Editora FIOCRUZ, 1996), 117–18.

4. Giralda Seyferth, "Construindo a Nação: Hierarquias raciais e o papel do racismo na política de imigração e colonização," in *Raça, Ciência e Sociedade*, ed. M. C. Maio and R. Ventura Santos (Rio de Janeiro: Ed. Fiocuz-CCBB, 1996); and Lilia Moritz Schwarcz, *O espetáculo das raças: Cientistas, instituições e questão racial no Brasil, 1870–1930* (São Paulo: Companhia das Letras, 1993). See also Sílvio Romero, *História da literatura brasileira: Contribuições e estudos gerais para o exato conhecimento da literatura brasileira*, ed. Nelson Romero, 7th ed., 5 vols. (Rio de Janeiro: Livraria J. Olympio Editora, 1980); and Francisco José de Oliveira Vianna, *Evolução do povo brasileiro*, 2nd ed. (São Paulo: Companhia Editora Nacional, 1933). Freyre dialogues directly with these texts and sets himself in opposition to them.

5. Dain Borges, "'Puffy, Ugly, Slothful and Inert': Degeneration in Brazilian Social Thought, 1880–1940," *Journal of Latin American Studies* 25 (1993); Borges, "The Recognition of Afro-Brazilian Symbols and Ideas, 1890–1940," *Luso-Brazilian Review* 32, no. 2 (1995).

6. The classical definitions of *culture* proposed by Edward Burnett Tylor and later by Ward Goodenough, though cited in contemporary anthropological literature merely as historical references, nevertheless still strongly influence the non-scientific uses of the word, as evidenced by the entries for "culture" in the latest editions of the *American Heritage Dictionary of the English Language* and the *Novo Dicionário Aurélio da Língua Portuguesa*.

7. For a discussion on the limits of ostensive definition as a strategy for learning the "meaning" of a word (i.e., its use), see Ludwig Wittgenstein, *Philosophical*

Investigations, trans. G. E. M. Anscombe, 3rd ed. (Englewood Cliffs, N.J.: Prentice Hall, 1958), 28–33.

8. Wittgenstein, *Investigations*, 28, emphasis in original.

9. Franz Boas, *Anthropology and Modern Life* (New York: Dover, 1986), 12.

10. For the intellectual background against which Freyre's work was produced, see Dain Borges, "Review Essay: Brazilian Social Thought of the 1930s," *Luso-Brazilian Review* 31, no. 2 (1994).

11. Boas, *Anthropology*, 22–25, 29.

12. Boas, *Anthropology*, 27–28, 37.

13. Boas, *Anthropology*, 36, 47–51, 58.

14. Boas, *Anthropology*, 65–71.

15. Boas, *Anthropology*, 92.

16. Boas, *Anthropology*, 138, emphasis in original.

17. Freyre, *Masters and the Slaves*, xxvii, emphasis in original.

18. When Freyre uses the term *ethnicity*, he is in fact referring to race. The contemporary definition of *ethnicity*—as social groups with relative cultural homogeneity, sharing a history and a common origin, in direct opposition to a strictly racialist designation of human groups—is an elaboration reached only recently in modern anthropology and one that has roots in the paradigm of cultural relativism. To avoid ambiguity, in this chapter the term *ethnicity* will always be utilized in the Freyrean sense.

19. Freyre, *Masters and the Slaves*, 8.

20. Freyre, *Masters and the Slaves*, 5.

21. Ricardo Benzaquen de Araújo, *Guerra e paz: Casa-Grande & Senzala e a obra de Gilberto Freyre nos anos 30* (Rio de Janeiro: Editora 34, 1994), 39.

22. Freyre, *Masters and the Slaves*, xxix.

23. Freyre, *Masters and the Slaves*, xxx.

24. Freyre refers in his footnotes to *The Political Evolution of Brazil* (1933), by Caio Prado Júnior; this text would become one of the most important Marxist references within Brazilian social thought.

25. Freyre, *Masters and the Slaves*, xxvii.

26. See Folha de São Paulo, "Céu & inferno de Gilberto Freyre," *Folha de São Paulo: Caderno Mais!* March 12, 2000.

27. Freyre, *Masters and the Slaves*, 348–49.

28. Élide Rugai Bastos, "Gilberto Freyre: Casa-grande & senzala," in *Introdução ao Brasil: Um banquete no trópico*, ed. Dantas Lourenço Mota (São Paulo: Editora SENAC, 1999).

29. Edson Nery da Fonseca collects eleven years of criticism of *The Masters and the Slaves*; these reviews offer an idea of the repercussion, not always positive, of Freyre's work: Edson Nery da Fonseca, *Casa-grande & senzala e a crítica brasileira de 1933 a 1944* (Recife: Companhia Editora de Pernambuco, 1985).

30. Dante Moreira Leite, *O caráter nacional brasileiro: História de uma ideologia*, 5th ed. (São Paulo: Editora Ática, 1992), 273–74; Carlos Guilherme Mota, *Ideologia da cultura brasileira (1933–1974): Pontos de partida para uma revisão histórica*, 5th ed. (São Paulo: Editora Ática, 1985), 61–62.

31. Leite, *O caráter nacional*, 270–72; Mota, *Ideologia*, 64.

32. Leite, *O caráter nacional*, 281; Mota, *Ideologia*, 59; Renato Ortiz, *Cultura brasileira e identidade nacional* (São Paulo: Brasiliense, 1985), 44. The typical elements of this type of criticism of *The Masters and the Slaves* are found in Maria Alice de Aguiar Medeiros, *O elogio da dominação: Relendo Casa-grande & senzala* (Rio de Janeiro: Achiamé, 1984).

33. Leite, *O caráter nacional*, 273.

34. Mota, *Ideologia*, 62.

35. Luiz Costa Lima, "A Versão solar do patriarcalismo: Casa-grande & senzala," in *A aguarrás do tempo: Estudos sobre a narrativa* (Rio de Janeiro: Rocco, 1989).

36. Araújo, *Guerra e paz*.

37. Lima, "A Versão solar do patriarcalismo," 205.

38. Lima, "A Versão dolar do patriarcalismo," 236.

39. Luiz Costa Lima, "O elogio do congraçamento," *Folha de São Paulo*, December 17, 2000.

40. Lima, "O elegio."

41. Araújo, *Guerra e paz*, 39.

42. Araújo, *Guerra e paz*, 103.

43. Araújo, *Guerra e paz*, 137.

44. George W. Stocking, *Race, Culture, and Evolution: Essays in the History of Anthropology* (New York: Free Press, 1968), 203.

45. Stocking, *Race, Culture and Evolution*, 201–3.

46. Stocking, *Race, Culture, and Evolution*, 214, emphasis in original.

47. Freyre, *Masters and the Slaves*, 157.

48. Freyre, *Masters and the Slaves*, 181.

49. Sebastião Vila Nova, *Sociologias & pós-sociologia em Gilberto Freyre: Algumas fontes e afinidades teóricas e metodológicas do seu pensamento* (Recife: Fundação Joaquim Nabuco; Editora Massangana, 1995), 74–75.

50. Gilberto Freyre, *Como e porque sou e não sou sociólogo* (Brasília: Editora Universidade de Brasília, 1968), 45. Gilberto Freyre, *Tempo morto e outros tempos; trechos de um diário de adolescência e primeira mocidade, 1915–1930* (Rio de Janeiro: José Olympio, 1975), 79.

51. Bastos, "Gilberto Freyre." See also Élide Rugai Bastos, "Gilberto Freyre e a questão nacional," in *Inteligência Brasileira*, ed. Ricardo Antunes, Vera Ferrante, and Reginaldo Moraes (São Paulo: Brasiliense, 1986).

52. Georg Simmel, *On Individuality and Social Forms: Selected Writings* (Chicago: University of Chicago Press, 1971), 70.

53. Such a claim can be found in Bastos's collaboration to *Folha de São Paulo*, "Céu & inferno de Gilberto Freyre."

54. All these perspectives were recently published in *Folha de São Paulo*; see note 55.

55. In this respect, see Araújo, *Guerra e paz*, 153–84.

56. See Gilberto Velho, "Unidade e fragmentação em sociedades complexas," in *Projeto e metamorfose: Antropologia das sociedades complexas* (Rio de Janeiro: Jorge Zahar Editor, 1994).

II

FACTS

4

❧

Brasiliana: Published Works and Collections

José Mindlin and Cristina Antunes
Translation by Elizabeth A. Marchant

Published works, both individual and collective, have served as essential agents in the forging of Brazil's national identity as well as in the preservation of the country's historical record. The great cumulative mass of written material on Brazil, often termed *Brasiliana*, with its wealth of factual and interpretive data on national conditions and development, has bolstered an ever-growing and increasingly nuanced awareness of Brazilian national identity. Here, beyond texts of singular importance, the value of *Brasiliana* derives from its content rather than its style or form. This chapter surveys significant publications and collections that have formed a basis for Brazilian studies over the past two hundred years.

Brazil's identity has drastically changed over the course of history. From modest beginnings in the sixteenth century as an agricultural colony of Portugal, Brazil has become a modern, highly urbanized giant with a population of more than 170 million. In land area, it is now the sixth-largest country in the world. Like the United States, it has a predominant national language, is geographically well integrated, and has a strong sense of national individuality. The corpus of *Brasiliana* reflects these changes, constantly reinterpreting Brazil's collective reality and reinterpreting its national identity. Defining the country's cultural reality today, as in the past, is a challenge. Despite its complexity and contradictions, however, Brazil has been united by the Portuguese language, strengthened by a shared historical experience, and distinguished by racial and multicultural amalgamation. Thus, we can speak of Brazilianness, of a coherent Brazilian society, and of a national identity.

Intellectuals throughout history have contributed to these currents of thought in forms that reflect their perspective and vision, reaffirming or refuting prior visions and emphasizing different aspects of Brazilian reality: tradition and modernity, continuity and change. Gathering and interpreting facts related to Brazil was generally pursued within a literary tradition until the 1870s; since then, scientific methods of investigation and analysis have becoming increasingly influential. Among the diverse intellectuals who studied and interpreted Brazil, creating the most significant synthesis of national reconstruction, are Francisco Adolpho de Varnhagen, with his *História Geral do Brasil*, published in 1850, reflecting the gaze of the Portuguese colonizer; João Capistrano de Abreu, with *Capítulos da História Colonial* (1907; *Chapters of Brazilian Colonial History, 1500–1800*, 1997), with a scientific preoccupation that privileges the people and their ethnic makeup; Gilberto Freyre, with *Casa-Grande & Senzala* (*The Masters and the Slaves*, 1933), a sociological history that reconsiders Portuguese colonization and traditional Brazil; Sérgio Buarque de Holanda, with *Raízes do Brasil* (1936), who seeks to know Brazil in its singularity; Raimundo Faoro, with *Os Donos do Poder* (1958), a rereading of Brazil's history through the influence of Max Weber; Nelson Werneck Sodré, Marxist theorist, with his *História da Burguesia Brasileira* (1964); Caio Prado Júnior and the historical materialism in *A Evolução Brasileira* (1966); Florestan Fernandes, with a classical sociological training, representing Marxist thought in his *A Revolução Burguesa no Brasil* (1975).

EARLY *BRASILIANA*

The colonial period—which lasted at a minimum until 1808, when the Portuguese court relocated to Rio de Janeiro, or at a maximum until independence, in 1822—should be separated from all that happened thereafter, for it is only with the declaration of independence that the existence of Brazil as a nation truly began. In colonial Brazil, the practice of collecting books was dominated by private collectors and by the Jesuits in their seminaries and schools because of the responsibility they bore for teaching from the primary level to advanced studies in philosophy. Portugal thought that the colonies should serve only for agriculture, exploration, and commerce. The books that arrived in Brazil from Europe passed through the sieve of censorship, which confiscated all that represented an affront to faith or morality. The printing of new books in Portugal depended on the concession of licenses. Beginning in 1750, under the Marquês de Pombal, censorship took on a political aspect, denying the printing license to many manuscripts and thus favoring the appearance of clandestine editions, printed with false indications of their place of publication and publishers. After the expulsion of the Jesuits in 1759, other religious orders—Franciscan, Benedictine, and Carmelite—already in Brazil took on a pronounced role in teaching. They had schools annexed to their convents, advanced courses of study for training friars, and excellent libraries. Rubens Borba de Moraes, one of the great scholars of rare books about Brazil, traces an excellent panorama of the formation of Brazilian thought in the colonial period and the situation of books and libraries in the country, in his work *Livros e Bibliotecas no Brasil Colonial.*

By the eighteenth century, increasing development in the colony, especially urbanization, produced a richer environment for intellectual production and consumption. A large number of Brazilian students were already in the universities of Coimbra and Montepelier. The study of philosophy and the sciences was beginning to develop through formal educational institutions; private institutions, such as libraries; bookstores; and gatherings such as public lectures and literary salons. The academy movement, which drew together members spread across the wealthiest centers of the colony—principally, Pernambuco, Bahia, and Minas Gerais—was the first attempt at organizing intellectual activities in Brazil. It indicated a certain cohesion in the country, a taste for poetry and things of the mind. Although most expressions of the academies were effected in mere academic acts in honor of a particular person or event, some of them, such as the Academia dos Renascidos, had not only literary but also historical and scientific purposes. Wills and inventories of the period tell of books and small libraries in private hands in various colonial captaincies. Some literary manifestations show that Brazil possessed orators, prose writers, and poets of great quality. For example, *Triunfo Eucharistico* (1733) and *Aureo Throno Episcopal* (1749), by Brazilian authors and printed in Portugal, relate events that took place in the captaincy of Minas Gerais. By the mid-eighteenth century, Brazilian students introduced the first notions of French liberal thought, and the independence of the United States influenced Brazil's patriotic ambitions to a significant degree.

The nineteenth century in Europe marked the beginning of the improved technology of book publication, especially with the manufacture of paper and the mechanics of the press. Printing presses were automated, and the production of books increased considerably, resulting in larger print runs and the expansion of the periodical press. The need arose to satisfy the tastes of a public that looked to the book more for its ideas than for its beauty of form. The growing facility of communication, travel, and emigration led to an almost simultaneous universalization of technical innovations and the standardization of the book in the various countries of Europe. In Brazil, the taste for reading grew, and the most published works were novels (national and in translation), travel writings, and periodicals. Simple popular texts were the most sought after, and the French influence was reflected in the Brazilian translations of *folhetins* (pamphlets or chapbooks). But the Brazil that for centuries was tied more to Europe than to any other continent and had almost zero internal cultural communication had no press until 1808 with the transfer of the Portuguese court to Rio de Janeiro due to the invasion of Portugal by Napoleon Bonaparte.

BRASILIANA IN THE NINETEENTH CENTURY

The transfer of the Portuguese royal court from Lisbon to Rio de Janeiro protected the honor of the Braganza dynasty and preserved the Portuguese empire from French intervention. The presence of the Portuguese crown in Rio de Janeiro from 1808 to 1821, the opening of Brazil's ports to world trade in 1808, and Brazil's declaration of independence from Portugal in 1821 resulted in some significant changes in Brazilian politics and culture. During this period, the corpus of *Brasiliana* expanded as intellectuals, government officials, and foreign visitors conducted their business and confronted new opportunities and challenges. Once installed, the court found that it needed a printing office and thus created the Imprensa Régia for the publication of official documents (decrees, royal letters, charters, etc.). In 1808 there appeared in print an unofficial biweekly gazette mostly concerned with what was happening in Europe but also containing American news, obituaries, and commercial advertisements: the *Gazeta do Rio de Janeiro*, so called until 1821, when it changed its name several times until becoming the *Diário Oficial*, today merely an organ for publishing official acts. Nevertheless, over its existence—from 1808 to 1822—the Imprensa Régia published a significant quantity of literary and scientific works, such as the first Brazilian edition of *Marília de Dirceo*, by Tomás Antônio Gonzaga (1810); the *Observações sobre a Franqueza da Indústria, e Estabelecimento de Fábricas no Brasil*, by José da Silva Lisboa (1810); the *Ensaios Morais* (Moral Essays, 1811), by Alexander Pope; and the *Memórias Históricas do Rio de Janeiro* (1820).

The creation of secondary education in Rio de Janeiro and Bahia came in the same period (1808) as did the founding of the Biblioteca Real in 1811, which became public in 1814. This library contained the books of the Royal Library, brought from Portugal by Dom João VI and transported to Brazil in various stages, forming what is today the Biblioteca Nacional (National Library) in Rio de Janeiro. The coming of the court to Rio de Janeiro led to changes in the self-perceptions and worldviews of educated Brazilians.

The first Brazilian province to develop its own publishing activity independent of Rio de Janeiro was Bahia, where the Portuguese Manual Antônio de Silva Serva, having immigrated to Salvador in 1797, installed a printing establishment in 1811. After his death in 1819, the Tipografia de

Silva Serva became known as the Tipografia Viúva Serva. The newspaper *Idade de Ouro do Brasil* was published at this press beginning on May 14, 1811, with the intention of presenting political facts and news without any reflection on them and, as such, continued until 1823, the date of its last issue. Silva Serva, whose press survived until 1846, launched in 1812 the first Brazilian literary magazine—*As Variedades ou Ensaios de Literatura*—and published many works on religion; some on law and medicine; and a few on history, politics, and literature.

Some important periodicals appeared in the nineteenth century in various disciplines but especially in history and literature. The *Correio Brasiliense*, the first Brazilian newspaper, was published in London to escape censorship. Under the direction of Hipólito José da Costa, it circulated between 1808 and 1822 and dealt with Brazilian issues in various fields. Also printed in London between 1811 and 1819, *O Investigador Português em Inglaterra* focused on Brazil in particular, being a perfect example of the courtly press, the only kind permitted in this period. Even at the end of the century, three important illustrated magazines were published outside the country: *O Novo Mundo*, a magazine with high-caliber literary content edited in New York between 1871 and 1879 under the direction of José Carlos Rodrigues, who would come to direct the *Jornal do Comercio*, one of the oldest Brazilian newspapers; Alexandre Mello Moraes's *Echo Americano*, published in London between 1871 and 1872 and also circulated in Portugal; and the *Revista Moderna*, edited fortnightly in France beginning in 1897 by Martinho de Arruda Botelho, a Brazilian millionaire residing in Paris who gave a gold Patek Phillipe watch as a present to each subscriber.

Other periodicals emerging in the nineteenth century and deserving consideration were *O Patriota*, printed in Rio de Janeiro at the Imprensa Régia from 1813 to 1814 and founded by Manuel Ferreira de Araújo Guimarães, with the collaboration of men of letters; the pro-independence newspaper *Reverbero Constitucional Fluminense*, published from 1821 to 1832 by the Typographia de Moreira e Garcez; the *Revista Médica Fluminense*, published from 1835 to 1843; the women's magazine *A Marmota na Côrte*, published by Próspero Ribeiro and Paula Brito between 1852 and 1857, when it gave way to the magazine *A Marmota*, distributing lithographed fashion plates in Paris; the *Semana Illustrada*, founded by the draftsman and lithographer Henrique Fleiuss, published in Rio de Janeiro from 1861 to 1875 and dealing with the principal events of Brazilian life; and, finally, the *Revista Illustrada*, the principal illustrated Brazilian magazine, launched by Brazil's most famous caricaturist, Angelo Agostini, in January of 1876 and continuing until 1898, reaching a high circulation of four thousand. Ephemeral newspapers contributed to Brazilian cultural development and to the formation of a national political conscience. To cite only a few examples,

O Mosquito (1869) was a standout in the genre of illustrated satirical periodicals, and _O Mequetrefe_ (1875) brought together several masters of Brazilian caricature.

Brazil printed many books in Europe, principally in Portugal and France—by the Livraria Garnier, for example. The Garnier firm was founded in Paris in 1833 by brothers Auguste and Hyppolite under the name of Librairie Garnier Frères. A third brother, Baptista Luiz Garnier, came to Rio de Janeiro in 1844 and, in 1846, installed a branch, B. L. Garnier, which printed its editions both inside and outside the country. It was Garnier who introduced the French format (_in octavo_) to Brazil and who began to employ proofreaders and invest in the printed collections of authors such as José de Alencar and Machado de Assis. In sum, Garnier printed nearly 665 works by national authors, as well as many translations by Brazilian writers.

Other foreign publishers who established themselves in Brazil in the first half of the nineteenth century and who had an important role in the formation of the Brazilian editorial market were Pierre Plancher, who introduced the lithographic process in Brazil and published many political and administrative works in addition to the first Brazilian novella, _Statira e Zoroastes_, in 1826; J. C. Villeneuve, who bought Plancher's printing shop in 1832 and published Brazilian novels as well as translations of Victor Hugo and Alexander Dumas; and Edouard Laemmert, who inaugurated his printing establishment in 1838 and created the Tipografia Universal, for a long time the principal competitor of Garnier.

Among the Brazilian publishers who stood out in the period is Francisco de Paula Brito, who owned two printing establishments in 1833—the Fluminense and the Imparcial—and produced much for the common reader, striking a rich vein of female readership. In 1850 he founded the Imperial Tipografia Dois de Dezembro, a shareholding association that printed various periodicals and 372 nonperiodical publications. Two other relevant printers include José Maria Corrêa de Frias and Belarmino de Mattos, friendly rivals who had printing establishments installed in São Luís do Maranhão. They produced an enormous quantity of books printed with high technical and aesthetic standards, making the publishing production of Maranhão one of the best in the country in the second half of the nineteenth century. To give an idea of the Maranhense publishing market of the period, the Portuguese translation of Victor Hugo's _Les Misérables_ was published in São Luís in 1862, the same year that the original was published.

By the 1870s, the country had a generation of intellectuals concerned with studying, investigating, mapping, and explaining Brazilian reality. They were developing a self-knowledge of the country through the scientism that ruled the period, and they served to contribute to a precise definition of Brazil's national identity. By this time, historical institutes in various

Brazilian states began to publish their own magazines, important sources for the study of Brazilian history. The creation of the Instituto Histórico e Geográfico Brasileiro in Rio de Janeiro truly initiated historical reflection and research in Brazil. Standouts among them include the more than three hundred issues of the *Revista do Instituto Histórico e Geográfico Brasileiro*, published in Rio de Janeiro since 1839, with special issues dedicated to the congresses of História Nacional (National History); the *Revista do Instituto Arqueológico, Histórico e Geográfico Pernambucano*, published in Recife since 1863; the *Revista do Instituto Histórico e Geográfico da Bahia*, published in Salvador beginning in 1895; and the *Revista do Instituto Histórico e Geográfico de São Paulo*, begun in 1895. Also deserving mention are state historical archives, such as the Arquivo Público Mineiro and its *Revista do Arquivo Público Mineiro*, and the *Anais da Biblioteca Nacional*, first published in Rio de Janeiro in 1876.

If the arrival of the royal court in 1808 precipitated transformative changes in the evolution of Brazil's national identity, in part through the expansion of an increasingly nationalist *Brasiliana*, the end of the Brazilian empire and the declaration of a republic in 1889 ushered in a new era of *Brasiliana*, one that embraced modernity and science.

BRASILIANA AND THE NEW BRAZIL

In 1889, the republic was established by a bloodless military coup. Republicans sought to erase the vestiges of the nation's colonial and monarchic past and to construct a modern secular nation. The prospect of growth and progress quickened the pulse of forward-thinking Brazilians and foreigners, and the republican administrations labored to modernize Brazil's economic infrastructure and present attractive images of the new Brazil.

Still, Brazilian society was hierarchical, comprising an elite of rural and urban landholders, an emerging middle class that was overly heterogeneous and dependent on agrarian forces, and a great mass that lacked education and lived in ignorance. Conformity was the rule. But after World War I and the worsening of economic, political, and social problems, the question arose as to how to dynamize a society that was taking its first steps toward urbanization and industrialization—especially the cities of Rio de Janeiro, São Paulo, Belo Horizonte, and Porto Alegre—with the better part of the population still excluded from the basic right to knowledge. In that period, the wealthy families of northeast Brazil, following an old tradition, continued to send their children to study in Europe, while the sons of the wealthy southern and southeastern families began to go to the United States, where the entrepreneurial mentality was much more developed. This fact accentuated the differences between the Brazilian regions, especially with regard to industrialization and the immigration of European salaried workers to the plantations of the south after the abolition of slavery in 1888 and the decline of the northeastern cattle culture and the growth of coffee production in the Paraíba Valley, which resulted in the loss of economic supremacy for the north and northeast in relation to the south.

The federal government gave attention to the secondary and higher education systems, building on the foundation of various institutions of higher learning, such as the Real Academia Militar, the Laboratório Químico-Práctico, the Academia Médico-Cirúrgica, and the Academia Real dos Guarda-Marinhas. Specialized schools of law, medicine, and engineering would mushroom in first decades of the twentieth century, concentrating in Rio de Janeiro, São Paulo, and other state capitals. In 1920, the University of Rio de Janeiro was created as the first Brazilian university, bringing together the existing schools of law, medicine, and polytechnics. The University of Minas Gerais was founded in Belo Horizonte in 1927 and the University of São Paulo in 1934.

The majority of books published in Brazil came from typographies and from the offices of the newspapers and magazines, since their print shops were the establishments that printed everything. It was difficult to publish until the 1920s because of the lack of an established publishing tradition, and this job was more often in the hands of foreigners than in those of Brazilians. Even so, the beginning of the twentieth century saw the most beautiful magazine published in Brazil: *Kosmos*. Circulating from 1904 to 1909, it was in the line of French magazines with elaborate art nouveau covers. In 1907 the magazine *Fon-Fon* came out. With light articles and many illustrations that depicted daily life in Rio de Janeiro, it achieved great success among readers from all over the country. In the same year, Editora Vozes launched the *Revista de Cultura Vozes*, which positioned itself against positivist ideas and against the naturalist novels of the beginning of the century. On the initiative of Júlio Mesquita, there emerged in São Paulo in 1916 an important magazine that would come to have a long life and various phases: the *Revista do Brasil*, with its editorial line, carefully planned direction, and title appropriate to the nationalist fervor of the moment. In it were published the intellectuals of greatest expression. In parallel with the political unrest of the postwar era, a Brazilian artistic unrest showed itself in painting, sculpture, and literature and manifested itself in the realization of the Modern Art Week in São Paulo in 1922. Its participants expressed themselves mainly through the vanguard magazines, the majority of which were ephemeral. *Klaxon* was the first, with its revolutionary graphic presentation and nine issues running from May 1922 to January 1923. A collective statement made by members of the younger generation— including Gilberto Amado, Oliveira Viana, Ronald de Carvalho, Pontes de Miranda, and Alceu Amoroso Lima—and edited by A. Carneiro Leão was published as *À Margem da História da República* in 1924. These essays address various aspects of Brazilian identity and national problems.

In the meantime, the Brazilian publishing market began to solidify with Monteiro Lobato and the group who formed around him—Afrânio Amaral, Navarro de Andrade, Adolfo Lutz, Osvaldo Cruz, Artur Neiva, Emílio Ribas, Euclides da Cunha, and others—to address national problems. Lobato had founded Monteiro Lobato & Cia. Editores, which failed in 1924; but in 1927 he founded the Companhia Editora Nacional with Octalles Marcondes Ferreira. Lobato adopted aggressive methods of distribution, modified the format of books, improved their visual aspect, and invested in ample publicity for all of his releases. From then on publishers, being more concerned with fulfilling a social role, began to develop editorial projects with clear direction and better planning, giving the Brazilian publishing movement a constructed and continuous character until then only incipient. On the other hand, Brazilian intellectuals, who had already been considering Brazilian reality, were increasingly concerned with political ideologies, mainly those communist and fascist, and worried about the debate over the country's political problem. The first communist newspaper in Brazil was *O Debate*, published weekly in Rio de Janeiro. Directed by Adolpho Porto and Astrojildo Pereira, its first issue appeared in July 1917.

The revolution of 1930—which had its beginnings in a strong schism between the dominant elites of the great states of Brazil and principally involved Minas Gerais, Rio Grande do Sul, São Paulo, and Paraíba—did not signify a direct taking of power by a particular social class. The victors formed a heterogeneous picture as much from the social as from the political point of view, all united against the same adversary but with different interests. They were old oligarchs, interested in greater power and representing the dominant class of each region of the country; they were young civilians associated with the army lieutenants, forming the "civilian lieutenants" groups and interested in reforming the political system; they were high-ranking military officers defending the centralization of power; and they were the Democratic Party, mouthpiece of the traditional middle class and in favor of adopting the principles of the liberal state, which would guarantee its supremacy in the control of the government of São Paulo.

Aside from not breaking with the prevailing social organization, the revolution of 1930 provoked the emergence of great interest in Brazil, being largely responsible for the country's movement toward cultural unification. The influence of history on teaching and research, which had been in the hands of the Instituto Histórico e Geográfico Brasileiro, passed over to the universities. Under this influence, history moved to take in, aside from the merely political aspect, research on Brazilian reality from the economic, social, and mental point of view, thus drawing closer to the social sciences. The publishing market was moving out of the hands of immigrants and into those of young Brazilians. The print runs of fiction increased; excellent translations appeared; and the market for didactic books achieved enormous growth. During that era, the key concept was Brazilian reality, and the largest publishers were Companhia Editora Nacional, José Olympio, Martins, Globo, Irmãos Pongetti, and Amigos do Livro. As a reflection of the growth of the publishing market in Brazil, the Irmãos Pongetti founded the *Anuário Brasileiro de Literatura* in 1937, aiming to diffuse the movement of the market.

Important collections to the field of Brazilian studies were edited in that era as well: the *Coleção Brasiliana*, first edited by Fernando de Azevedo and published by the Companhia Editora Nacional beginning in 1931 in São Paulo; the collection *Documentos Brasileiros*, published in Rio de Janeiro by Livraria José Olympio Editora beginning in 1936, created and directed by Gilberto Freyre; and the collection *Biblioteca Histórica Brasileira*, published by Livraria Martins in São Paulo beginning in 1940. These series were designed as a sort of encyclopedia of *brasilidade*. Moreover, Azevedo and Freyre, along with Sérgio Buarque de Holanda and Caio Prado Jr., published their seminal interpretations of Brazilian society and culture in this same decade.

The democratic ideals brought from the United States by Brazilian intellectuals were widely embraced, but they had to face all at once the ire of the Catholic church and the authoritarianism resulting from the government of Getúlio Vargas. Vargas had assumed power in 1930 and retained it for fifteen years as head of the provisional government, elected president, and dictator. In 1933 liberal educators launched the Manifesto da Escola Nova, which defended individualism, advocated both the adaptation of the schools to regional characteristics and the primary role of free public instruction without gender distinction, and restricted religious instruction to private institutions. As such, the group's ideals threatened the two major strategic actors. The church, which was defending single-sex religious instruction, did not look favorably on an educational system that would exchange its prescriptive norms and orientation of behavior for the new stimuli of individual interests. Nor could it accept a free secular education for the public when the church itself actively participated in the business of private instruction. As for the authoritarian state, it could not admit in its structure support for liberty of choice, for decentralization, or for the differentiation that each region would imprint on its educational program.

However, the government was interested in forming a broader and more intellectually prepared elite, and it created the conditions for the emergence of real universities dedicated to instruction and research. Subsequently, universities proliferated in the country. Some European professors who came to be world famous in the fields of science, art, and literature, such as Claude Lévy-Strauss and Fernando Braudel, were contracted to work at the University of São Paulo. The concept of the university evolved. Formerly dispersed courses of study were being consolidated rather than being set as a mere collection of advanced courses, thereby better systematizing teaching and providing improved conditions for intellectual production.

During the Estado Novo, the publicity and printing of the government's works were controlled by the well-known DIP (Departamento de Imprensa e Propaganda), which answered directly to President Vargas and aggressively censored print media of all kinds, as well as radio, theater, and cinema. The DIP published, under government interests, the magazine *Cultura Política*, which Almir de Andrade founded in 1941 and directed from 1941 to 1945. Some magazines were linked directly or indirectly to leftist groups, whose main representative was the Brazilian Communist Party (Partido Comunista Brasileiro). Starting in 1946, the party published fortnightly *Divulgação Marxista*, which was edited by Calvino Filho and S. O. Hersen in Rio de Janeiro. *Fundamentos*, a cultural magazine founded by Monteiro Lobato in São Paulo, served as the official organ of the party from 1948 to 1955.

In the field of literature were the magazines *Clima*, a monthly cultural magazine published in São Paulo and created by the Grupo Clima— consisting of Antônio Cândido de Mello e Souza, Gilda de Mello e Souza, Décio de Almeida Prado, Paulo Emílio Salles Gomes, Ruy Galvão de Andrade, and Lourival Gomes Machado—with the first number coming out in May 1941; *Leitura: A Revista dos Melhores Escritores*, published in Rio de Janeiro beginning in 1942; *Letras Brasileiras*, an irregularly circulated magazine directed by Heitor Moniz, published in Rio de Janeiro by A Noite beginning in 1943.

From the 1950s on, Brazilian society experienced profound social change, with growing urbanization and increased industrial production. During the government of Juscelino Kubitschek, the growth of the automobile industry in São Paulo inaugurated a new era in Brazilian history, giving an enormous impulse to development. These alterations were accompanied by a political and cultural flowering and by the expansion of intellectual activities concerned with understanding the national reality.

Many magazines of the period came to reflect this concern. One example is the *Revista Brasiliense*. Edited bimonthly in São Paulo by Marxist historian Caio Prado Júnior, owner of the Editora Brasiliense, and directed by Elias Chaves Neto, the magazine was without political ties and was oriented by its own editors. It was published from the mid-1950s until the military coup in 1964. Marcelo Ridenti affirms that in the magazine, "which was marked by the centrality of the question of the national, emphasizing social, economic, and political problems, the world of the arts achieved a frequent presence beginning in 1960. Until then, the magazine carried at least one article per issue on cultural themes, but few on the living culture being produced in that period." Collaborators included Sérgio Buarque de Holanda, Sérgio Milliet, João Cruz Costa, Fernando Henrique Cardoso, Octávio Ianni, Florestan Fernandes, and Michel Löwy.

Other examples are the *Revista Brasileira de Política Internacional*, appearing in Rio de Janeiro in March 1958 and published quarterly by the Instituto Brasileiro de Relações Internacionais; *Trópico: Revista de Cultura e Turismo*, published by the Divisão de Expansão Cultural of the Departamento de Cultura of the Secretaria de Educação e Cultura do Estado de São Paulo beginning in 1950; and *Anhembi* magazine, directed by Paulo Duarte and published monthly beginning in 1950 for a total of 144 issues.

The popular press expanded in the 1960s. Magazines opened up to the cultural production of the moment, whether in theater, music, or the plastic arts. For example, the magazine *Realidade*, published by Editora Abril, well represents the new journalism of the period, with enormous circulation, audacious and profound reporting, and photo-essays on Brazilian reality. The magazine disappeared in the following decade.

Beginning in 1964, Brazil lived through decades of great political agitation, with long periods of severe repression having extremely negative impacts on the cultural area and the formation of new generations, then unaware of the country's real problems. The repression unleashed in December 1968, when the military dictatorship published Institutional Act No. 5, led to a prolonged lack of freedom of expression. Many magazines were closed, and artistic and cultural activities were hampered in an attempt to impede their involvement with political movements in opposition to the regime, thereby making the questioning of the existing order difficult. The lack of freedom of instruction weakened what could have been a rich development of the student body, and those who were truly interested in a broad cultural education became the exception rather than the rule.

A few academic magazines survived and were written by intellectuals linked to politics and the universities. Some of the periodicals circulated in only the university environment, but all thought about the national reality. Among the survivors are the already cited *Brasiliense* and *Tempo Brasileiro*, a quarterly magazine edited in Rio de Janeiro beginning in 1962 with a focus especially on philosophy and the social sciences and directed by Eduardo Portela, former director of the Biblioteca Nacional; *Estudos Sociais*, published quarterly and directed by Astrojildo Pereira—with the collaboration of Jacob Gorender as well as Jorge Miglioli, Armênio Guedes, Fausto Cupertino, Leandro Konder, Mário Alves, Nelson Werneck Sodré, and Rui Facó—was of the Marxist tendency, was tied to the Brazilian Communist Party, and saw nineteen issues between May 1958 and February

1964; *Revista Civilização Brasileira*, founded by Ênio Silveira in 1965 and edited by Moacyr Félix, published bimonthly in Rio de Janeiro by Editora Civilização Brasileira until 1968 with a high circulation of twenty thousand, and touched on historical, political, sociological, anthropological, and literary themes; *Problemas Brasileiros*, published monthly in São Paulo by the Conselho Técnico de Economia, Sociologia e Política, with its first issue in 1963; or, further, *Paz e Terra, Teoria e Prática*, and *Vozes*, all politicized and committed to progress, development, and democracy.

Other important magazines also emerged in this period, such as the *Revista Brasileira de Cultura*—published quarterly in Rio de Janeiro beginning in 1969 by the Conselho Federal de Cultura under the direction of Mozart de Araújo—aside from an alternative press that produced, among others, the pioneering *Pif-Paf*, Caetano Veloso's *O Sol*, and, principal among them, *O Pasquim*. In the form of a tabloid, this *Carioca* publication was begun in 1968 in weekly issues. Its editors were Tarso de Castro, Millôr Fernandes, and others who managed to maintain, with scant financial resources and great feints against censorship, a first-rate team of journalists from the international press. *O Pasquim* also relied on a cast of humorists, including Millôr himself, Ziraldo, Henfil, Claudius, Fortuna, and Jaguar. It was obligatory reading, a primer for a generation committed to the transformation of Brazilian society, and its print run could not keep up with the demand. Fortunately, democracy returned in 1984, but the damage caused by an authoritarian regime could not be undone overnight. During the twenty years of military dictatorship, the nation lost at least one generation of intellectuals and politicians, perhaps two.

BRASILIANA TODAY

Scholars of Brazil should keep in mind that this country has changed a great deal over the last two centuries. Considering the periods of the empire, the First Republic, the Vargas and Kubitschek eras, and the military regime, we should take into account that comparisons are difficult to make and can occasion incorrect interpretations. When we refer to the reign of Pedro II, we are speaking of a provincial country that looked permanently to Europe and, to a lesser extent, to the United States but with little experience of political, social, or economic organization. The republican regime gave great impetus to the country, being that the greater part of its growth occurred during the twentieth century.

In the last ten years, the number of books published in Brazil quintupled. Today it publishes as many titles as does France, Spain, Italy, or India. Print runs, however, are ten times smaller than those of these countries, making the retail price for the public higher. University presses are fertile, despite the lack of an ideal exchange with respect to the distribution of their publications. A recent example of the joint work of some federal universities is the release of the Coleção Nordestina in April 1999. Bringing together the universities of Ceará, Rio Grande do Norte, Paraíba, Pernambuco, Alagoas, Sergipe, and Bahia, the collection emerged with the idea of republishing literary and scientific works of the northeastern region that effectively contributed to the panorama of Brazilian thought.

Some institutions, such as the Fundação Joaquim Nabuco and the Editora Massangana, located in Recife, produced a significant quantity of books valuable for Brazilian Studies. These are distributed in various collections such as the series *Abolição, Estudos e Pesquisas, Descobrimentos, Documentos, Monografias,* and *Obras de Consulta,* among others. The Editora Itatiaia of Belo Horizonte offers a valuable contribution with collections such as the *Reconquista do Brasil* and the *Biblioteca de Estudos Brasileiros.*

Brazil's libraries are growing and new libraries are being formed, but the country needs a larger network of public and school libraries, not to mention bookstores. Presently, it has twenty-one hundred bookstores and only four thousand public libraries. They are concentrated in urban middle-class areas and downtown areas, and their numbers are decreasing at a dizzying rate in the poorest urban areas and in rural zones.

For those specialists interested in Brazilian Studies, we recommend a visit to the largest public library, the Biblioteca Nacional, which in 1908 acquired the building in which it remains today. It is part of the architectural complex of Cinelândia in Rio de Janeiro, which includes the Teatro Municipal, the Museu de Belas Artes, and the Assembléia Legislativa. Augmented by donations and acquisitions, its holdings include over nine million items. Today it is one of the greatest national treasures of Brazil and one of the best libraries in the world. It possesses the largest existing collection of the national periodical press, with a total of five million fascicles. Anyone has access to its holdings; Brazilian as well as many foreign researchers make use of it. The old Instituto Nacional do Livro (National Book Institute)— today called the Departamento Nacional do Livro—is part of the Fundação Biblioteca Nacional and produces co-editions, promotes national and international expositions, and is responsible for registering authorial rights. In January 2002 the Biblioteca Nacional launched the catalog *Brasiliana,* with texts explaining documents from its nearly nine million holdings and reproducing nearly five hundred of them. According to the Biblioteca Nacional, this publication is one of its most important since the appearance in 1881 of the *Catálogo da Exposição de História do Brasil,* a work fundamental to the study of Brazilian bibliography. Also in Rio de Janeiro is a small gem that deserves a visit—the Biblioteca do Gabinete Português de Leitura. Another good library is that of the Fundação Casa de Rui Barbosa.

In São Paulo, there is the Biblioteca Municipal Mário de Andrade, with good but relatively few holdings for such a city. On the other hand, the Instituto de Estudos Brasileiros (Institute of Brazilian Studies), located on the campus of the University of São Paulo, has a beautiful library and archive that bring together different collections. Among them are the Brasiliana de Yan de Alemeida Prado and the library of Mário de Andrade, whose holdings are an authentic memory of Brazilian modernism. Various publications come out of the institute, including the *Revista do Instituto de Estudos Brasileiros*, irregularly published since 1966.

Our private library (Biblioteca José Mindlin) is also located in São Paulo. Though undisciplined, it retains a certain logic and is not a simple accumulation of books. It comprises principally *Brasiliana*, including history, travel writing, natural history, and literary and social studies. Over the years, we have managed to collect documents, books, manuscripts, literary originals, and a good collection of periodicals (approximately nine hundred titles). The library itself comprises a total of more than forty thousand titles. Because of physical limitations and the necessities of document preservation, the library is not open to the public, but as we are able, we readily receive the specialists who seek us out.

Other libraries, of course, deserve to be consulted in accordance with the interests of scholars: the university libraries, those of the public archives, the academies of letters, the historical institutes, and those of foundations. We have a Sistema Integrado de Bibliotecas, located at the University of São Paulo, that brings together information about the holdings of a good portion of Brazil's online libraries.

At present, the number of periodicals published in Brazil is immense and quite varied. Besides an informative globalized press, some publications persist in the study of Brazilian culture and aspects that refer to the national identity. Aside from this is a new vehicle, the digital press, which is beginning to flourish, bringing with it new perspectives.

Given that it would be impossible to describe in detail the innumerable publications that contribute to the formation of the Brazilian mentality, we must close the current overview, which is much more indicative than exhaustive. Excess information can be more inconvenient than can a restricted report. Our principal aim is to introduce interested scholars to the world of Brazilian themes, utilizing the sources described here as a point of departure for more ample and more profound explorations with the aid of the bibliography that follows.

Another aim is to show that Brazilian studies and the aforementioned publications reveal a wide-ranging concern with the country as a whole. When they deal with only a single region, they always look to be part of a whole that gives readers an idea of what Brazil is so that they can sense how its citizens are but one people, immigrants or natives, all identified as partners in the construction of a great country. Speaking one language, without dialects, Brazilians cultivate respect for regional particularities, cheering themselves with their successes and seeking to cooperate in the solution of their problems. They can say, without being overly prideful or panglossian, that they are all happy to be Brazilians and are committed to examining and strengthening their national identity.

BIBLIOGRAPHY

Magazines and Newspapers

Álbum Imperial. São Paulo. Directed by Couto de Magalhães. Began in January 1906, first as a bimonthly; after 1908, a monthly; articles on Brazilian history and literature and other themes.

Anais da Biblioteca Nacional. Rio de Janeiro. Published by the Biblioteca Nacional; irregular; first number dated 1876.

Análise e Conjuntura. Quarterly. Published in Belo Horizonte by the Fundação João Pinheiro. First number dated January–April 1986.

Anhembi. São Paulo. Directed by Paulo Duarte. Monthly; began in 1950 and continued until November 1962; 144 issues.

Bahia Ilustrada. Rio de Janeiro. Monthly, directed by Anatólio Valladares; first number dated 1917.

Brasil/Brazil. Revista de Literatura Brasileira/A Journal of Brazilian Literature. Published in Porto Alegre in collaboration with the Center of Portuguese and Brazilian Studies, Providence, Rhode Island; first number dated 1988.

Brasiliense. Published bimonthly by Editora Brasiliense, São Paulo, October 1955 to February 1964. Edited by Caio Prado Júnior and Elias Chaves Neto; 51 bimonthy issues.

Brazilea. Revista Mensal de Propaganda Nacionalista. Rio de Janeiro. Directed by Arnaldo Damasceno Vieira and Álvaro Bomilcar; first issue January 1917. Emphasizes sociology, art, the sciences, and economics. Collaborators include F. C. Hoehne, Emiliano Pernetta, Nestor Victor, Fabio Luz, Afonso Celso, Lima Barreto, Jackson de Figueiredo, Humberto de Campos, Rodolpho Theophilo, Padre Antônio Carmelo, among others.

Cadernos Brasileiros. Directed by Afrânio Coutinho. Published three times per year by the Associação Brasileira do Congresso pela Liberdade da Cultura, Rio de Janeiro. Emphasizes history, politics, the sciences, literature, and sociology; since 1959.

Ciência e Cultura. Organ of the Sociedade Brasileira para o Progresso da Ciência, São Paulo. Began in 1948; three issues per year.

Ciência e Trópico. Recife. Published by Editora Massangana, Fundação Joaquim Nabuco; biannual; began in 1973.

Clima. Monthly cultural magazine. Established in São Paulo by Clima and directed by Lourival Gomes Machado. First issue May 1941; 16 issues published.

Correio Brasiliense. Published in London by Hipólito José da Costa between 1808 and 1822. Republished in facsimile by Imprensa Oficial do Estado de São Paulo.

Cultura. Official publication (arts, theater, cinema, music, and literature) of the Ministério de Educação e Cultura, Brasília; first issue, 1971. Published three times per year.

Cultura Política. Rio de Janeiro. Cultural magazine launched in 1941 and maintained by the Vargas government. Published by DIP, under the direction of Almir de Andrade, 1951–1954.

O Debate. First communist magazine in Brasil. Published weekly in Rio de Janeiro; directed by Adolpho Porto and Astrojildo Pereira; first issue, July 1917.

Diário de Pernambuco. Published in Recife since November 7, 1825; emphasizes conservative viewpoint.

Diógenes. Biannual publication, dedicated to the study of man, of the Universidade de Brasília, under the auspices of the Conselho Internacional de Filosofia e Ciências Humanas, with the cooperation of UNESCO; first issue, 1981.

Divulgação Marxista. Directed by Calvino Filho and S. O. Hersen; first issue, 1946. Published every two weeks in Rio de Janeiro with the objective of promoting Marxism.

Documentos Históricos. Rio de Janeiro. Published by the Biblioteca Nacional and the Ministério de Educação e Saúde since 1928.

D. O. Leitura. Published monthly in São Paulo by the Imprensa Oficial do Estado since June 1982.

Echo Americano. Published in London between 1871 and 1872 under the direction of Alexandre Mello Moraes.

Edições Cadernos Culturais. Uma Revista de Cultura do Nordeste para o Brasil. Published in Recife, Pernambuco, under the direction of Aluízio Furtado de Mendonça. First issue carries no date; second issue dated February 1975.

Estudos Avançados. Quarterly publication begun in 1987 of the Instituto de Estudos Avançados da Universidade de São Paulo; directed by Alfredo Bosi. Focuses on the social sciences, philosophy, history, and culture.

Estudos Sociais. Marxist publication, directed by Astrogildo Pereira with the collaboration of Jacob Gorender; published from May 1958 to February 1964; circulation 2,000–3,000.

Fon-Fon. Illustrated magazine, begun in Rio de Janeiro in 1907; emphasizes daily life in Rio.

Fundamentos. Cultural magazine of the Brazilian Communist Party, published in São Paulo from 1948 to 1955.

Fundamentos. Revista de Cultura Moderna. Founded by Monteiro Lobato in 1948 and published in São Paulo. Sections on economics, science, literature, theater, and the plastic arts.

Gazeta do Rio de Janeiro. Published in Rio de Janeiro by Imprensa Régia since 1808.

Humanidades. Publication of the Universidade de Brasília and Shell do Brasil. Focuses on history, politics, sociology, anthropology, literature, and the arts.

Idade de Ouro do Brasil. First issue appeared May 14, 1811; continued until June 24, 1823. Printed in Bahia by Tipografia de Silva Serva. Written by Diogo Soares da Silva and Father Inácio José de Macedo, both Portuguese.

O Investigador Português em Inglaterra. Printed in London, 1811 to 1819.

Jornal do Commércio. Printed by Pierre Plancher in Rio de Janeiro, beginning October 1, 1827.

Klaxon. Published in São Paulo between 1922 and 1923. Vanguard magazine associated with the Semana de Arte Moderna.

Kosmos. Exquisitely designed magazine that circulated between 1904 and 1906. Contributors included, among others, Olavo Bilac, Arthur Azevedo, José Veríssimo, Gonzaga Duque, Raul Pederneiras, Félix Pacheco, Coelho Neto, Capistrano de Abreu, and Euclides da Cunha.

Leitura. A Revista dos Melhores Escritores. Published in Rio de Janeiro, beginning in 1942, with special emphasis on literature.

Letras Brasileiras. Irregular magazine published in Rio de Janeiro by A Noite. First issue in 1943 under the direction of Heitor Moniz. Emphasis on Brazilian letters and the influence of intellectuals on the formation of national identity.

Malasartes. Art magazine published in Rio de Janeiro under the direction of Cildo Meireles, Waltércio Caldas, Carlos Vergara, Bernardo de Vilhena, Carlos Zílio, Ronaldo Brito, José Resende, Luiz Paulo Baravelli, and Rubens Gerchman. First issue September–November 1975.

A Marmota. Women's magazine; formerly *A Marmota na Côrte,* until 1857.

A Marmota na Côrte. Women's magazine published by Próspero Ribeiro e Paula Brito, Rio de Janeiro, between 1852 and 1857.

O Mequetrefe. Began publication in Rio de Janeiro in 1875 under the direction of Lins de Albuquerque with collaboration by Cândido de Faria, Antônio Alves do Vale, Aluízio de Azevedo, Olavo Bilac, and Raimundo Correia, among others.

O Mosquito. Subtitled *Jornal Caricato e Crítico;* began circulation in Rio de Janeiro in 1869. Collaborators include Angelo Agostini and Rafael Bordalo Pinheiro. Absorbed other magazines until ceasing publication in 1877.

Muda. Magazine of literature and poetry. Contributors include Paulo Leminski, Wally Salomão, Régis Bonvicino, Carlos Ávila, and Erthos Albino de Souza, among others.

O Novo Mundo. Published in New York from 1871 to 1879 under the direction of José Carlos Rodrigues.

O Pasquim. Weekly tabloid, published in Rio de Janeiro; established in 1968. Editors: Tarso de Castro, Millôr Fernández, and others.

O Patriota. Printed in Rio de Janeiro by Imprensa Régia from 1813 to 1814.

Paz e Terra. Victim of dictatorship; beginning in 1966, nine issues were published.

Pif-Paf. The humor section in this publication is the longest lasting with the exception of that in the weekly *O Cruzeiro.*

Problemas. Published by the Comité Central of the Brazilian Communist Party, 1947 to 1957; almost entirely translations with no space given to discussions of Brazilian reality.

Problemas Brasileiros. Monthly publication of the Conselho Técnico de Economia, Sociologia e Política, São Paulo; first issued in April 1963.

Realidade. Published in the mid-1960s by Editora Azul, São Paulo.

Reverbero Constitucional Fluminense. Published by Typographia Moreira e Garcez, Rio de Janeiro, 1821–1823.

Revista Americana. Monthly magazine in Rio de Janairo that circulated between 1909 and 1919. Founded by Araújo Jorge of Itamarati under the sponsorship of the Barão do Rio Branco. Contributors include Joaquim Nabuco, Euclides da Cunha, Oliveira Lima, Silvio Romero, and José Oiticica e Araripe Júnior.

Revista Brasileira de Cultura. Quarterly magazine established in 1969 in Rio de Janeiro by the Conselho Federal de Cultura, under the direction of Mozart de Araújo. Among the collaborators are Ariano Suassuna, Gilberto Freyre, Rodrigo Mello Franco de Andrade, Octávio de Faria, Luís da Câmara Cascudo, and Peregrino Júnior.

Revista Brasileira de Política Internacional. Quarterly issued by the Instituto Brasileiro de Relações Internacionais, Rio de Janeiro, since March 1958.

Revista Brasiliense. Bimonthly magazine directed by Elias Chaves Neto. The editorial board includes Álvaro de Faria, Caio Prado Júnior, Catulo Branco, Edgard Cavalheiro, E. L. Berlinck, Heitor Ferreira Lima, João Cruz Costa, Nabor Caires de Brito, Paulo F. Alves Pinto, Paulo Dantas, and Sérgio Milliet.

Revista Civilização Brasileira. Founded by Ênio Silveira in 1965 and edited by Moacyr Félix. Published bimonthly in Rio de Janeiro by Editora Civilização Brasileira until 1968. Focus on history, politics, sociology, anthropology, and literature.

Revista da Academia Brasileira de Letras. Rio de Janeiro; established 1910.

Revista da Academia de Letras da Bahia. Salvador; established 1930.

Revista da Academia Paulista de Letras. Monthly; published in São Paulo beginning in November 1937.

Revista de Antropofagia. São Paulo. Literary magazine. Began as a monthly directed by Antônio de Alcântara Machado (10 issues, 1928–1929). Became a weekly (one page in the *Diário de São Paulo*), with some irregularity, directed by Raul Bopp and Jaime Adour da Câmara.

Revista de Cultura Vozes. Petrópolis, Rio de Janeiro; Editora Vozes, beginning in 1907.

Revista do Arquivo Municipal de São Paulo. Established in 1934 under the direction of Alfredo Luzzi Galliano; later directed by Mário de Andrade.

Revista do Arquivo Público do Rio Grande do Sul. Porto Alegre; first issue published in 1921.

Revista do Arquivo Público Mineiro. Established in 1896; published in Ouro Preto until 1898, when it moved to Belo Horizonte.

Revista do Brasil. São Paulo (beginning in 1916) and Rio de Janeiro (beginning in 1926). Monthly publication directed by Júlio Mesquita, L. P. Barreto, and Alfredo Pujol, 1916–1918. From 1918 to 1925, directed by Monteiro Lobato with collaborators Lourenço Filho, Afrânio Peixoto, and Amadeu Amaral. In 1926–1927, published every two weeks, directed by Pandiá Calógeras, Afrânio Peixoto, Alfredo Pujol, and Plínio Barreto, with Rodrigo de Mello Franco de Andrade as editor in chief. In 1938 became a monthly directed by Otávio Tarquínio de Souza.

Revista do Globo. Porto Alegre; Editora Globo.

Revista do Instituto Arqueológico, Histórico e Geográfico Pernambucano. Recife, since 1863.

Revista do Instituto de Estudos Brasileiros. São Paulo; IEB-USP. First appeared in 1966; irregular.

Revista do Instituto Histórico e Geográfico Brasileiro. Rio de Janeiro; since 1839. Publishes special issues dedicated to national history congresses.

Revista do Instituto Histórico e Geográfico da Bahia. Salvador; since 1895.

Revista do Instituto Histórico e Geográfico de São Paulo. São Paulo; since 1895.

Revista do Livro. Rio de Janeiro, Instituto Nacional do Livro, Ministério de Educação e Cultura. Quarterly, established in 1956.

Revista do Norte. Ciências, Letras, Artes e Ofícios. Recife, Pernambuco, under the direction of José Maria C. de Albuquerque; first issue dated April 1942.

Revista do Serviço do Patrimônio Histórico e Artístico Nacional. Rio de Janeiro; issued by the Ministério da Educação e Saúde beginning in 1937; after 1945, published by the Fundação Nacional Pró-Memória.

Revista Illustrada. The leading illustrated magazine of the period; published in Rio de Janeiro from 1876 to 1898 under the direction of Angelo Agostini.

Revista Médica Fluminense. Rio de Janeiro, 1835–1843.

Revista Moderna. Directed by Martinho de Arruda Botelho; published in France, beginning in 1897.

Semana Illustrada. Founded by Henrique Fleuiss; published in Rio de Janeiro, 1861–1875.

SPHAN. Began in 1979 with an issue numbered 0; edited by the Instituto do Patrimônio Histórico e Artístico Nacional (IPHAN). From number 6 forward it was edited by the Secretaria do Patrimônio Histórico e Artístico Nacional (SPHAN).

Staden-Jahrburch. Beiträge zur Brasilkunde. São Paulo, Instituto Hans Staden. Annual publication in German focusing on science and general topics; established in 1953.

Suplemento Literário de Minas Gerais. Belo Horizonte, beginning in 1966. In 1994 name changed to *Suplemento.*

Tempo Brasileiro. Quarterly magazine published in Rio de Janeiro, beginning in 1962, under the direction of Eduardo Portela.

Trópico. Revista de Cultura e Turismo. Published by the Divisão de Expansão Cultural do Departamento de Cultura, Secretaria de Educação e Cultura do Estado de São Paulo; first issue appeared in 1950.

Collections

Abolição. Recife: Fundação Joaquim Nabuco, Editora Massangana (1980s).

Biblioteca de Divulgação Cultural. Rio de Janeiro: Ministério de Educação e Cultura, Instituto Nacional do Livro.

Biblioteca de Divulgação Cultural. Rio de Janeiro: MEC (1950s).

Biblioteca de Estudos Brasileiros. Belo Horizonte, Minas Gerais: Editora Itatiaia.

Biblioteca de Letras e Ciências Humanas, Série Estudos Brasileiros. São Paulo: T. A. Queiroz (1980s).

Biblioteca Histórica Brasileira. São Paulo: Livraria Martins (1940).

Biblioteca Pedagógica Brasileira. Brasiliana. Série Grande Formato. São Paulo: Companhia Editora Nacional (1950s).

Os Cadernos de Cultura. Rio de Janeiro: Ministério de Educação e Cultura (1952).

Coleção Brasil. Análise e Crítica. Rio de Janeiro: Editora Forense Universitária.

Coleção Brasiliana. São Paulo: Companhia Editora Nacional (1931).

Coleção Coroa Vermelha. Estudos Brasileiros. São Paulo: T. A. Queiroz (1980s).

Coleção Debates. São Paulo: Perspectiva (1960s).

Coleção de Estudos Brasileiros (Série Cruzeiro e Série Marajoara). Bahia: Livraria Progresso (1950s).

Coleção Documentos Brasileiros. Rio de Janeiro: José Olympio (1936). Created and directed by Gilberto Freyre.

Coleção Ensaio. São Paulo: Conselho Estadual de Cultura (1950s).

Coleção Estudos Brasileiros da C.E.B. Rio de Janeiro: Casa do Estudante do Brasil, 1945.

Coleção Estudos Históricos. São Paulo: Hucitec (1980s).

Coleção LTC de Estudos Brasileiros. Rio de Janeiro: Livros Técnicos e Científicos (1970s).

Coleção Nordestina. Launched in April 1999 by the federal universities of Ceará, Rio Grande do Norte, Paraíba, Pernambuco, Alagoas, Sergipe, and Bahia.

Coleção Pensamento Político. Brasília: Universidade de Brasília (1980s).

Coleção Pensando a História. São Paulo: Editora Contexto (1980s).

Coleção Retratos do Brasil. Civilização Brasileira, INL (1960s).

Coleção Roteiros do Brasil. Rio de Janeiro: Editora Nacional (1960s).

Coleção Temas Brasileiros. Rio de Janeiro: Editora Conquista (1970s).

Coleção Temas Brasileiros. Brasília: Universidade de Brasília (1980s).

Coleção Textos e Documentos. São Paulo: Conselho Estadual de Cultura (1950s).

Coleção Vida Brasileira. Rio de Janeiro: MEC.

Descobrimentos. Recife: Fundação Joaquim Nabuco, Editora Massangana.

Documentos. Recife: Fundação Joaquim Nabuco, Editora Massangana.

Encontros com a Civilização Brasileira. Rio de Janeiro: Editora Civilização Brasileira; directed by Ênio Silveira and Moacyr Félix. First issue appeared in July 1978. Focus on history, politics, sociology, anthropology, economics, and so on.

Estudos Brasileiros. São Paulo: O Livro (1920s).

Estudos Brasileiros. Rio de Janeiro: Paz e Terra (1970s).

Estudos Brasileiros. São Paulo: Hucitec (1970s).

Estudos Brasileiros. Recife: Fundação Joaquim Nabuco, Editora Massangana.

Estudos e Pesquisas. Recife: Joaquim Nabuco, Editora Massangana.

Monografias. Recife: Fundação Joaquim Nabuco, Editora Massangana.

Obras de Consulta. Recife: Fundação Joaquim Nabuco, Editora Massangana.

Problemas Políticos Contemporâneos. Rio de Janeiro: José Olympio, 1934.

Reconquista do Brasil. Belo Horizonte, Minas Gerais: Editora Itatiaia.

BOOKS

Abreu, João Capistrano de. *Capítulos de história colonial.* 5th ed. Brasília: Editora da UnB, 1963.

Biblioteca Nacional, Rio de Janeiro. *Brasiliana.* Rio de Janeiro: Biblioteca Nacional, 2002.

———. *Catálogo da Exposição de História do Brasil.* Rio de Janeiro: Biblioteca Nacional, 1881–1882.

92 *José Mindlin and Cristina Antunes*

Faoro, Raimundo. *Os donos do poder*. 2nd ed. Rev. and exp. São Paulo: Editora da Universidade de São Paulo, 1975.

Fausto, Boris. *História do Brasil*. 2nd ed. São Paulo: Editora da Universidade de São Paulo, Fundação do Desenvolvimento da Educação, 1995. (Didática, 1)

Fernandes, Florestan. *A revolução burguesa no Brasil*. 3rd ed. Rio de Janeiro: Guanabara, 1987.

Freyre, Gilberto. *Casa grande & senzala*. 25th ed. Rio de Janeiro: José Olympio, 1987.

Gonzaga, Tomás Antônio. *Marília de Dirceo*. New ed. Rio de Janeiro: Impressão Regia, 1810.

Holanda, Sérgio Buarque de. *Raízes do Brasil*. 17th ed. Rio de Janeiro: José Olympio, 1984.

Lisboa, José da Silva. *Observações sobre a franqueza da indústria, e estabelecimento das fábricas no Brasil*. Rio de Janeiro: Impressão Regia, 1810.

Machado, Simão Ferreira. *Triunfo Eucharistico, exemplar da Christandade Lusitana em publica exaltação da Fé na solemne Transladação do divinissimo Sacramento da Igreja da Senhora do Rosario, para hum novo Templo da Senhora do Pilar em Villa Rica, corte da capitania das Minas, Aos 24 de Mayo de 1733.* . . . Lisboa: Officina da Musica, 1734.

Martins, Ana Luiza. *Revistas em revista*. São Paulo: EdUSP, FAPESP, Imprensa Oficial, 2001.

Mello e Souza, Antônio Cândido de. *Formação da literatura brasileira (momentos decisivos)*. 2nd ed. São Paulo: Martins, 1964.

Moraes, Rubens Borba de. *Livros e bibliotecas no Brasil colonial*. Rio de Janeiro: Livros Técnicos e Científicos; São Paulo: Secretaria de Cultura, Ciência e Tecnologia, 1979.

Pizarro e Araújo, José de Souza Azevedo. *Memorias históricas do Rio de Janeiro e das provincias annexas á jurisdição do Vice-rei do Estado do Brasil, dedicadas a El-Rei Nosso Senhor D. João VI. Por Joze de Souza Azevedo Pizarro e Araujo, Natural do Rio de Janeiro.* . . . Rio de Janeiro: Impressão Regia, 1820.

Pope, Alexandre. *Ensaios moraes de Alexandre Pope em quatro epistolas a diversas pessoas traduzidos em portuguez pelo Conde de Aguiar*. With notes by José Warton and by the translator. Rio de Janeiro: Imprenssão Regia, 1811.

Prado, Caio, Jr. *A revolução brasileira*. 7th ed. São Paulo: Brasiliense, 1987.

Reis, José Carlos. *As identidades do Brasil de Varnhagen a FHC*. 2nd ed. Rio de Janeiro: Fundação Getúlio Vargas Editora, 1999.

A revista no Brasil. São Paulo: Editora Abril, 2000.

Ridenti, Marcelo. "A memória, a mídia e a história em revista." In *D. O. Leitura*. São Paulo: IMESP, July 2001.

———. "Por uma cultura nacional e popular: Brasiliense, anos 60." In *D. O. Leitura*. São Paulo: IMESP, July 2001.

Silva, Francisco Ribeiro da. *Aureo throno episcopal, collocado nas minas de ouro, ou Noticia breve da creação do novo Bispado marianense, da sua felicissima posse, e pomposa entrada do seu meretissimo, primeiro Bispo, e da jornada, que fez do Maranhão, o excellentissimo, e reverendissimo senhor D. Fr. Manoel da Cruz, Com a Colleção de Algumas obras.* . . . Lisboa: Officina de Miguel Menescal da Costa, Impressor do Santo Officio, 1749.

Sodré, Nelson Werneck. *História da burguesia brasileira*. 4th ed. Petrópolis: Vozes, 1983.

Statira e Zoroastes. Rio de Janeiro: Imperial Typographia de Plancher, Impressor-Livreiro de S. M. O Imperador, 1826.

Varnhagen, Francisco Adolpho de. *História geral do Brasil*. 7th ed. 5 vols. São Paulo: Melhoramentos, 1962.

5

❦

Forging Future Citizens in Brazilian Public Schools, 1937–1945

Carmen Nava

The script for the classroom play calls for each elementary student to portray an individual state in Brazil and to recite a short verse about the state's beauty and richness. Then, for the high point of the drama, the script calls for "an older female student" to make a dramatic entrance to center stage and to fling her arms open to show the Brazilian flag emblazoned on her long white tunic (figure 5.1). The Brazilian Flag then invites the states (students) to join hands in a circle as she recites a poem about national unity.

> You speak the same beloved and eloquent language
> And only one credo do you recite, with ardent faith . . .
> Uniting us all, in a loving union,
> Only one symbol, one unique flag . . .
> Firmly united, holding each other's hands . . .
> How indestructible we make our Brazil![1]

This play, entitled *The Sacred Union*, appeared in a Brazilian school textbook from the early 1940s. The learning objective of this activity was more elaborate than the rote memorization of state names and geographic features. By acting out the classroom play, the children were to rehearse adult patriotic responsibilities of overt loyalty and civic participation. Specifically, the children were to act out the unification of Brazil's states into a unified nation. Students embodied the states of the union and thereby became active nationalist agents.

The Estado Novo (New State) dictatorship of Getúlio Vargas crafted a version of nationalism in the mold of its "new" political ideology, and

Figure 5.1.   The feminine figure, described in the public school civics play as an "older student," is rendered with an aura and a Christlike posture. Clothing a body that is sexless, the gown harkens to an allegorical past and avoids reference to contemporary world. But the image of the Brazilian flag on the actress's costume, revealed at the climax of the play, transforms Brazil from an abstract idea to something real. *Source*: João Barbosa de Moraes, *Dramatizações cívicas* (Rio de Janeiro: Livraria Jacinto [194?]), 13–20.

civics lessons such as *The Sacred Union* delivered the content of Estado Novo nationalism to Brazilian schoolchildren. The student protagonists in this play, as well as the students in the audience, were cast as actors in a performance of Vargas's nationalist political ideology.[2] British sociologist Benedict Anderson defines *nation* as an "imagined political community" distinguished from other imagined political communities "not by their falseness but by the style in which they are imagined."[3] In the same way that nationalism imagines a nation into being, gender imagines masculine/feminine into being and race imagines us/other into being. The authoritarian Estado Novo (1937–1945) provides a fascinating case to explore this process of reinventing—or reimagining—a nation where race and gender served as both literal and figurative components of the nationalist discourse. At this moment, Brazil was a complex multiracial society undergoing dramatic political, economic, and social change. Official school textbooks and mandated educational activities such as plays, parades, and choral singing may be treated as a specialized form of *Brasiliana* that presented the official version of nationalism to schoolchildren in an age-appropriate manner.[4] This chapter looks not just at the content of the material but also at what schoolchildren were supposed to do with the representations they encountered. The lessons gave schoolchildren lines to recite and roles to play, but students were supposed to do more than read the curriculum—they were supposed to apply what they had learned and become loyal citizens and productive workers. It was not so much a question of being as it was one of doing and being seen doing.[5]

EXAMINING VARGAS'S VERSION OF BRAZILIAN NATIONALISM

The version of Brazilian nationalism examined in this chapter belongs within the context of the long and continuously evolving narrative of Brazilian nationalisms. This scholarly historical approach debunks Vargas's claim of exclusive legitimacy. Nationalism sees itself as being natural or innate, but that is myth. As British philosopher Ernest Gellner argues, we must "turn the tables on nationalism-as-seen-by-itself."[6] The historical perspective exposes the myth by documenting how the nationalisms change over time. Estado Novo school textbooks reveal a significant but little-studied example of the behind-the-scenes workings of Brazilian nationalism.[7] The primary sources for this historical study—classroom textbooks for the elementary and secondary levels—were written by private parties and published by commercial enterprises. As a sort of commodified curriculum, they served not only a growing market of public school classrooms but also as a new mass medium in printed form.[8] During the Estado Novo, classroom texts promoted Brazilian nationalism through a repetition of certain formulas that had been screened by publishers, and increasingly by state and federal evaluators, for appropriateness of textual and visual content.[9] Textbooks used during the Estado Novo are a distinguishable document set since the federal government under Vargas began its objective of reviewing "all" textbooks for public school use.

Some brief comments are needed here to establish the historical moment. In 1937, Getúlio Vargas and his supporters declared a "New State," tearing down the remaining shreds of the liberal ideology of the First Republic (1889–1930) and replacing it with a newly centralized vision of the Brazilian nation and Brazilian nationalism. Vargas employed a renovated nationalism to advance the new economic and political agenda between 1937 and 1945 and to consolidate popular support among the citizenry.[10] Vargas faced many domestic challenges to national unity, especially centrifugal forces of regionalism. In the citizen, Vargas sought to overcome loyalty to local identities, which had prevailed before, and to replace it with loyalty to the nation and his administration. The Estado Novo discourse presents Vargas's nationalism as a new, "organic nationalism" based on objectivity and good sense. Further, the discourse argued that the new state was authentically Brazilian, unlike the previous republic.[11] Elsewhere, scholars have examined the corporatist and paternalistic politics of the Estado Novo and documented the "contradictions and paradoxes" in its cultural policies.[12] Suffice it to say that Vargas reinterpreted *brasilidade* (Brazilianness) and then promoted it ambitiously.

It is important to stress that the Vargas regime promoted a strengthened sense of paternalistic national identity on a mass scale. The federal government broadcast a message of national unity to the fullest extent of the national populace, repeatedly and in multiple media. For example, the administration employed new radio technologies to broadcast the *Brazil Hour* to Brazilians throughout the national territory. In another example, the administration monitored and legislated about carnival and the composition of original samba songs.[13] Through these other cultural initiatives, the administration was protecting or enhancing national culture, but it was also exercising new control through censorship and selective repression. Children in public schools became important targets in Vargas's nationalist campaign: the regime established ambitious new goals to inculcate appropriate patriotic values in the hearts and minds of the nation's youth. As minister of education Gustavo Capanema argued,

> When we assert that education will function at the service of the state, we mean that [education], far from being neutral, should take part, or better, should adopt a philosophy and follow a list of values, should strictly follow the system of moral, political, and economic directives which constitute the ideological base of the nation, and . . . be under the supervision, the control, and the defense of the state.[14]

Public schools were an important new venue for the centralized government campaign led by Vargas to legitimize his New State. Physical education, vocational, and academic curricula promoted group activities that emphasized the ideal of national unity. In the official jargon of the era, Vargas and his supporters sought to "remove the obstacles which impeded the action of government."[15] The stated goal was national rejuvenation and economic progress. In this case, unschooled Brazilian children were an obstacle to the realization of Vargas's vision for the nation.

While a full discussion of public education policy during the Estado Novo falls outside the scope of this chapter, it important to establish here that what children read—indeed the educational experience of schoolchildren in Brazilian public schools—was legislated to an unprecedented extent under Vargas's Estado Novo.[16] In Vargas's vision, the new scientific and democratic public education would produce a generation of Brazilians who saw themselves as "moral, political, and economic units" who worked toward national goals.[17] During the Estado Novo, the federal government began to produce lists of approved texts in an attempt to standardize national instruction. The National Commission for Textbooks ordered that after January 1, 1940, all textbooks would be subject to approval by Ministry of Public Education and Health before they could be used in a public school.[18] Inadmissible content included criticism of the regime, disrespect of national tradition, incitement of class struggle, destruction of religious sentiment, and "pessimism or doubt as to the future power of the Brazilian race."[19] After Brazil declared war on the Axis powers on August 13, 1942, criteria for evaluating textbooks shifted to reflect new political contingencies—textbooks that advocated fascism in general or Hitler or Mussolini in particular were thereafter banned.[20] Civic education, or "moral and political instruction" as it was also called, was made mandatory by the constitution of 1937. Instead of a specific discipline, civic education was mandated as an educational practice that was to permeate all scholastic activities in all types of schools, and all teachers were responsible for transmitting these values and ideas.[21]

In examining civics material, this chapter goes beyond chronicling the pro-Vargas nationalism to reveal how this particular form of *Brasiliana* represented gender and race to Brazil's multiracial coeducational student body. When using gender as a category of analysis, historian Joan Scott's definition of the term is pivotal. Scott asserts that the core of her definition "rests on an integral connection between two propositions: gender is a constitutive element of social relationships based on perceived differences between the sexes, and gender is a primary way of signifying relationships of power."[22] Both parts of Scott's definition bear out in the present chapter. Barbara Weinstein makes a helpful clarification that the point is not that the institution (here, the Vargas administration) imposed an image on a population that had no prior gender constructions. Rather, Vargas's nationalism "served to elaborate, formalize, and institutionalize difference" in ways that were advantageous to the administration.[23] Additionally, rigid barriers between masculine and feminine gender roles served the purposes of the institution without regard to their correspondence to reality. So this chapter contributes by documenting the particular form that Brazilian patriarchalism took under Vargas.[24] The very examination that reveals patterns in the construction of gender meanings also reveals patterns in the constructions of race.

In multiracial societies such as Brazil, promoters of national identity have necessarily grappled with long-standing racial tensions, and they have constructed the idea of nation partly through an interpretation of what racial differences mean. In devising an approach to the race constructs in the documents under review, we must acknowledge that the Vargas administration created its political rhetoric in the context of an ongoing national dialogue about race in Brazil. Scholars have analyzed patterns in how Europeans and Brazilians discuss notions of race (difference in genetics, physiognomy, psychology, intelligence, morality, etc.), comparing people in Brazil to people in Europe and comparing peoples in Brazil.[25] These notions of difference contain assumptions of hierarchy that we can identify as being religious, social, gendered, as well as racial.[26] Clearly, European intellectuals influenced Brazilian social thinkers, but as historian Dain Borges argues, the "weak science" of race and degeneracy theories provided Brazilian thinkers with a "creative matrix for social vision" that could respond to European scientific debates but also acknowledge positive traits in Brazilian culture.[27] Somewhere between the pseudoscientific approach of the eugenists and Gilberto Freyre's "lyrical picture" of Brazilian society, Estado Novo rhetoric acknowledges no racial problem and instead portrays Brazil as a white European country.[28] Although the Estado Novo ideology does not deny the reality of the indigenous and African presence in Brazil, it does refer to the nation as being white or soon-to-be white. Jeffrey Lesser argues that a single, unitary national identity never existed in Brazil; this chapter examines how the Vargas regime tried to make it exist by tinkering with the nation's collective memory.[29]

Constructs of gender and race were woven together into the fabric of the nationalist message, giving texture and body to Vargas's nationalism. The assumption was that conceptions of race and gender are not natural entities but "constructs, not absolutes but relative, situational . . . engendered by historical process of differentiation."[30] In some examples of the curricular materials, constructs of gender stand out in relief; in others, race. But both aspects are present. Thus, the cover of the book *Civic Plays* illustrates happy, attentive children participating in various ways in the educational activity, a class play (figure 5.2). The illustrator carefully depicts boys and girls involved in the activity, suggesting full participation from all students— all white students, that is. The children on the stage are acting; the children in the audience are spectating. By performing appropriate roles, they are rehearsing patriotism that reduces the ambiguity of Brazil's regionalist tensions to the certainty of unity.[31] The play they perform, and the image of the nation that the textbook illustration creates, was explained through a gendered and racialized vocabulary.

GENDER IN THE IDEA OF THE BRAZILIAN NATION

As in other nation-states, gender undergirded the structure of social hierarchy of Brazil. As the present case illustrates, gender as a signifier of power is omnipresent in constructions of nationalism and national identity.[32] The

Figure 5.2.   The cover of the textbook portrays a well-appointed school auditorium as an appropriate venue for the civics play. The schoolchildren onstage wear historical costumes while the children in the audience—both girls and boys—wear elementary school uniforms. Note the active stance of the boy actor and the demure stance of the girl actor. *Source*: João Barbosa de Moraes, *Dramatizações cívicas* (Rio de Janeiro: Livraria Jacinto [194?]).

familiar gender formula of the dominant masculine and the subordinate feminine, with the feminine occasionally being placed "on a pedestal," appears frequently in the textbook lessons. In perhaps the most prominent example of this formula, phrases such as *Pátria* (Fatherland) and *Mãe-Pátria* (literally Mother-Fatherland or Mother-country) refer to the idea of the Brazilian nation. The way that this language refers to the male and female parents reveals how national identity functioned as a relational concept rather than as an essence.[33] *Pátria* is a grammatically feminine term often defined as "nationhood" or "Fatherland." The Latin root of the word, *pater*, indicates that the nation belongs to or is possessed by the father. Diana Taylor emphasizes that in the concept of *Pátria*, the idea of nation has been "constructed in patriarchy."[34] This is not to say that the Vargas administration invented this idea but rather that it employed this trope effectively, with a prime example being the rhetorical strategy of referring to

Vargas as the "Father of the Poor." Marit Melhuus and Kristina Stolen argue "gender differences... appear to take on commanding significance in the conceptualization of differences and the ordering of inequalities other than gender."[35] This point is salient considering the emphasis that the Vargas administration gave to inculcating patriotism in the nation's public school children.

Reference to *Pátria* and *Mãe-Pátria* in the civic education curriculum reinforced the parent-child model for nation-citizen relations. The idea of nation was gendered to encourage schoolchildren to identify it with the unquestionable good of Mother. In one lesson, *Pátria* is equated with "Mother" and "Love" on one hand and "Unity" on the other.

> United, we will learn to love you as our beloved Mother!
> United, we will learn to defend you as our just Mother!
> United, we will learn to exalt you as Mother pure and good!
> United, we will fight to raise you even higher and make you happier![36]

The text instructs children to love and defend the Mother-country. The reference to Mother-country sought to make a connection in the children's mind between appropriately respectful behavior in the family and home and an appropriately loyal attitude of patriotism for Vargas's New State. Instilling such paternal loyalty to the state in the hearts and minds of school-age Brazilians helped the nationalists distance modern Brazil from the backwardness of the nation's past (especially its practice of slavery). If devotion to the state would subsume differences of race, then the new national "family" would be harmonious and unified.

The transference of the child's love for Mother to the nation was presented as a duty. This requirement was introduced to the child in school-book lessons such as the following: "It is my duty to be a patriot, as it is my duty to be a good son."[37] "Good son" and "good citizen" were thus made into related values. A good son behaves toward the nation as he behaves toward his Mother and family. In another text, a list of important civic duties exhort children to "venerate the *Pátria*," sing the national anthem "with enthusiasm," and "adore your mother."[38] Yet another lesson makes the equation patently clear: "Bad son, bad citizen! Good son, good citizen![39] Children in the nation/family were taught that good citizenship starts at the home and that the proper relationship of the individual to the state is one of deference. The male-determined pattern of social hierarchy was the model for the construction of the national family—that is, the nation.[40]

Some textbook lessons focus on inculcating loyalty to the *Pátria*/ Motherland at home, as something one was born into. As one lesson phrases it, *Pátria* is the "first world of the civilized man."[41] Or,

> Patriotism is the profound and noble sentiment that the citizen feels for his *Pátria*. It is the moral patrimony that is born in the cradle and that the father bequeaths to his son in the cultivation of traditions and veneration of ancestors.[42]

In this lesson, the father's role is to instill the patrimonial sentiment in the child starting from infancy, continuing to inculcate the veneration of traditions and ancestors in an unbroken line. Here, it is the masculine parent who passes patriotic values to the next generation.

Textbook lessons directly addressed the proper relationship between nation-state and citizen and consistently dictated the same kind of authoritarian and patriarchal relationship. In one primary school text, a son asks his father,

> "What is government, Dad?" The father replies, "[Government] is an organization that directs and orients the destiny of the country, attending to its needs and its progress. Everybody needs a guide, a *governador*, a *diretor* who determines a smooth running of things."[43]

An authoritarian and paternalistic version of government and society emerges from this text. Students were taught that they needed a strong, presumably masculine, leader to maintain social equilibrium and guarantee progress.

School textbooks made the Estado Novo synonymous with the *Pátria*. In the most common theme, the president himself, Getúlio Vargas, was presented as an inspired, heroic figure for the schoolchildren to venerate. In one lesson, students are taught that Vargas united the "Great Brazilian Nation" and restored Brazil's "direction in the pursuit of glory and national unity." Immediately following the chapter "I Believe in the Creator!" is a chapter entitled "I Believe in the Unifier of Brazil!"

> Getúlio Vargas united Brazil, he unified the Nation and gave the great Brazilian mosaic an orientation of healthy continuity . . . under a perspective of order and progress, on the road to success for the Glory of the most beautiful hopes, the most beautiful dreams, the purest aspiration of National Unity.
> Oh, Brazil has become Brazil!
> . . . and because of this: I believe in Getúlio Vargas—Unifier of Brazil![44]

Employing the technique of repetition, this lesson hammers on the theme of *united, unified, unity, unifier*. Getúlio Vargas is the agent of unification and, as such, deserves veneration.

These lessons catechized students about a social hierarchy where Vargas, as head of state, comes directly after God: reverence, even more than respect, was called for. Another text, one winning official recommendation in the state of São Paulo, emphasizes Vargas's activities regarding the decision to declare war against the Axis powers. "President Getúlio Vargas, superior as always, followed the people and declared war."[45] Although Vargas is "superior" vis-à-vis other national leaders, he is presented as if he acted as any good democratic leader must by following the wishes of his constituency. Later, Vargas is described as a "serene but decisive commander. He is a man of personal courage and a patriotic Brazilian. A friend of his people...impartial, just and good." Despite the fact that this text had been praised for "avoiding ornate patriotic language," it is actually consistent with the treatment that most texts accord Vargas.[46] The state is portrayed as an extension of family structure, with Vargas acting as the father.[47] The image of Vargas as the national father figure had wide implications. This ideology depicts workers as children who not only require protection by the state but also need the personal intervention of the national father.[48]

"ADVANCING THE NATION" THROUGH PATRIOTIC LABOR

The Vargas administration articulated explicit new goals for Brazilian public education that addressed the exigencies of the domestic acceleration of industrialization and the looming war overseas.

> Education will act, then, not in the sense of preparing man for just any action in the society, but precisely in the sense of preparing him for necessary and defined action, so that he comes to constitute a moral, political, and economic unit, which helps advance the nation. The individual, thus prepared, will...pursue a certain course. He will work to construct the nation, in its material and spiritual elements, conforming to the lines of a precise and steady ideology.[49]

Apparently, this rhetoric, although blunt and not sentimental, responded to the popular sector's growing desire to belong to the nation.[50] The ideal worker was unit produced by renovated public education. Assuming such a vision, specifically who served the nation through which kinds of work? Vocabulary that uses the male as generic is suggestive. Another observable pattern in the textbook lessons is that they describe appropriate forms of work for patriotic Brazilians in masculine versus feminine terms. If meanings of gender vary according to the historical moment, then the construction of idealized work roles reflects the efforts of the Vargas administration to maneuver the nation out of the depression and into an advantageous position during World War II. These representations of nation were intended for public school children, including the offspring of the burgeoning class of factory workers.[51] When examining Estado Novo textbooks for representation of work for the nation, constructions of gender predominate over constructions of race.

In a section on the citizen and government, a textbook lesson promotes the idea that the type of work or profession is a free choice for Brazilian citizens and that the federal government "protects" the family, work, and education. But to enjoy these privileges, the Brazilian citizen needs to meet certain obligations:

All should work, since work is a social duty.
All should contribute military service, since to guard national security and to be prepared for it is a patriotic duty.
All should respect the authorities, because in this respect is the guarantee of order and progress.[52]

Intended for schoolchildren of the third grade, this lesson communicates implicit messages about gender as well as explicit ones about patriotic duty. Patriotic duty through military service is only prescribed for males. A few texts utilize the more inclusive term *people* to call young Brazilians to serve their country.

The land is great and rich; the people are strong and capable of great deeds. But the country, still new, cannot demonstrate all the development it will have one day. For this it will need the new generations, the children and youth of today. Understand your duty. Be worthy of your *Pátria* and your people. Devote yourself to study and work![53]

The central idea is that work is a social duty and the nation has an acute need for Brazilians to carry out that duty. Thus, free choice of profession or work is actually limited according to certain roles for either gender, and only the male roles are treated. The masculine role is thus legitimated, and the feminine role is implicitly marginalized.

Regarding ideals of masculine work, the civic lessons evoke a martial spirit most frequently. Another of the ubiquitous lists of civic duties cites as the first duty of a patriotic young Brazilian,

Love Brazil more than anything in life and Brazilians more than any others on Earth. Venerate your *Pátria*, your soldiers, and sailors.[54]

In the hearts and minds of young Brazilians, the Motherland should be venerated above "anything in life." Other lessons use phrases such as "sacrifice in carrying out one's duty" and "zeal in the defense of the national territory" to describe appropriate nationalist values.[55] Soldiers are presented as national heroes by virtue of their occupation.[56] The soldiers embody the state as the "container of national identity and aspiration." In claiming that position, the military male/state guards the Mother-country.[57] Uncertainty before war and then overt participation in war on the side of the Allies made this call to arms vital. The line of communication from textbook to teacher to student was charged with this wartime message. Interestingly, in spite of the war, the textbook lessons call for women to carry out their social duty in the home.

Which part were women to play in the national society? Which territory or territories were assigned to women?[58] Didn't a looming war dislodge some part of the traditional gender hierarchy? These textbooks reserve the economic, social, and cultural space of "the nation" for masculine actors—except for the home, where feminine actors are assigned.[59] Thus, textbooks from the Estado Novo period cast women's fundamental social responsibility—and patriotic responsibility—as educating their children in the home. One text is explicit, saying that "only in this way will the woman have cooperated for the great national victory—the education of the man of tomorrow."[60] Thus, women were honored *in their place*.[61] Women's ideal traits are uniformly described as virtues such as generosity and love, and the only appropriate role for women is that of homemaker. This was a portrayal of ideal behavior: mothers were pure and watched over their families, raising their daughters to serve the nation by growing up to be happy homemakers. When they became full-grown adults, these Brazilian citizens would revere their Motherland as they revered their own mothers and as they would expect to be revered by their children. Feminine role models are practically absent in lessons on Brazil's history and national traditions. A rare lesson on a heroine appears in a textbook for elementary students.[62] Here a naval battle between a Portuguese vessel and a pirate ship in 1714 is recounted to provide an example of heroism—in this case, one woman's heroism. The comprehension question at the end of the lesson asks about naval terminology but nothing about the woman's accomplishments or women's accomplishments in general. Lessons in moral and civic education that present "our illustrious men" feature a gallery that includes men and omits women.[63]

Although the Estado Novo encouraged some notable changes in the industrial relations system, the textbook lessons do not question established roles for men and women. This set of traditional gender roles comprise a nostalgic view of the bourgeois family in which men worked at industrial labor, the professions, or the military while women served as mothers and homemakers, outside the wage-labor system. The mother/homemaker plays her part by ministering to the needs of the family. For example, in an illustration that accompanies a lesson entitled "Occupations," the father animatedly converses with his offspring at the family table while the mother hovers in the shadows of the kitchen doorway.[64] Though she is in the background of the frame, her performance of the prescribed role is featured. In this image we see a visual representation of a real woman executing her duty by adhering to the prescribed social norms. The pre-scribed role for Brazilian women to demonstrate their patriotism by pre-siding over the nuclear family—a role that overidealized the experiences of many Brazilian women and ignored the expanding employment op-portunities in industry—is presented with a force and a consistency that must have been influenced by traditionally hierarchical Catholic values. Through the textbook lessons, the schools, as an agency of the state, pro-mote the established gender order as being "natural" to a generation of Brazilian schoolchildren who would see dramatic change in economic, po-litical, social, and cultural relations.[65]

EMBODYING THE NATION

The hierarchies of race and gender are often inextricable when the idea of the Brazilian nation is represented in human form. In the lessons, the major characters are cast according to race and gender formulas and include (in rough order of assigned importance) the Brazilian white male, the Brazil-ian male *mestiço*, the Brazilian white female, and the African male and the Indian male (African and Indian females did not figure prominently). Al-though the lessons theoretically acknowledge the contribution of the three races to the homogenized Brazilian, in actuality the rhetoric marginalizes black images in favor of whitened or white images.[66] In a comparable way, the generic Brazilian male was supposed to represent both the masculine and the feminine but actually reinforced the gender hierarchy. Numer-ous scholars have explored and documented the process of *branqueamento* (whitening) in Brazil, where value is given to one's "becoming white." To approach an understanding of *branqueamento*, some scholars have an-alyzed assumptions in certain cultural products that address the sexual aspect of race and gender constructions, such as novels and commercial advertising. Like many of these adult-oriented cultural products, the child-oriented public school textbooks use and support assumptions of race and gender in terms of whitening. Unlike adult consumer products, though, the textbooks omit reference to sexual relations. Textually repressing the sexual aspect of whitening results in a message that equates whitening with one's properly memorizing and frequently reciting civic commandments.[67]

The Brazilian flag appears as a frequent and significant motif in both textual and visual curricula, and the inanimate object is personified in gender and racial terms. *The Sacred Union* was intended to be part of the commemoration of Flag Day. In this play, the flag that symbolizes the nation is portrayed as being feminine and phenotypically European (see figure 5.1). The body of the nation as presented in both text and visual image is young, European, and feminine. This is not an illustration of a woman or a mother but an image of the *Pátria*. The body is feminine and not masculine, inverting the traditional hierarchy but retaining the feminine (image of the flag) on a figurative pedestal. The body is white, not black or mulatto or *mestiço*. Here the textbook advocates the greater value of the white. Gender and race in the image enhance the image's pedagogic impact on young children.

In the same textbook, the Brazilian flag is central in another play, called *Nossa Raça* (Our Race; or, Our People). Intended for upper-level elementary students studying Brazilian history, this play makes reference to the flag as a masculine figure (figure 5.3).

A certain understanding of race is explicit in the lesson. In the play, the actors number four: the Brazilian, the Portuguese Race, the Black Race,

Figure 5.3.   This illustration appears in the text of a civics play called *Our Race*. Composed of adult masculine figures—not elementary schoolchildren—the allegory represented in the illustration would have been difficult to cast and stage. However, this allegorical image serves to reinforce the lesson that the three races of Brazil have merged into an ideal, new, *Brazilian* race. *Source*: João Barbosa de Moraes, *Dramatizações cívicas* (Rio de Janeiro: Livraria Jacinto [194?]), 39.

and the Indigenous Race. The text of the play calls for each actor to recite a fifteen-line poem. For the dramatic finale, the stage directions call for the student actors portraying the three historical races to fraternally embrace while the actor portraying the Brazilian (the new race) proclaims,

> The three races joined together
> To produce a superb and noble new type,
> Thus forming the Brazilian race.[68]

The dialogue of the play upholds the idea of national unity in terms of racialized population groups where the three races—European, indigenous, and African—join together to form a new and improved race. The lesson instructs students that the new type is "superb" and "noble."

In this identity-making process, individual difference and social inequalities "disappear in the staging of a singular body."[69] The message is eugenic but optimistic. We can imagine how the students who participated in this classroom play would rehearse this particular version of Brazilian identity until they knew it by heart. The message of unity-through-eugenics was projected in a society that Europeans then regarded as "dysgenic" and that social scientists today describe as rural, racially mixed, and illiterate.[70]

The accompanying illustration does not depict the action described in the play's dialogue but instead uses the flag as a visual image to inculcate the lesson on a metaphoric level. The torso of the Brazilian, a masculine adult figure, emerges triumphantly (and surrealistically) from the Brazilian flag. Underneath the Brazilian/flag, three races appear as adult males, rendered in identifiable sixteenth-century attire. The Portuguese is portrayed in a bold stance in the center. The Indian is depicted in a loincloth, grasping a lance. Unlike the other two ethnic types, whose bodies and faces were rendered realistically, the African appears with a naturalistic body (albeit posed with arms held stiffly at his side and wearing a slave's short pants), but the face is rendered in what appears to be the minstrel's blackface makeup.[71] The Brazilian is portrayed from the waist up, nude, with a confident expression and with muscular arms crossed on his chest. The figure bears a remarkable facial resemblance to president Getúlio Vargas. Race and nation conflate into the Brazilian to constitute an unequivocal visual parable (though one no longer feasible to produce on an elementary classroom stage). The illustration supports the text of the lesson: in Brazil, the historical races have blended to form a new, noble, and whitened racial ideal. Throughout this textbook, Afro-Brazilian and indigenous children rarely appear as subjects in the text or the illustrations, and *mestiços* are rendered white. The lessons admonish young Brazilian citizens to conceptualize the nation as being unified in spite of racial differences. But even as the textbooks present a whitened racial ideal, the textbook authors acknowledge the reality of the nation's "triple ethnicity."[72]

"Ethnic Types" is the title of a chapter in a secondary-school geography text.[73] The content of the chapter is divided with subject headings: "The majority of Brazilians descend from Europeans"; "*Mestiços* constitute an important element of the population"; "The Black element in the Brazilian population"; "The indigenous lived isolated from civilization"; and "The Asian element is little represented." The lesson defines ethnic terminology such as *caboclo, mamaluco, gaúcho,* and *cafuso* and cites the 1940 census for its statistical information. The text characterizes African Brazilians as being "generally strong," though "superstitious" and interested in "fetishist rites." *Mestiços* and whites are portrayed differently.

> The *mestiço*, which is an authentic Brazilian historical creation, stands alone before the almost-pure white, for whom the *mestiço*, sooner or later, will be mistaken.[74]

The text of this lesson communicates a eugenic message through its emphasis on the white European type, as if desired biological traits could be bred into Brazilians and destructive inherited traits eliminated.[75] The lesson include an illustration to reinforce this concept (see figure 5.4). The official nationalism describes diversity but advocates uniformity.

The elements of the illustration include the title "Brazil," an outline map of the country, and human figures (all masculine), with a narrative caption below the illustration. The five figures purportedly illustrate the demographics presented in the caption:

> More than half of the population of our country is constituted of individuals who are white, descendents of Europeans. *Mestiços* account for about thirty percent and blacks less than ten percent.[76]

Representing half of the nation's citizens, the white figure towers over the other types like a giant. The smaller, *mestiço* figure has dark skin but distinguishable features; the figures of the other nonwhite ethnic types appear with indistinguishable features. In the most literal interpretation, the illustration can be seen as a kind of bar graph of national population superimposed over an outline of the national territory for visual effect. However, an alternative reading of the illustration features the figures labeled *Mestiços,* Blacks, *Indios,* and *Diversos* occupying an increasingly distant background while the figure labeled Whites dominates the foreground. Either way the book's author (whose initials appear in the illustration) seems to conclude that the population of Brazil is whitening and that this trend is constructive. This illustration reinforces the central lesson of the text: Brazil is a white European country.

A população brasileira

Mais de metade da população de nosso país é constituída por indivíduos de côr branca, descendentes de europeus. Os mestiços correspondem a cêrca de 30 % e os negros a menos de 10 %.

Figure 5.4. The authors layer a visual metaphor on top of the ostensibly empirical demographic data by placing the figure representing the white majority in the foreground. This reinforces the lesson's thesis that Brazil is a white nation. *Source:* Aroldo de Azevedo, *Geografia do Brasil. Tomo Primeiro. A Terra. O Homen. A Economia,* 16th ed. (São Paulo: Companhia Editora Nacional, 1948), 102.

CONCLUSION

As one part of his effort to rapidly modernize Brazil in the face of turbulent world politics and complex social and political challenges at home, Getúlio Vargas executed an ambitious public education campaign to forge allegiance to the Brazilian state in the hearts and minds of Brazilian schoolchildren. In targeting public schoolchildren, centralizing control over the civics curriculum content, and then mandating adherence to it throughout the country, Vargas's nationalist campaign stands out from those of previous administrations and set a precedent for subsequent administrations. Supporters of the regime appealed to young Brazilians, who "would fly in airplanes . . . and enjoy the advantages of electricity and radio," to embrace the Estado Novo's "rational education" and work to transform the nation's "disunity" into national unity in "a unique historical moment."[77] Still, the

Vargas administration expressed its policies and nationalist ideals in a society where most privileged children attended private schools and most
children who did attend public school were poor and stayed for only a few
years.[78] The representations did not reflect reality. This chapter has shown
that in the textual content and visual images of public school textbooks,
formulas of gender and race in large part constitute the nationalism for
schoolchildren that in turn became a foundation for Vargas's larger policy
initiatives.

In representing the nation in a way that was advantageous for the state,
"getting the history right" was less important.[79] The idea of the nation—its
past and future—was described in racial and gendered terms that reinforced the established social hierarchy. Thus, whether discussing Brazil's
historical patrimony or presenting a list of civic commandments, the curriculum constructed gender ideals wherein the feminine ideal was to serve
the nation by staying at home and the masculine ideal was to serve the
nation through labor and public service. The curriculum presented racial
ideals wherein there was no racial problem—Brazil was a white nation
or would soon be white. While the curriculum acknowledged differences
in gender and differences in race in Brazilian society, it made distinct use
of both. With gender, the perceived differences were used to rationalize
and promote separateness of and the hierarchical relationship between the
masculine and the feminine. On the other hand, with race, the differences
between white, black, and *mestiço* were acknowledged and the hierarchy remained unchanged, but the separate identities were fused into a whitened
ideal. As we have seen, the representations of gender and race in Estado
Novo public school civics textbooks were not innocent, transparent, or
true.[80]

The public school textbooks show that the educational approach during
the Vargas administration prioritized inculcating allegiance to the state
over open inquiry and liberty. Although the Vargas regime gave new attention to public education in Brazil, these changes were not installed as a
result of consensus in society but rather as a form of social control.[81] De-
viation from the scripted version of nationalism was not acceptable. Still,
the authoritarian nationalism that Vargas prescribed is a layer on top of the
fundamental nationalist discourse. The historical approach helps to identify the myths of the nationalism, including the internal myth that says that
nationalism is natural.

Vargas's project to promote Brazilian national identity through the public
school curriculum illustrates both continuity and change in the ongoing
evolution of Brazilian national identity. The newly aggressive nationwide
reach of the federal government disbursed a version of the Brazilian nation
that was packaged as new to a new clientele. But the content was not in fact
new. The state delivered to the children of the nation's multiracial men and

women a consistently patriarchal and whitened image of the nation and called on the children to act patriotically as adults. This form of nationalism conflated the distance between the child and the abstract nation by labeling the Brazilian nation a family. It obscured the multiplicity of regional, ethnic, and racial difference by labeling the Brazilian nation *unified*. The facts were presented to the schoolchildren with an authoritarian rhetoric that argued that this form of nationalism was among the highest truths. The promise of nationalism was perpetual subservience to the national father. The question arises, did these future citizens, forged in Estado Novo schools, act out their role?

NOTES

1. João Barbosa de Moraes, *Dramatizações cívicas* (Rio de Janeiro: Livraria Jacinto, 194?), 13–20.

2. Diana Taylor, *Disappearing Acts: Spectacles of Gender and Nationalism in Argentina's "Dirty War"* (Durham, N.C.: Duke University Press, 1997), 27. Also see Mary Kay Vaughan, "The Educational Project of the Mexican Revolution: The Response of Local Societies (1934–1940)," in *Molding the Hearts and Minds: Education, Communications, and Social Change in Latin America*, ed. John A. Britton (Wilmington, Del.: Scholarly Resources, 1994), 105–27.

3. Benedict Anderson, *Imagined Communities: Reflections on the Origin and Spread of Nationalism* (New York: Verso, 1991), 6.

4. Compare with chapter 4 of this volume, José Mindlin and Cristina Antunes, "*Brasiliana*: Published Works and Collections."

5. Taylor, *Disappearing Acts*, 92.

6. Ernest Gellner, *Nations and Nationalism* (Ithaca, N.Y.: Cornell University Press, 1983), 48–49.

7. Carmen Nava, "Patria and Patriotism: Nationalism and National Identity in Brazilian Public Schools, 1937–1974" (PhD diss., University of California, Los Angeles, 1995); and Nava, "Lessons in Patriotism and Good Citizenship: Nationalism and National Identity in Public Schools during the Vargas Administration, 1937–1945," *Luso-Brazilian Review* 35, no. 1 (Summer 1998): 39–66. Compare with Robert M. Levine, *The History of Brazil* (Westport, Conn.: Greenwood Press, 1999), 106.

8. Steven Selden, *Inheriting the Shame: The Story of Eugenics and Racism in America* (New York: Teachers College Press / Columbia University, 1999), 63.

9. Until the Estado Novo, Brazilian school textbooks were largely unregulated, which meant that school texts varied greatly in composition and distribution. Decreto Lei 1.006 (December 30, 1938) ordered that after January 1, 1940, all textbooks would be subject to approval by Ministry of Public Education and Health (MESP) before they could be used in a public school. See Brasil, MESP, "Ministerio de Educação e Cultura: Trinta Anos de Organização e Situação Atual," *Documento de trabalho* 3, no. 6 (1968). In the samples I examined, I looked for evidence of official approval or adoption and/or an award.

10. Ludwig Lauerhass Jr., *Getúlio Vargas e o triunfo do nacionalismo brasileiro* (Belo Horizonte: Itatiaia; and São Paulo: Editôra da Universidade de São Paulo, 1986);

Lúcia Lippi Oliveria, Mônica Pimenta Velloso, and Angela Maria Castro Gomes, *Estado Novo: Ideologia e poder* (Rio de Janeiro: Zahar Editores, 1982); Robert Levine, *Father of the Poor?* (Cambridge: Cambridge University Press, 1998).

11. Oliveira, *Estado Novo*, 4–5.

12. See Randal Johnson, "Regarding the Philanthropic Ogre: Cultural Policy in Brazil, 1930–1945/1964–1990," in *Constructing Culture and Power in Latin America*, ed. Daniel H. Levine (Ann Arbor: University of Michigan Press, 1993), 311–56; Riorden Roett, *Brazil: Politics in a Patrimonial Society* (Westport, Conn.: Praeger, 1992); Howard J. Wiarda, *Corporatism and National Development in Latin America* (Boulder, Colo.: Westview, 1981).

13. On radio and nationalism, see Joseph Straubhaar, "The Electronic Media in Brazil," in *Communication in Latin America: Journalism, Mass Media, and Society*, ed. Richard R. Cole (Wilmington, Del.: Scholarly Resources, 1996), especially 220–22; and Philo C. Wasburn, *Broadcasting Propaganda: International Radio Broadcasting and the Construction of Political Reality* (Westport, Conn.: Praeger, 1992). On samba and carnival, see William Rowe and Vivian Schelling, *Memory and Modernity: Popular Culture in Latin America* (London: Verso, 1991), 135; Roberto DaMatta, *Carnavais, malandros e heróis: Para uma sociologia do dilema brasileiro* (Rio de Janeiro: Editora Guanabara, 1990); Claudia Mattos, *Acertei no milhar: Samba e malandragem no tempo de Getúlio* (Rio de Janeiro, 1982); and Alison Raphael. "Samba and Social Control: Popular Culture and Racial Democracy in Rio de Janeiro" (PhD diss., Columbia University, 1980).

14. Gustavo Capanema, "Discurso lido na solenidade comemorativa do primeiro centenário da Fundação do Colégio Pedro II no dia 2 de dezembro de 1937," in *Panorama de Educação Nacional: Discursos do Presidente Getúlio Vargas e do Ministro Gustavo Capanema* (Rio de Janeiro: MESP, 1937), 16.

15. Vanderlei Ramos de Moraes, "A Era de Vargas: Uma Decada de Educação, 1930–1940. Contribuições para o Estudo da História da Educação no Brasil" (master's thesis, Universidade Federal, Rio de Janeiro, 1978), 43.

16. Nava, "Patria and Patriotism," 46–64. See Walter Jerome José Davila, "Perfecting the Race: Education and Social Discipline in Brazil's Vargas Era, 1930–1945" (PhD diss., Brown University, 1998); David K. Plank, *The Means of Our Salvation: Public Education in Brazil, 1930–1995* (Boulder, Colo.: Westview, 1996); Edward Reisner, *Nationalism and Education since 1789: A Social and Political History of Modern Education* (New York: Macmillan, 1925); and Fernando de Azevedo, *Brazilian Culture: An Introduction to the Study of Culture in Brazil* (New York: Macmillan, 1950), 470–76.

17. MESP, "Plano Nacional de Educação. Questionario para um Inquerito. 1936," 1–2.

18. The director of the research institute of the Ministry of Education under Vargas, Lourenço Filho, believed that the lack of regulation of school textbooks meant that many texts currently in use were actually "defective." Lourenço Filho to W. W. Charters, June 22, 1942, Archivo Historico do Instituto Nacional de Estudos Pedagógicos (Ministério de Educação e Cultura, AHINEP), Brasília DF.

19. Decreto Lei 1.006 (December 30, 1938).

20. Marinete dos Santos Silva, *A Educação Brasileira no Estado-Novo* (São Paulo: Editorial Livramento, 1980), 42. Textbooks from before this date often employed

styles and content inspired by the fascist movements in Germany and Italy, and Brazilian education bureaucrats studied Nazi pedagogy.

21. Article 131. "Moral and Civic Instruction" was first established in 1925 as part of the final exam of the first year of secondary school. Brasil, Decreto 16.782-A (January 1925). See Maury Rodrigues Cruz, *Antecedentes e perspectivas da educação moral e cívica no Brasil* (Curitiba: Editora da Universidade Federal do Paraná, 1982), 96.

22. Joan W. Scott, "Gender as a Useful Category of Historical Analysis," *American Historical Review* 91, no. 5 (December 1986): 1053–75.

23. Barbara Weinstein, "Unskilled Worker, Skilled Housewife: Constructing the Working Class Woman in São Paulo, Brazil," in *The Gendered Worlds of Latin American Women Workers*, ed. John D. French and Daniel James (Durham, N.C.: Duke University Press, 1997), 95. Original emphasis. On the paulista case, see Theresa R. Veccia, "My Duty as a Woman: Gender Ideology, Work, and Working-Class Women's Lives in São Paulo. Brazil, 1900–1950," in French and James, *The Gendered Worlds*; and Joel Wolfe, *Working Women, Working Men: São Paulo and the Rise of Brazil's Industrial Working Class, 1900–1955* (Durham, N.C.: Duke University Press, 1993).

24. French and James, *Gendered Worlds*, 16.

25. Lilia Moritz Schwarcz, *The Spectacle of the Races: Scientists, Institutions, and the Race Question, 1870–1930* (New York: Hill and Wang, 1993); Thomas E. Skidmore, *Black into White: Race and Nationality in Brazilian Thought* (Durham, N.C.: Duke University Press, 1993); Nancy Lays Stepan, *The Hour of Eugenics: Race, Gender, and Nation in Latin America* (Ithaca, N.Y.: Cornell University Press, 1991); Richard Graham, *The Idea of Race in Latin America, 1870–1940* (Cambridge: Cambridge University Press, 1990); Dain Edward Borges, "'Puffy, Ugly, Slothful, and Inert': Degeneration in Brazilian Social Thought, 1880–1940," *Journal of Latin American Studies* 25, no. 2 (May 1993): 235–56; Borges, "Review Essay: Brazilian Social Thought of the 1930s," *Luso-Brazilian Review* 31, no. 2 (Winter 1994): 137–50; António Sérgio Alfredo Guimarães, "Racism and Anti-racism in Brazil: A Postmodern Perspective," *Racism and Anti-racism in World Perspective*, ed. Benjamin P. Bowser (Thousand Oaks, Calif.: Sage, 1995).

26. Robert Stam, *Tropical Multiculturalism: A Comparative History or Race in Brazilian Cinema and Culture* (Durham, N.C.: Duke University Press, 1997), 1.

27. Borges, "'Puffy, Ugly, Slothful,'" 239, 256. Also see Simon Schwartzman, *A Space for Science: The Development of the Scientific Community in Brazil* (University Park: Pennsylvania State University Press, 1992).

28. Dzidzienyo calls Freyre's approach a "lyrical picture" of race in Brazilian society. Anani Dzidzienyo, "Brazil," *International Handbook on Race and Race Relations*, ed. Jay A. Sigler (New York: Greenwood, 1987), 23. Compare with chapter 3, José Luis Passos and Valéria Torres, "Gilberto Freyre's Concept of Culture in *The Masters and the Slaves*." Also see Gilberto Freyre, *The Masters and the Slaves: A Study in the Development of Brazilian Civilization* (Berkeley: University of California Press, 1986); Jeffrey Needell, "Identity, Race, and Modernity in the Origins of Gilberto Freyre's *Oeuvre*," *American Historical Review* 100, no. 1 (February 1995): 51–77; Borges, "'Puffy, Ugly, Slothful,'" especially 253; and, in a special issue focusing on Freyre with guest editor Joel Wolfe, *Luso-Brazilian Review* 31, no. 2 (Winter 1994).

29. Jeffrey Lesser, *Negotiating National Identity: Immigrants, Minorities, and the Struggle for Ethnicity in Brazil* (Durham, N.C.: Duke University Press, 1999), 3.

30. Stam, *Tropical Multiculturalism*, 44.

31. Murray Edelman, *Constructing the Political Spectacle* (Chicago: University of Chicago Press, 1988), 3.

32. See Mark E. Kann, *On the Man Question: Gender and Civic Virtue in America* (Philadelphia: Temple University Press, 1991); Dana D. Nelson, *National Manhood: Capitalist Citizenship and the Imagined Fraternity of White Men* (Durham, N.C.: Duke University Press, 1998); Richard Trexler, *Sex and the Conquest: Gendered Violence, Political Order, and the European Conquest of the Americas* (Ithaca, N.Y.: Cornell University Press, 1995).

33. Ferguson, *Representing "Race,"* 81.

34. Taylor, *Disappearing Acts*, 77.

35. Marit Melhuus and Kristi Anne Stolen, *Machos, Mistresses, and Madonnas: Contesting the Power of Latin American Gender Imagery* (London: Verso, 1996), viii.

36. J. Antunes Mattos, *Creio no Brasil* (Porto Alegre: Sul Editora, 1942), 25.

37. Arthur De Vasconcelos, *Pró Juventude Brasilero* (São Paulo: Melhoramentos, 1943), 17.

38. Federico Villar, *Faze assim: Breviario moral e cívico* (Rio de Janeiro: Oficinas Graficas Laemmert, 1940), 63.

39. João Lemos, *O evangelho da juventude brasileira: Educação pessoal, moral e cívica* (author's edition, 1945), 67. The Portuguese reads, "Mau filho, mau cidadão! Bom filho, bom cidadão!"

40. Darien Davis, *Avoiding the Dark: Race and the Forging of National Culture in Modern Brazil* (Brookfield, Vt.: Ashgate, 1999), 9.

41. Lemos, *O evangelho*, 67.

42. Silvio Coelho, *Educação moral e cívica* (Rio de Janeiro: Zelio Valverde, 1940), 80.

43. Luiz Amaral Wagner, *Nosso Brasil: Para o 4o grau primário* (São Paulo: Nacional, 1938), 138–72. See Nava, "Patria and Patriotism," 69.

44. Mattos, *Creio no Brasil*, 166.

45. Morel Marcondes Reis, *Contos brasileiros: Livro de leituras cívicas para classes adiantadas de cursos primários* (Rio de Janeiro: Francisco Alves, 1943), 12.

46. Reis, *Contos brasileiros*, 4, 14.

47. The Estado Novo propounded a series of regulations to bolster "traditional" families. In 1939, Vargas proposed funding special programs for the "health of mothers and children" by placing a tax on single adults and married couples without children. Wolfe, *Working Women*, 72–73.

48. Wolfe, "Father of the Poor," 87.

49. MESP, "Plano Nacional de Educação. Questionario para um Inquerito. 1936," 1–2.

50. Davis, *Avoiding the Dark*, 28.

51. These images, designed for Brazilian elementary school children, contrast with those that had been exported to the adult cosmopolitan audience at international expositions in the last quarter of the nineteenth century. See Ingrid E. Fey and Karen Racine, eds., *Strange Pilgrimages: Exile, Travel, and National Identity in Latin America, 1880s–1990s* (Wilmington, Del.: Scholarly Resources, 2000).

52. Erasmo Braga, *Leitura III: Para o 4o Ano Escolar* (São Paulo: Melhoramentos, 1942), 178.

53. Braga, *Leitura III*, 252.

54. Villar, *Faze assim*, 63.

55. Coelho, *Educação moral e cívica*, 80.

56. Coelho, *Educação moral e cívica*, 82–83.

57. Taylor, *Disappearing Acts*, 38.

58. Jill K. Conway, Susan C. Bourque, Joan W. Scott, "Introduction," in *Learning about Women: Gender, Politics, and Power* (Ann Arbor: University of Michigan Press, 1989).

59. Linda Steiner, "Construction of Gender in Newsreporting Textbooks, 1890–1990," *Journalism Monographs* 135 (October 1992): 2.

60. Coelho, *Educação Moral e Cívica*

61. Taylor, *Disappearing Acts*, 33–34.

62. Braga, *Leitura III*, 142–47.

63. Boaventura Ribeiro da Cunha, *Surto moral e cívico nacional* (typed manuscript, AHINEP, 1938), 17.

64. Braga, *Leitura III*, 42.

65. Nellie P. Stromquist, ed., *Women and Education in Latin America: Knowledge, Power and Change* (Boulder, Colo.: Rienner, 1992), 5.

66. Davis, *Avoiding the Dark*, 58–59.

67. Ella Shoat and Robert Stam, *Unthinking Eurocentrism: Multiculturalism and the Media* (New York: Routledge, 1994), 220.

68. Moraes, *Dramatizações Cívicas*, 35, 39.

69. Taylor, *Disappearing Acts*, 121.

70. Nancy Lays Stepan, "Eugenics in Brazil, 1917–1940," in *The Well-Born Science: Eugenics in Germany, France, Brazil, and Russia*, ed. Mark B. Adams (Oxford: Oxford University Press, 1990), 111.

71. See Joseph Baskin, *Sambo: The Rise and Demise of an American Jestor* (New York: Oxford, 1986); and Wayne Martin Mellinger, "Postcards from the Edge of the Color Line: Images of African American in Popular Culture, 1893–1917," *Symbolic Interaction* 15, no. 4 (1992): 413–33. Also see John J. Johnson, *Latin America in Caricature* (Austin: University of Texas Press, 1980).

72. Cunha, *Surto moral*, 15.

73. Aroldo de Azevedo, *Geografia do Brasil. Tomo Primeiro. A Terra. O Homen. A Economia.* 16th ed. (São Paulo: Companhia Editora Nacional, 1948). Though its publication date falls after the end of the Estado Novo, I include it because of the likelihood that its earlier editions were in use between 1937 and 1945.

74. Azevedo, *Geografia do Brasil*, 101–11.

75. Selden, *Inheriting the Shame*, 71.

76. Azevedo, *Geografia do Brasil*, 102.

77. Da Cunha, *Surto moral*, 21, 40.

78. Davila, "Perfecting the Race," 12–13.

79. Eric Hobsbawm, *On History* (New York: New Press, 1997), 270.

80. Taylor, *Disappearing Acts*, 21.

81. Davila, "Perfecting the Race," 4.

III

SIGHTS

6

The Visual Imaging of Brazilian Identity

Ludwig Lauerhass, Jr.

PATHS TO THE GLOBAL VILLAGE

By the time of Brazil's independence in 1822 the geographic vision of the world was reasonably clear in broad outline and in much detail, at least to an educated few. Yet, views of its component parts were often dim, imprecise, and unevenly distributed. Most people still had little sense of the world beyond their immediate surroundings, and opportunities for travel—expensive, arduous, and time-consuming as it was—seldom came. Visual images had long been available in the form of prints and book illustrations, but these were in scant circulation and were often unreliable renderings based on written descriptions rather than firsthand observation. The literate public continued to rely on printed texts for their visions of home and foreign lands, and, of course, most people could not read at all. The visually knowable world that we now take for granted did not yet exist.

As the nature of life changed over the course of the nineteenth and twentieth centuries, so did people's images of themselves and their neighbors, even their most distant neighbors. Along with expanding agriculture, industrialization, growing populations, greater mobility, the spread of democratic institutions, rapidly advancing technology, scientific discovery, and the emergence of a more highly interdependent global economy came demands for a clear and precise knowledge about the world. Governments needed accurate assessments of the resources and societies within their domains, and a host of commercial, cultural, and scientific needs could be met only with improved, more widely distributed visual images, in addition to statistical data. In Brazil such demands for national imaging were given a dramatic initial impulse when the royal court of Portugal was transferred to Rio de Janeiro in 1808, in the face of Napoleon's invasion of the Iberian Peninsula.

By the time of the centennial celebration of Brazilian independence in 1922, the electronic/media age in which we now live was well under way. In fact, most of the technological paths leading us toward what Marshall McLuhan has described as our life in a "global village" or "simultaneous happening" had been discovered. Photography, the telegraph, sound recording, wireless transmission, and motion pictures were then commonplace, and radio, talking pictures, and television were only a few years off. Advances in typography, photo reproduction, printing, and paper manufacture significantly reduced publication costs, allowing for greater production and wider distribution of printed materials than what had ever been seen before. By the end of the twentieth century telecommunications, the computer, and the Internet linked even the remotest corners of Brazil with one another and with the outside world. Brazilians could readily see themselves, as could others, within the broad context of a rapidly changing world. Visual images not only recorded Brazil's progress and modernization but also helped to chart its direction.

COLONIAL ANTECEDENTS

With the exception of a brief period of Dutch occupation in northeastern Brazil in the seventeenth century, artists were not readily available to document the progress of Portuguese exploration and settlement during colonial times (1500–1808). Accurate imagery was rare. The earliest firsthand accounts lacked illustration, and those that followed—by Hans Staden (figure 6.1), André Thevet, and Jean de Léry—were illustrated in Europe from their textual descriptions.[1] Images as well as texts were often corrupted and reused by other writers (figure 6.2). Manipulation of imagery was frequent and made to achieve desired effects. Image makers were often propagandists and sensationalists rather than objective recorders. Certain themes, such as cannibalism and the existence of monsters, were popularized in collections of voyages such as those with engravings by Theodore de Bry (figures 6.3, 6.4). Fact commingled with distortion, objectivity with prejudice, and reality with fantasy. Brazilian Indians often looked like seminaked Europeans with feathers in their hair, and neighboring Peruvian Incas even appeared in the works of Jorge Juan and Antonio de Ulloa dressed in togas and housed in Renaissance palaces (figure 6.5).[2]

Figure 6.1. A crude woodcut of warring Indian tribes from the mid-sixteenth-century Account by Hans Staden. Note placement in rear of four heads on pikes. *Source*: Hans Staden, *Hans Staden, the True History of His Captivity, 1557* (London: G. Routledge & Sons, 1928).

Figure 6.2. A nineteenth-century revision of the Staden image (fig. 6.1) in a steel engraving. Among other changes, the heads on pikes have been moved to the forefront of the compound. *Source*: Ferdinand Denis, *Brésil* (Paris: Firmin Didot, 1837).

Figure 6.3. The imagery of Brazilian cannibalism was popularized in the collections of American voyages published by Theodor de Bry at the end of the sixteenth century. *Source*: *L'Amérique de Théodore de Bry* (Paris: Editions du Centre National de la Recherche Scientifique, 1987).

Figure 6.4. De Bry spread the notion that Brazil was inhabited by monstrous creatures on land and sea, and in the air. *Source*: *L'Amérique de Théodore de Bry* (Paris: Editions du Centre National de la Recherche Scientifique, 1987).

Figure 6.5. Indian civilization in the Americas was praised by conveying Inca nobles in European dress, living in Renaissance palaces. *Source*: Jorge Juan and Antonio de Ulloa, *Voyage historique de l'Amérique Meridionale* (1752).

In the late eighteenth century a new European spirit of enlightenment encouraged empirical research and exploration. While its impact was not generally felt in Brazil until after the arrival of the court in 1808, the groundwork for new approaches to visual documentation was being laid by scientific travelers such as Alexander von Humboldt. One of the most prominent figures of this age, he spent a five-year period in the Americas, though not in Brazil, from 1799 to 1804. He set new standards for the visual presentation of geographic, natural, social, and historical data along with travel accounts and scientific studies. His work had a profound influence in contemporary scientific communities and among the broader educated public. His books were issued and reissued throughout the century in many editions and translations and served as models for his successors to follow.

UR-IMAGES OF BRAZIL: A GOLDEN AGE OF VISUAL DOCUMENTATION

In the first half of the nineteenth century Brazil became an active focus of scientific exploration and social analysis. Under royal and later imperial

Figure 6.6.   Greater visual accuracy came only with the illustrated travel accounts by European scientists, such as Spix and Martius, in the early nineteenth century. Here, Europeans are portrayed reacting to the splendor of Brazilian nature by artists who accompanied the expeditions. *Source*: Johann Baptist von Spix and Karl Friedrich Philip von Martius, *Reise in Brasilien* (Munich: Lindauer, 1823).

sponsorship, leading European observers came to study Brazil's exotic landscapes, natural resources, and rich ethnic variation. They traveled much of the country and produced a descriptive panorama of its regional differences and distinctive national characteristics. Their illustrated travel accounts and scientific publications have long stood among the century's most important geographical, biological, and anthropological contributions. Foremost among these interpreters of Brazil were Prince Maximilian of Wied-Neuwied, the great botanist Karl F. P. von Martius, the zoologist Johann Baptist von Spix (figure 6.6), painters Moritz Rugendas and Jean Baptiste Debret, and the journalist Charles Ribeyrolles (working with the photographer Victor Frond). (See also figures 6.7–6.13.)[3]

All were concerned with both the accuracy and the artistic quality of their visual documentation. Together they published hundreds of images, reproduced as striking engravings and lithographs—many hand-colored—in sumptuous, large-format albums or atlases. Many single images, whether of physical or human-made landmarks, social or ethnic types, or examples of flora and fauna, were so memorable that they served as founding images or Ur-images that would be perpetuated in a variety of later

Figure 6.7. A popularized version of the scene in fig. 6.6 with great loss of detail and dramatic intensity. *Source*: Ferdinand Denis, *Brésil* (Paris: Firmin Didot, 1837).

renderings by other artists, printmakers, and photographers. A few of the images attained near-iconic status as conveyors of national identity. The power that made them memorable sprang from their context associated with a sense of Brazilianness—from subjects such as palm trees, Sugarloaf Mountain, masters and slaves, forest Indians, or coffee plantations—and from their artistic excellence. For some, popularity was immediate and continued; for others, it was revived and re-revived following interludes of obscurity.

Prince Maximilian, followed by Spix and Martius, visited Brazil's major settled areas, including urban centers, mining districts, and agricultural regions, as well as the hinterlands that connected them. Their enormous collections of plant and animal species, deposited in European and American institutions, engendered decades of scientific research. The monumental *Flora Brasiliensis*, initiated by Martius in the 1840s and completed with the aid of seventy-five other botanists in 1906, was published in forty large volumes, and it alone contained nearly four thousand botanical illustrations. His traveling companion Spix published separate works on Brazilian fish, birds, reptiles, and mammals, and together Spix and Martius produced excellent maps and well-illustrated descriptions of varied aspects of Brazilian life. Martius even wrote studies on local music and linguistics. He became an influential member of the Brazilian Institute of Geography and History (founded in 1839) and was one of the first to suggest that writing of Brazil's history should be approached from the perspective of racial and cultural fusion—European, African, and Indian.

The German Moritz Rugendas and the Frenchman Jean Baptiste Debret were the most talented *costumbrista* painters to visit the Americas in the nineteenth century. The legacy of their physical and social images formed the core of what became Brazil's golden age of visual documentation. Both traveled widely, on their own or as part of scientific expeditions, sketching what they observed. Their work was often tinged with a romantic flair, depicting heroic Indians or dramatic historical scenes, but they also sought to capture the nuances of the exotic society in which they worked. As he did later in Argentina, Chile, Peru, and Mexico, Rugendas sketched urban scenes, landscapes, Native Americans, and black slaves (figure 6.8). Debret left an even more detailed anthropological record, portraying all levels of society, from the royal court to the slave ship. He was particularly in tune to occupational activities and to the treatment and punishment of slaves. The work of each was published in Paris with large lithographic reproductions and a text of a *voyage pittoresque* (figure 6.9).

Figure 6.8.   The importation, treatment, and occupational activities of African slaves were frequent subjects of early nineteenth-century illustration. *Source*: Johann Moritz Rugendas, *Voyage pittoresque dans le Brésil* (Paris: Mulhouse, Engelman, 1835).

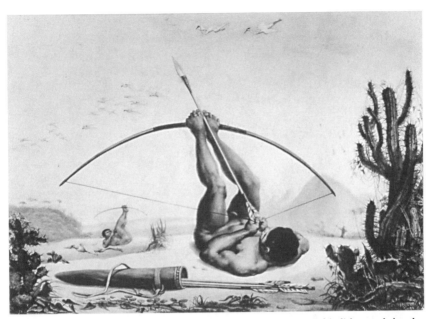

Figure 6.9. Brazilian Indians, while accurately depicted, as in this lithograph by the French artist Jean Baptiste Debret, were also idealized and captured in dramatic poses. *Source*: Jean Baptiste Debret, *Voyage pittoresque et historique au Brésil* (Paris: Firmin Didot, 1834).

Figure 6.10. A steel engraved altered version of the image in fig. 6.9, issued by the same publisher, Firmin Didot. *Source*: Ferdinand Denis, *Brésil* (Paris: Firmin Didot, 1837).

Figure 6.11.   A modern photograph of an Indian striking a pose similar to that in figures 6.9 and 6.10, with a bow shooting at birds in the sky. *Source*: Jean Manzon, *Flagrantes do Brasil* (Rio de Janeiro: Bloch, 1950), 120.

The age of these great plate atlases concluded in 1861 with the publication, again in Paris, of Charles Ribeyrolles's *Brasil pittoresco*. This work, unlike those that preceded it, was reproduced from photographs rather than sketches. Victor Frond, who traveled with Ribeyrolles, was the first documentary photographer to attempt a panoramic documentation of Brazilian society similar to that done earlier by painters of equal anthropological and geographic value. The images convey the combined qualities of photographic accuracy with the artistic rendering made by several lithographers. The work opens with portraits of the imperial family and follows with scenes of Rio de Janeiro (figures 6.12 and 6.13), Petrópolis, Minas Gerais, and Bahia. Original plates from this volume—like those from the atlases of Maximilian, Spix and Martius, Rugendas, and Debret—are still highly prized and sold regularly in the antiquarian print market. They, along with reproductions of varying quality, commonly adorn the walls of houses and public buildings in Brazil today, thus perpetuating their role as iconic Ur-images.

Figure 6.12.   The aqueduct in Rio de Janeiro has served as an icon of the urban landscape since the late eighteenth century. Here it is shown in an 1850s lithograph made from a photograph by Victor Frond. *Source*: Charles Ribeyrolles, *Brasil pittoresco: Album de vistas* (Paris: Lemmercier, 1861).

Figure 6.13.   The Rio aqueduct in a 1920 *National Geographic* photograph. *Source*: *National Geographic Magazine* 38, No. 3 (September 1920).

THE FIRST MASS-MARKET BOOKS

Although the large-format lithographic atlases were expensive and beyond the reach of the general public, many of their images were quickly copied and widely distributed, at times by the same publisher. In Paris, for example, Firmin Didot, who issued the first edition of Debret, produced a series of some forty volumes under the general title *L'Univers Pittoresque—Histoire et description de tout le peuple*. Didot's aim was to create a verbal and visual encyclopedia of all major countries and areas of the world as they were known in the 1830s. In this endeavor he commissioned texts and culled visual images from a range of existing sources. Ferdinand Denis wrote the volume on Brazil, which was translated into German, Italian, and Portuguese and illustrated by ninety-two plates taken from Hans Staden through the nineteenth-century scientific and artistic documentalists.[4] These images often appeared with modifications, which were in turn passed on to future generations of copyists, who at times severely corrupted them. Plates from this series and their descendant variations (figures 6.6, 6.7, 6.8, 6.9, 6.10, 6.11) are, like the originals that inspired them, still widely circulated and sold as both books and separate prints.

By midcentury, as part of a general expansion of the book-publishing industry, visual imagery of Brazil proliferated. Journalists, diplomats, businessmen, missionaries, and independent travelers of all sorts joined the corps of sponsored scientists and artists in producing illustrated texts. Among these second-generation accounts were those of two American Methodist ministers. Initiated in 1845 as *Sketches of Residence and Travel in Brazil* by the Reverend Daniel P. Kidder, who had traveled to many parts of Brazil distributing Bibles and recording his firsthand impressions, the work was later revised and augmented by his colleague James C. Fletcher, who traveled an additional three thousand miles, including areas not reached by Kidder. Their collaborative project *Brazil and the Brazilians* became enormously popular, appearing in nine editions published in New York, Boston, Philadelphia, and London over a twenty-two-year period from 1857 to 1879.[5] In fact, it served as the major source of information about Brazil in North America and England in the latter half of the nineteenth century. The work included 150 steel engravings depicting Brazilian life and nature—some made from original sketches and daguerreotypes and others copied from a variety of Ur-images. Some images, such as the portraits of emperor Dom Pedro II (figures 6.14, 6.15, 6.16), were revised from one edition to another. Now considered a classic, the work has been translated into Portuguese and is kept in print to this day.

Figure 6.14.   The visual images of Brazil's Emperor Pedro II changed with his advancing age. Here he appears as an adolescent to illustrate a work on Brazil by Daniel P. Kidder. *Source*: Daniel P. Kidder, *Sketches of Residence and Travels in Brazil* (London: Wiley and Putnam, 1845).

Figure 6.15.   In 1879, the emperor appears in his old age. *Source*: James C. Fletcher and D. P. Kidder, *Brazil and the Brazilians*, 9th ed. (Boston: Little Brown, 1879).

Figure 6.16.   One of many caricatures of Pedro II in Brazil's active and relatively free press. *Source*: Rafael Bordallo Pinheiro, *Album das glories* (Lisbon: 1880–1883).

THE COMING OF PHOTOGRAPHY

The advent of photography was one of the great revolutions of the nineteenth century—so much so that William Ivins, former curator of prints at the New York's Metropolitan Museum of Art, could claim with a measure of truth that "the histories of techniques, of art, of science, and of thought can be divided into their pre- and post-photographic periods."[6] From the 1840s on, many of the changes in values, attitudes, and ideas were related to photography. Even though they were subject to manipulation, photographic images conveyed a greater sense of reality and immediacy than those made by the hand of artists. Photographs were accurate; they portrayed what was seen, and seeing was believing. The new pictorial process was also faster and cheaper, and early in the twentieth century it could be practiced by anyone with a widely affordable Kodak camera. It democratized the entire realm of image production. Everyone could be the photographer as well as the subject of photographic images.

Photography spread quickly to Brazil as it did to most parts of the world. The first photographs—daguerreotypes—debuted in France in 1839, and the technology came to Brazil a year later. In the following decades European photographers worked throughout the country, where they were joined by Brazilians who readily mastered the new medium. Such names as Stahl, Mullock, Frisch, Gaensly, Coutinho, Ferrez, Riedel, Pacheco, Leuzinger, Militão, Gutierrez, and Malta reflected the cosmopolitan nature of their growing profession. Emperor Dom Pedro himself became an enthusiastic practitioner and collector of photography, and by the turn of the century more than two hundred photo studios had flourished in Rio de Janeiro alone. Tens of thousands of images in all forms—daguerreotypes, albumen and silver prints, postcards, and lantern slides—gained popularity among locals and tourists alike. Brazilians and foreigners could tap these ever-changing aspects of Brazil's national identity. While photographers recorded events and publicized the new, they often repeated Ur-images, presenting them with clarity and a sense of reality. One photographer, Militão Augusto de Azevedo, produced a "then and now" album comparing his 1862 photographs of São Paulo street scenes with ones taken in 1887 of the same scenes. The photographic work of Marc Ferrez, a second-generation Brazilian of French ancestry whose father, Zeferino, had come to Brazil as a member of the French Artistic Mission in the 1810s, gained international recognition for its exceptional aesthetic merit and its documentary value. His long career, from the 1860s until his retirement in 1914, coincided with a period of urbanization and economic expansion during which coffee culture and the wealth it created came to symbolize Brazil and the growing dominance of São Paulo within this development. The rubber boom added a further and still more exotic cast to the country's shifting identity.

Ferrez's photos, like the novels of Machado de Assis, captured the dynamics of emerging urban lifestyles. From his base in Rio de Janeiro Ferrez was well positioned to become a major national as well as local observer, reaching out to São Paulo, Minas Gerais, Bahia, Pernambuco, Paraná, and Rio Grande de Sul. His portraiture ranged from the imperial family to street vendors and his photographic views from idyllic landscapes to scenes of industrial and agricultural activity. He often received governmental commissions to record elements of the modernization process—for example, the building of the Brazilian navy; the construction of railroads; and the architectural documentation of Rio's newly carved out main boulevard, the Avenida Central (now the Avenida Rio Branco). Ferrez also gave due attention to the reinterpretation of Ur-images, such as Sugarloaf Mountain, Guanabara Bay, and the waterfalls of Tijuca Forest (figure 6.17). He was Brazil's transitional image maker par excellence, perpetuating established icons within the context of national progress.[7]

The work of Augusto Malta took up where Ferrez's left off, both in time and in professional approach. Rather than become a commercially astute artistic photographer like Ferrez, who successfully blended realism with impressionistic interpretation, Malta became Rio's premier photojournalist

Figure 6.17.   Natural icons of Rio de Janeiro, such as Corcovado and Sugarloaf Mountains, shown in this turn-of-the-century photograph by Marc Ferrez, became common identifiers of the city at home and abroad. *Source*: Gilberto Ferrez, *Photography in Brazil, 1840–1900* (Albuquerque: University of New Mexico Press, 1990).

of the first half of the twentieth century. He served the municipal government as an official photographer from 1903 until 1936, producing a corpus of more than thirty thousand photographs. Less concerned with aesthetic refinement, he had a great sense of the newsworthy and chronicled the accelerating pace of Rio's development. He conveyed the animation of city life—the movement of its streets, markets, cafés, political demonstrations, and beaches. He caught the drama of large-scale urban renewal. He photographed the hydraulic demolition of Castelo Mountain and the extensive shoreline landfilling that followed. He documented the damage from storms and floods as well as many of the city's public works projects. New forms of entertainment, the racetrack, movie theaters, and the modern carnival attracted his camera eye. Many of his images found their way into the growing mass market, either as printed postcards or as magazine and book illustrations. For Malta the image of Brazilian identity was almost exclusively urban. He publicized the new Brazil, the land of the future (figure 6.18).[8]

Figure 6.18. Many photographs of Rio have aimed to show the city as a bustling, modernizing metropolis. Here is a parade poised in front of the Monroe Palace at the edge of the bay. The serpentine sidewalk designs were also a distinguishing mark of the city. *Source: Fotografias do Rio de ontem: A. Malta* (Rio de Janeiro: Prefeitura da Cidade do Rio de Janeiro, [n.d.]), 13.

THE GROWTH OF MASS-MARKET PRINTED IMAGES

Advances in printing technology together with lowered costs expanded the mass market for images as well as for written material in the decades that spanned the twentieth century. From midcentury such popular news magazines as the *Illustrated London News* and *Harper's Weekly* led the way. A Brazilian monthly, *O Novo Mundo: Periódico Illustrado do Progresso da Edade*, followed their model in the 1870s. This magazine was published in New York under the direction of the Brazilian journalist José Carlos Rodrigues, who later edited Rio's leading newspaper, *O Jornal do Comércio*. Aimed at a Latin American, primarily Brazilian, readership, *O Novo Mundo* augmented its general international coverage with a special emphasis on the progress of the United States and on developments within Brazil. It was "an illustrated journal, depicting popular, historical, and other events of the day by engravings executed in the best style of modern art and printed with the utmost typographical skill."[9] These images were state-of-the-art wood engravings of the time, mostly made from photographs, the standard means of reproduction until the 1890s. Brazilian subjects included portraits of Indians and leading figures of the day—such as Dom Pedro II, the Duque de Caxias, Machado de Assis, and the Visconde do Rio Branco—as well as urban and natural landscapes such as forests and the Paulo Affonso Falls (the Brazilian Niagara; figures 6.19, 6.20).

The Brazilian government turned to photographic imagery as part of a propaganda effort to project a positive view of the national identity to the world at large. In preparing for Brazil's participation in the Universal Exposition of 1889, held in Paris, the Baron of Rio Branco produced an *Album de vues de Brésil* to accompany a text on Brazil revised from the French Encyclopedia.[10] His expressed intent was to present a view of contemporary Brazil, like that of the album of Ribeyrolles and Frond three decades earlier. Its coverage, however, was to be more comprehensive, especially with respect to urban scenes from different parts of the country. The ninety-four images were reproduced from photographs sent from Rio. Most were by Marc Ferrez, but a few prephotographic classic views by Rugendas and Prince Maximilian were also included. Although for some photos the standard wood-engraving technology was utilized, most were reproduced by the newer, halftone process, which conveyed the realistic sense of an actual photograph. Thus, the artistry of Ferrez and the publicizing of Brazilian development began to reach an international audience.

Varieties of visual images, from halftones to caricature, played a growing role in the popular press, with Brazil again following worldwide trends. Beautifully produced monthlies such as *Kosmos*, *Renacença*, and *Ilustração Brasileira* heralded the modernization of the country, blending current-event analysis with serious commentary on literature and the arts.

Figure 6.19. Like *Harper's Weekly* and the *Illustrated London News*, Brazilian editor José Carlos Rodrigues featured photographs rendered as wood engravings in his magazine *O Novo Mundo* in the 1870s. Seen here is a view of Paulo Affonso Falls, the "Niagara of Brazil." *Source*: *O Novo Mundo* (July 23, 1873).

Figure 6.20. Forest Indians are shown in this 1926 photograph from the *National Geographic Magazine*. Similar imagery appears to this day. *Source*: *National Geographic Magazine* 49, no. 4 (April 1926).

Reportage and articles on historical and cultural themes by some of Brazil's leading intellectuals were interspersed with high-quality photographs and other artwork. Subjects ran the gamut from the inauguration of the Avenida Central to scenes of slavery by Rugendas. Other magazines, such as the *Revista da Semana, Vida Fluminense,* and *Don Quixote,* were noted primarily for their caricature. They were dominated by immigrant artists such as Angelo Agostini and Bordallo Pinheiro (figure 6.16), who approached contemporary society and politics in a satiric vein, using humor to achieve another, often metaphoric level of reality. As national symbols, a jocular version of the emperor was replaced by an abstract heroic female image of "the republic" in her Phrygian cap. Seriocomic treatment brought the public into a highly visualized world of the country's issues, problems, successes, and failures.[11]

VIEWS OF BRAZIL ABROAD

In the first quarter of the twentieth century photo-illustrated books, magazines, and travelogues grew rapidly popular both abroad and in Brazil. Geographic societies, government institutions, commercial publishers, and travel lecturers all increased their imaging activities. Vastly improved reproductions were able to sharply delineate the visual variations and commonalities of national identity from one country to another. Heightened nationalism and cultural curiosity ensured an expanding market for imagery that encouraged comparative study of superiority and inferiority, modernity and backwardness, and above all a search for the exotic. American and European publishers turned out dozens of illustrated books on South America, including ones on Brazil. For these the publishers often acquired standard sorts of photo images from in-country photographers, who tended to perpetuate a growing body of stereotypic national views. While most volumes were issued singly, others appeared in publishers' series such as D. Appleton's South American Handbooks or T. Fisher Unwin's South America Series. *Brazil,* by Pierre Denis, in this latter series formed part of an encyclopedic effort to follow the "march of progress" in all countries of Latin America. A new breed of professional travel writers, such as Frank Carpenter, added their accounts to those of prominent figures such as Theodore Roosevelt, whose photo-illustrated *Through the Brazilian Wilderness* brought a vision of the unexplored interior to the English-speaking public. Marie Robinson Wright's *The New Brazil: Its Resources and Attractions, Historical, Descriptive, and Industrial,* with its 417 illustrations and large format, was an especially notable country survey.[12]

No product fulfilled this need more than *National Geographic* magazine. In the 1920s the magazine captured a vivid picture of the modern-primitive dichotomy of Brazilian identity in two of its issues. One focused on Rio de Janeiro, the other on the Amazon. Rio is shown and described—in forty-five pages with thirty-nine photos—in all of its natural glory and recent urban development. The standard identifiers are there: palm trees, vistas of the bay, beaches, Sugarloaf Mountain, Corcovado, the aqueduct (figures 6.12 and 6.13), the Avenida Rio Branco, and the Botanical Gardens. The picture is enlivened with scenes of daily life and occupational types. The author concludes that Rio is a fairyland that "will stand preeminent in beauty among the habitations of man." Coverage of the Amazon is even more extensive—eighty-five pages including one hundred photos. Here the magazine is really in its element, exploring "the earth's mightiest river," its "greatest forest," and a basin of 2,700,000 square miles much of which is still "terra incognita." Here are tropicalism and primitivism to the extreme, with images of Indian and white lifestyles on the river and in the jungles. The Amazon also gave ample opportunity to photograph the dark-hued, bare-breasted native women who became staple fare of the *Geographic* (figure 6.20). For imagery the magazine relied on its own contract writers and photographers, supplemented by others from local sources.[13]

The flow of official publications on Brazil and the rest of Latin America gained momentum. From its inception in 1889, the Bureau of American Republics, renamed the Pan American Union in 1910, issued sporadic and later monthly bulletins on its member states. Coverage emphasized the area's commercial, agricultural, and industrial development and its economic ties to the United States. The heavily illustrated *Bulletin of the Pan American Union* served as a major source of data and imagery until its demise in 1947. Typical of articles on Brazil was "São Paulo—the Heart of Coffee Land." Four years later, the May 1922 issue was devoted entirely to a "Commemoration of the Centennial Anniversary of Brazilian Independence." Scholars, diplomats, and even Kermit Roosevelt, Theodore's son, joined forces to contribute pieces on Brazilian history, investment opportunities, U.S.-Brazilian friendship, and the country's prospects for the future. These texts were visually enriched with sixty-one illustrations, including one by Rugendas and two by Debret.[14]

The media breakthroughs of stereographs and lantern slides brought additional imagery to an evermore visually oriented public. The stereopticon with its collections of cards became a common feature of American parlors, and droves of spectators were drawn to a new form of educational entertainment—the travelogue. From the turn of the century through the 1940s, companies such as Keystone and Underwood produced hundreds of thousands of stereo images, with their three-dimensional effect. Brazil, like most countries of the world, was well represented in these collections, and the spectacular features of the Brazilian landscape were well suited to this type of display. The word *travelogue* was coined by the American

Figure 6.21.   The natural glory of Rio's Guanabara Bay with Sugarloaf Mountain to the right of center was captured for a Burton Holmes travelogue in this 1911 photograph in which Holmes himself is a featured subject. *Source*: Genoa Caldwell, ed. *The Man Who Photographed the World* (New York: Harry Abrams, 1977).

Burton Holmes, who traveled the world capturing the exotic with photographs that he then projected from lantern slides with commentaries in widespread series of lectures, some of which were published in book form. His first trip to Brazil in 1911 resulted in dramatic images from the bay of Rio to Iguaçu Falls (figure 6.21).[15]

BRAZILIAN MAGAZINES IN THE TWENTIETH CENTURY

The accelerating advance of magazine publishing in Brazil from the 1920s through the end of the century accompanied both a growing readership in an evermore literate public and a proliferation of images that conveyed

Figure 6.22.   At home and abroad Carmen Miranda offered a personification of the animated Brazilian spirit in the 1930s and 1940s. *Source: A Revista no Brasil* (São Paulo: Abril, 2000), 31.

national identity. Such images reflected the growing importance of nationwide popular culture, which received further stimulus from films and television. The different media were mutually supportive in spreading and reinforcing Brazilian identity. Celebrity was paramount. In the 1930s and 1940s Carmen Miranda came to rival president Getúlio Vargas as a cover subject and symbol of *brasilidade* at home and, thanks to Hollywood, far outstripped his recognition abroad (figures 6.22, 6.23, 6.24). Later, in the 1950s and beyond, World Cup superstar Pelé became the quintessential image of Brazilian domestic and international success (figure 6.25). More recently, Xuxa (Maria de Graça Meneghel), a one-time romantic interest of Pelé, became the most ballyhooed national female presence. She parlayed her exposure as a children's television show host into a mythic figure of Brazilian celebrity. She is known throughout the world and is one of the country's richest women. On the weekly *Manchete* alone she has graced six covers (figures 6.26). New magazine titles constantly appear—some to last for decades, others for only a few issues. Many are geared to general readers, others to particular audiences—women, sports enthusiasts, moviegoers, children, nature lovers, homemakers, and numerous others. Many have projected a special sense of Brazilianness, and most have become visual in their appeal. Circulation overall has increased tremendously.

Figure 6.23.   Brazil's president Getúlio Vargas (1930–1945, 1950–1954) was a common image of the nation as the wily "Father of the Poor." Often he was the subject of inventive caricature. *Source*: *A Revista no Brasil* (São Paulo: Abril, 2000), 15.

Figure 6.24.   Vargas was depicted in idealized form as a visionary of the new Brazil. *Source*: *A Revista no Brasil* (São Paulo: Abril, 2000), 92.

Figure 6.25. Pelé (center) led Brazil to World Cup victory in soccer, becoming an international icon as well as a national hero of Brazilian popular culture. _Source_: _A Revista No Brasil_ (São Paulo: Abril, 2000), 98.

Illustrated magazines of two major types set the style for the further spread of natural imagery. The first began with _O Cruzeiro_ (1928–1975, 1977–1983) and culminated with _Manchete_ (1952–). These were large-format products similar to _Life_ and _Look_. Originally, _O Cruzeiro_ used photos as simple illustrations, but early in the 1940s, followed by _Manchete_ in the 1950s, it developed a new form of visual language in which sequenced photos carried a storyline. These were combined with interpretive reporting and at times with commentary by noted writers on aspects of Brazilian reality. The second of these types, dominated by _Veja_ (1968–) and _Isto É_ (1976), were weekly news digests with analytic articles patterned after _Time_. Less focused on imagery, they proved to be less vulnerable to the visual competition mounted by television, which ultimately undermined the viability of _O Cruzeiro_, _Life_, and other magazines of that genre. By the year 2000 _Veja_, with a circulation of 1.7 million per issue, ranked fourth in the world among news magazines. By comparison, the viewership of TV Globo, the world's fourth-largest television network, numbered over 50 million. _Veja_

Figure 6.26.   Here with Xuxa, his one-time romantic interest, Pelé is featured on the cover of a leading Brazilian monthly, *Manchete*. The symbolic image of black and white racial harmony is echoed by the clothes they wore for this photo. *Source*: *Manchete*, Special Issue, No. 2, 522 (July 2001).

and *Isto É* remain important for the spread of national imagery because of the high level of their readership. Their role was often as the creators of new images as well as perspectives on the old. The *Cruzeiro* issue commemorating the fourth centennial of Rio serves as an example, blending a variety of new and historical photographs with Ur-images by Debret and others.[16]

A rather special niche for Brazilian identity has focused on the mystique of Brazilian sensuality. Regardless of underlying reality, Brazil has acquired a reputation at home and abroad for sexual openness. The general-interest magazines regularly portray the country as a tropical paradise populated by nearly nude carnival revelers and Copacabana bathing beauties in their dental-floss bikinis (figures 6.27, 6.28). Other magazines, targeting a largely male audience, offer high-quality photo spreads featuring local and foreign women in various stages of undress. By far the most successful of these has been the Brazilian version of *Playboy* (1978–), which by 1990 had become

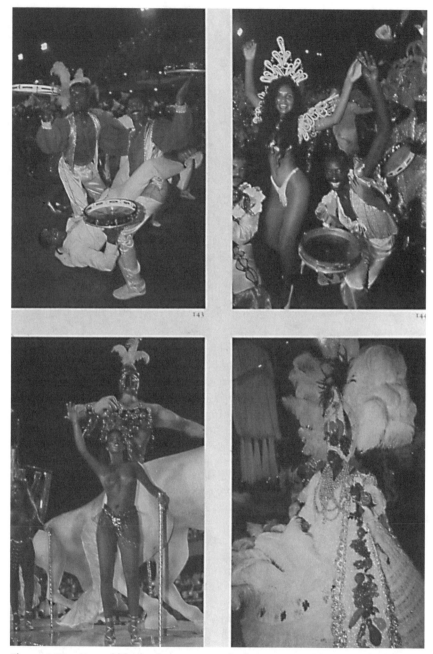

Figure 6.27. It would be hard to overstate the importance of Brazilian carnival as a national image, conveying beauty, exuberance, and a relaxed attitude toward sex. *Source:* José Inácio Parente and Patrícia Monte-Mór, *Rio de Janeiro: Retratos da cidade* (Rio de Janeiro: Interior Produções, 1994), 132.

Figure 6.28. Rio's beach scene is a strong national image, with its famous bikinis, immortalized by "Garota de Ipanema." *Source*: José Inácio Parente and Patrícia Monte-Mór, *Rio de Janeiro: Retratos da cidade* (Rio de Janeiro: Interior Produções, 1994), 142.

Figure 6.29. Sonia Braga epitomized the Brazilian image of the *Morena* as seen here with José Wilker in the film, *Dona Flor and Her Two Husbands. Source*: *Dona Flor and Her Two Husbands*. Produced by L.C. Barreto. Rio de Janeiro, 1978.

the country's leading monthly with a circulation of 1.2 million. With its winning combination of good local writing and imagery, together with translations and international coverage of beautiful women, the Brazilian *Playboy* outsells all of the magazine's foreign editions. Many of Brazil's most famous actresses and television stars, including Sonia Braga, Maite Proença, and Bruna Lombardi, have appeared totally nude in the magazine's pages, enhancing the image of the Brazilian woman as being modern, liberated, and free-spirited. In addition, Sonia Braga came to epitomize the Brazilian ideal of the sensuous *morena* in films and television series, especially in the film adaptations of Jorge Amado's *Gabriela, Clove and Cinnamon*, and *Dona Flor and Her Two Husbands* (figures 6.29).

THE PROGRESS OF BOOK ILLUSTRATION

By the 1990s the quality of Brazilian book publishing and photo reproduction, which had been improving since World War II, reached a level of international standard. Brazilian publication output today is ninth in the world. Illustrated works of all kinds, many with images of the constant and shifting elements of national identity, are prominently displayed in local bookshops. Photographic books such as Jean Manzon's *Flagrantes do Brasil* (Snapshots of Brazil; fig. 6.30) and Erich Eichner's compilation of photographic documentation on Rio de Janeiro were intended to capture the essence of the country, with its wealth of regional variation and social contrast from modern to primitive coexisting in the 1940s (figures 6.11, 6.26, 6.32, 6.33, 6.34, 6.35, 6.36). Forty years later Carlos Guilherme Mota and Adriana Lopez presented a collection of "fragments of memory" in *Brasil revisitado: Palavras e imagens* (Brazil Revisited: Words and Images), in which they ask "Who are we?" and follow a five-hundred-year historical quest for the "imaginary Brazilian" in paintings, engravings, lithographs, prints, and photographs.[17] Brazilians in ever greater numbers have been searching for their national identity in the array of visual sources available to them.

Two examples of such national portraiture stand out. The first originally appeared as a series of drawings by Percy Lau in the *Revista Brasileira de Geografia* in the 1940s (fig. 6.31). They were then published in book form as *Tipos e aspectos do Brasil* (with translations into English, Spanish, French, and Esperanto).[18] Numerous editions followed, and the work has been kept in print to this day by the Brazilian Institute of Geography and Statistics. Arranged by geographic region, the illustrations depict each area's most prominent landscape features and human types—both ethnic and occupational. Emphasis throughout is on the persistence of traditional

Figure 6.30.   Here a black fisherman is caught in a strikingly similar pose to the image of a northeastern cowboy in fig. 6.31. *Source*: Jean Manzon, *Flagrantes do Brasil* (Rio de Janeiro: Bloch, 1950).

Figure 6.31.   Compare this image of a northeastern cowboy with figure 6.30. *Source*: *Tipos e Aspectos do Brasil* (Rio de Janeiro: Instituto Brasileiro de Geografia e Estatística, 1956), 46.

ways of life, giving a sense of the timeless to Brazilian development that was more appropriate to the 1940s than it was to the present. Many of Lau's images have become well-recognized renditions of Brazilian forests, river life, cowboys, coffee lands, palm trees, and black Bahian food vendors (figure 6.35).

The second example recently appeared as the fourteen-volume *Mostra do Redescobrimento* (Exposition of Rediscovery). Maintaining that "the visual arts were always present in the cultural identity of the Brazilian people," this monumental work was published to accompany exhibits mounted in celebration of the five-hundredth anniversary of the discovery of Brazil (1500–2000). A visual encyclopedia of national identity and development, the work surveys Brazilian art from its archaeological past to the present. Individual volumes, all with text in English and Portuguese, are devoted to major stylistic eras, such as Baroque or nineteenth century, or to special types, such as black or Indian art. All genres are covered, from sculpture to photography, and artists range from the academic to the popular. Also

Figure 6.32.   Harmony of Indians, whites, and blacks—"three strong races"—became a highly promoted national image in the 1930s and 1940s, as captured here by the French photographer Jean Manzon. *Source*: Jean Manzon, *Flagrantes do Brasil* (Rio de Janeiro: Bloch, 1950).

Figure 6.33. Rio's Municipal Theater is a prime symbol of national achievement on the level of high culture. *Source*: *Cidade e arredores do Rio de Janeiro* (Rio de Janeiro: Livraria Kosmos, [194?]), 87.

included, whether for their design or historical significance, are products of material culture of interest. Together the volumes present a panorama of *brasilidade* and illustrate the iconic status of many images. With respect to this project, Rio's mayor Luis Paulo Conde pointed out that Brazilian cultural plurality is never static and will always demand more and newer portraits. Moreover, in a country that constantly reviews its history and its diversity, rediscovery is a permanent, enlightening process. To reach their identity in the present, Brazilians must always reevaluate their past, and visual images provide a major key in this effort.[19]

No image, or set of images, in twentieth-century Brazil has been more indicative of the country's shifting national identity than that of Brasília. Even the name conjures up a new national essence and sense of purpose. Long planned—provision for relocating the federal capital from Rio to the central plateau was made in the first republican constitution of 1891— the national dream of men such as president Juscelino Kubitschek, urban planner Lúcio Costa, and architect Oscar Niemeyer was finally implemented in the 1960s. Brasília is actually the country's third capital. Each one

Figure 6.34. The statue of Christ atop Rio's Corcovado Mountain has become a local and national icon, blending a sense of the city with traditional religiosity. *Source: Cidade e arredores do Rio de Janeiro* (Rio de Janeiro: Livraria Kosmos, [194?]), 117.

Figure 6.35. The Bahian good seller conveys a strong image of Afro-Brazilian identity. *Source: Tipos e aspectos do Brasil* (Rio de Janeiro: IBGE, 1956), 111.

Figure 6.36.   The innovative modernism of Brazilian architecture is best expressed in the signature public buildings by Oscar Niemeyer in Brasília. *Source*: Júlio Katinsky, *Brasília em três tempos: A arquitetura de Oscar Niemeyer na capital* (Rio de Janeiro: Revan, 1991), 42.

reflected a distinct visual reality: Salvador da Bahia, colonial times from the mid-sixteenth century until 1808; Rio de Janeiro, royal, imperial, and republican centrality and progress from 1808 to 1959; and Brasília, from 1959 on, the hope for a dynamic and diversified future. Brasília was to grow into this symbolic identity over the last decades of the century. The city was a futuristic representation of what many hoped the country would become. At the same time Brazilian identification with Rio has not diminished. If anything, it has grown, and even Salvador has experienced a resurgence of identity as a center of an increasingly appreciated Afro-Brazilian culture. Thus, the overlay of official visual images continues and becomes more complex as time goes on.

PERSISTING CONTRASTS

A generation ago the French anthropologist Roger Bastide called Brazil the "Land of Contrasts."[20] It is certainly inevitable that a country as vast as Brazil in land area and in population (Brazil ranks fifth in both) should

Figure 6.37. Along with progress, the nagging persistence of poverty was dramatically filmed by *Life* photographer Gordon Parks in 1961 in his photo study of a Rio de Janeiro *favela* (slum). *Source*: Gordon Parks, *Flavio* (New York: W. W. Norton, 1978).

remain a land of contrasts and a continual source of distinction. In fact, it was recently tagged as a type of "Bel-India," combining Belgium's high level of development with the poverty of India. The visual images of national identity have not failed to seize upon this dichotomy. The dark side of modernization, as well as its notable achievements, have been made dramatically evident by foreign and local observers. In the 1960s the poetic American photojournalist Gordon Parks captured the tragic sense of life in Rio's *favelas* (hillside shantytowns) as he focused on a young boy, Flávio. The pages of *Life* and the book that followed brought to the world's attention this contrast of urban progress and Brazilian poverty in the midst of natural beauty (figures 6.37, 6.38).[21] A variation on the theme, but in a rural setting, was photographed toward the end of the century by Brazil's foremost poetic image maker of his generation, Sebastião Salgado. In a series of shocking pictures, he decried the antlike exploitative drudgery of pit miners who were surrounded by the Amazonian "earthly paradise" (figure 6.39). Thus, the contrast of images of national identity continues, as it has in the past, in an effort to balance the antagonisms that Gilberto Freyre saw at the formative core of Brazilian culture.

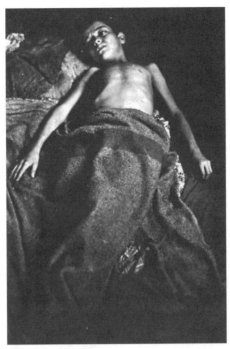

Figure 6.38.   *Life* photographer Gordon Parks focused his story on the figure of a slum child, Flávio, whom he was able to revisit in later years. *Source*: Gordon Parks, *Flavio* (New York: W. W. Norton, 1978).

Now, at the end of nearly two centuries of independent life, Brazil's identity has been highly visualized. The imaging of its rich cultural distinctiveness continues to accelerate as it keeps pace with the vast changes occurring within society. Newer media of film and television have ignited an exponential explosion of visual images. Brazil today differs quantitatively and qualitatively from the Brazil of the 1960s, the 1930s, the early twentieth century, and the nineteenth century. Brazil has been transformed from a predominantly rural, agriculturally based, highly regionalized provincial country into one that has been profoundly urbanized and industrialized, with a culture that has become national at the same time that it has become cosmopolitan. These same trends, of course, have been common to many countries of the world. Brazil, though, is a rare case, like that of the United States, which has been able to maintain national control over a vast area and a large population. In addition to increasingly effective governmental operations, official nation-building efforts and the strengthening of distinctive countrywide popular culture have led to a great sense of cohesiveness in Brazil as in the United States. The massive volume of visual imagery

Figure 6.39. A lament for human exploitation was circulated internationally in Sebastião Salgado's poignant photos of open-pit gold miners in the Amazon in the 1990s. *Source*: Sebastião Salgado, *An Uncertain Grace* (New York: Aperture, 1990).

portraying national progress as blended with icons from a usable national past has been essential to this successful development process.

NOTES

1. For brief descriptions of their published texts and illustrations, see Rubens Borba de Moraes, *Bibliographia Brasiliana* (Los Angeles: UCLA Latin American Center Publications, 1983), 467–73, 830–37, 857–61.

2. Borba de Moraes, *Bibliographia Brasiliana*, 249–51, 445–48.

3. Borba de Moraes, *Bibliographia Brasiliana*, 252, 524–29, 544, 737, 754, 829–30.

4. Borba de Moraes, *Bibliographia Brasiliana*, 256–59.

5. Borba de Moraes, *Bibliographia Brasiliana*, 434.

6. William M. Ivins Jr., *Prints and Visual Communications* (Cambridge, Mass.: MIT Press, 1953, 1982), 116.

7. On the history of photography in Brazil, see Gilberto Ferrez, *Photography in Brazil, 1840–1900* (Albuquerque: University of New Mexico Press, 1990); Pedro Vasquez, *Fotógrafos pioneiros no Rio de Janeiro* (Rio de Janeiro: Dazibao, 1990).

8. Fernando Ferreira Campos, *Um fotógrafo, uma cidade: Augusto Malta, Rio de Janeiro* (Rio de Janeiro: Maison Graphique, 1987); Ferreira Campos, *Fotografias do Rio de ontem: A. Malta* (Rio de Janeiro: Prefeitura da Cidade do Rio de Janeiro, n.d.).

9. *O Novo Mundo*, unnumbered *prefácio*, October 23, 1874. This periodical was published in New York, 1871–1879.

10. Rio Branco, Baron, *Album de vues de Brésil* (Paris: Lahure, 1889).

11. On these and other Brazilian magazines, see *A revista no Brasil* (São Paulo: Editora April, 2000).

12. Pierre Denis, *Brazil* (London: T. Fisher Unwin, 1911); Theodore Roosevelt, *Through the Brazilian Wilderness* (New York: Scribners, 1914); Marie Robinson Wright, *The New Brazil* (Philadelphia: George Barrie and Sons, 1907).

13. Harriet Chalmers Adams, "Rio de Janeiro, in the Land of Lure," *National Geographic Magazine* 38, no. 3 (September 1920): 165–210; Albert W. Stevens, "Exploring the Valley of the Amazon in a Hydroplane," *Geographic Magazine* 49, no. 4 (April 1926): 353–420; and W. L. Schurz, "The Amazon, Father of Waters," *National Geographic Magazine* 49, no. 4 (April 1926): 445–63.

14. *Bulletin of the Pan American Union* 46, no. 6 (June 1918): 720–47; *Bulletin of the Pan American Union* 54, no. 5 (May 1922): 433–537.

15. Genoa Caldwell, ed., *The Man Who Photographed the World: Burton Holmes Travelogues, 1886–1938* (New York: Abrams, 1977), 12, 186–93.

16. *O Cruzeiro: Edição comemorativa do IV centenário* (November 1965).

17. Jean Manzon, *Flagrantes do Brasil* (Rio de Janeiro: Bloch, 1950); *Cidade e arredores do Rio de Janeiro: A jóia do Brasil* (Rio de Janeiro: Livraria Kosmos, n.d.); Carlos Guilherme Mota and Adriana Lopez, *Brasil revisitado: Palavras e imagens* (São Paulo: Editora Rios, 1989), 9.

18. *Tipos e aspectos do Brasil* (Rio de Janeiro: IBGE, 1956).

19. *Brasil + 500: Mostra do redescobrimento* (São Paulo: Associação Brasil 500, 2000), x.

20. Roger Bastide, *Brasil: Terra de contrastes* (Sao Paulo: Difel, 1976).

21. Gordon Parks, *Flavio* (New York: Norton, 1978).

7

❦

Cinematic Images of the Brazilian Indian

Robert Stam

Pedro Alvares Cabral arrived on the shores of present-day Brazil in 1500, laying claim for Portugal to what he called land of the *Vera Cruz* (True Cross). This chapter examines the cinematic representations of the encounter between European and indigenous peoples in Brazil from early silent film through the documentary and fictional films of the 1990s. The portrayals of the Indian as being romantic, patriotic, and tropicalist constitute an important theme in Brazil's developing sense of national identity, culminating with the documentary and fictional films of the 1990s. Whether constant or changing, images of the Indian have formed an important part of Brazil's heritage of cultural distinctiveness. Appropriately chosen films drawn from the successive periods of Brazilian cinema illustrate the various incarnations of the "Indianness" constructed by the Brazilian cinema, viewed against a comparative backdrop of U.S. cinema and culture. I adopt a cultural studies approach, which considers film as part of a larger, discursive continuum that includes other arts and media such as popular music and television.[1]

In Brazil and the United States, colonization led to the occupation of vast territories and the dispossession of indigenous peoples, whether by *bandeirantes* (explorers and traders from São Paulo) or "pioneers." An implacable ethnocide decimated the indigenous peoples in North and South America, which scholars estimate at sixty million in the late 1400s.[2] Of this number, roughly five million resided in present-day Brazil and another five million in what is now the United States. A popular song of the 1990s by Caetano Veloso titled "Manhata" uses the figure of an indigenous woman to suggest associations between indigenous culture in North and South America. An excerpt from the lyrics goes as follows:

A canoe
Crossing the morning from North to South
The goddess of legend on the prow
Everyone looks in her direction
Feeling the taste of the wind
Singing through the windows
The sweet name of the young woman. Manhata, Manhata, Manhata
Meanwhile, a whirlpool of money
A light Leviathan, sweeps the entire world.[3]

The young woman in the song is a palimpsest: she is at the same time Eve, the Statue of Liberty, a native American woman, and a native Brazilian woman—specifically, a Tupi woman, since Caetano calls her a *cunha*, the Tupi word for "young woman." The identification of the *cunha* with the name "freedom" suggests a link between native peoples—the Iroquois, the Tupinamba—and Enlightenment notions of freedom. Caetano Brazilianizes and nasalizes the indigenous word for "Manhattan" to make it *Manhata*, evoking both *Manha* (morning) and Manhattan. The wordplay creates a magical cross-epochal temporality that mingles the time when Indians canoed across the Hudson and the contemporary world of Wall Street and globalization conjured up by the "whirlpool of money sweeping the world."[4]

THE INDIAN IN EARLY BRAZILIAN CINEMA

From its beginnings at the turn of the twentieth century, Brazilian cinema has performed variations of the themes first set down by literary Indianism in the nineteenth century. The period of silent film offers a marked contrast between American and Brazilian cinema. American cinema developed a schizophrenic discourse, depicting the Indian as both noble victim and bloodthirsty savage, with the discourse of conquest and "manifest destiny." Brazilian filmmakers, many of them immigrants, did not stress conquest but rather gave cinematic prolongation to the romantic Indianist tradition while shying away from representations of black Brazilians, who become a kind of structuring absence in silent cinema. Although no Brazilian film of the first few decades of the twentieth century advances an explicitly racist perspective—there is no Brazilian *Birth of a Nation* (1914–1915)—one is struck by the frequent adaptation of Indianist novels such as *O Guarani* (four versions in the silent period), *Iraçema* (three versions), and *Ubirajara* (one version), in contrast to the general slighting of Afro-Brazilian themes. Unfortunately, the mythification of the Indian involved an element of bad faith toward both Indian and black. By celebrating the fusion of an idealized noble Indian with an equally idealized noble European, novels such as *Iraçema* and *O Guarani* prettified the conquest and neglected the black.

Silent cinema celebrated the Indian as "brave warrior," as the naively good and deeply spiritual source and symbol of Brazil's nationhood. But this exaltation of the Indian was dedicated to the very group being victimized by a process of literal and cultural genocide. While the actual Indian was destroyed, marginalized, or eliminated through miscegenation, the remote Indian was idealized. The ambiguous compliment toward the Indian became a means of avoiding the vexing question of slavery. The proud history of black *quilombos* (runaway slave settlements) was ignored; the brave Indian, it was subtly insinuated, resisted slavery while blacks did not. The white filmmakers of the early twentieth century chose the safely distant and mythical Indian over the more problematically present black, victim of a slavery abolished just ten years before Afonso Segreto filmed the first Brazilian "views" in 1898.

In early Brazilian cinema, Indians were not allowed to represent themselves. Indeed, during the filming of the second adaptation of *O Guarani*, in 1926, the director, Vittorio Capellario, was interrogated by the police for showing Indians in his film when "there has been so much progress in the region."[5] Some Indian roles were performed by black actors such as Benjamin de Oliveira, the first Afro-Brazilian film actor. In the United States white actors such as Al Jolson performed in blackface, while in Brazil black actors performed, as it were, in "redface." Thus blacks played Indians in situations where neither black nor Indian had power over self-representation.

The Romantic Indian

While North American ideology tended to promote myths of separation and the doomed nature of love between white and Indian, Brazilian ideology promoted myths of fusion, transmitted by what Doris Sommer calls "foundational romances" of love between European and indigene.[6] For example, the romantic poets and novelists of the mid-nineteenth-century Indianist movement, such as José de Alencar, portrayed fusion through the marriage of the Indian Iraçema and the European Martins in the novel *Iraçema* or the love of the indigenous Peri and European Ceci in *O Guarani*. And while Brazilian literature promoted heterosexual romance—Indian men loving white women (*O Guarani*) or Indian women loving white men (*Iraçema*)—as being generative of the mestizo nation, American literature stressed male bonding between white frontiersmen and the native American male.[7] Nonetheless, it is hard not to discern the transnational resemblances of figures such as Pocahontas in the United States and Paraguaçu and Iraçema in Brazil.

Even today, Brazilian and North American cultural industries return obsessively to the theme of European-indigene romance. The 1990s brought us not only Disney's *Pocahontas* but also films such as *O Guarani* and television series such as *A Muralha* in Brazil. The Globo miniseries *A Invenção do Brasil* (The Invention of Brazil, 2000), by Guel Arraes and Jorge Furtado, is a witty mixed-genre study of Brazilian identity that tells a foundational fiction that precedes those of nineteenth-century romanticism, to wit the story of the romance between the Portuguese cartographer and the portrait painter Diogo Alvares (renamed "Caramuru" in Brazil) and the Indian princess Paraguaçu, the daughter of the chief of the Tupinambas in Bahia. Unlike Indianist novels, the Caramuru story is based on a real relationship, subsequently embroidered with legend.[8] As Janaina Amado points out, Caramuru and Paraguaçu represent symbolic parents of Brazil, which is why all the versions of their story reference their many descendants.[9] The story of Caramuru has been worked and reworked by many authors of diverse nationalities—Gabriel Soares de Sousa, Arthur d'Avila, Gregorio de Matos, Sebastião Rocha Pitta, Adolfo de Varnhagen, Arthur Lobo D'Avila, João de Barros, Claude d'Abbeville, Roberto Southey—but it became part of the Brazilian popular imaginary thanks to Frei José de Santa Rita Durão's epic poem *Caramaru* (1781). Caramuru and Paraguaçu have formed the theme for samba school presentations, and they were celebrated at Salvador's quincentennial carnival.

A Invenção do Brasil opens with a counterpoint of the perspectives concerning the arrival of the Portuguese, alternating the Portuguese view from the ships with the Tupiniquim view from the shore to suggest "who we—we Brazilians—are." The narrator relates how the Portuguese, looking through telescopes from the ships, were astonished by the verdant land and the naked beauty of the women, while the Tupiniquim, looking from the shore, were astonished by the overdressed and foul-smelling Portuguese. Each group brought its intertextual mythologies to the encounter: the Europeans imagined the Garden of Eden and Eldorado, and the Tupiniquim the "Land without Evil." *A Invenção do Brasil* brilliantly interweaves maps, paintings, archival footage, digital simulacra, and staged scenes, all backed up by highly syncretic music that evokes the "multination" cultures at the roots of Brazil. Anachronism is used to link Cabral to Neil Armstrong, Renaissance maps to satellite television, and the voyages of discovery to a theme park ride. At one point, the narrator appears in a helicopter over the coast of Brazil trying to rescue Diogo but laments that Diogo cannot be helped since "we're five hundred years too late."

The attempt at a contrapuntal, polyperspective approach sketched out in the overture sequence is compromised, unfortunately, by the predominance of a Eurocentric perspective throughout and the "redface" convention whereby non-Indians play Indian characters. The white narrator relays all the perspectives, and the narrative ultimately falls into "foundational fiction" mode. The historical and legendary love affair of Diogo and Paraguaçu recapitulates the gendered trope whereby European man plus indigenous woman equal Brazil (missing are both the indigenous man and African men and women). The entire series is imbued with a sexualized telos—one that obviously nourishes high ratings—whereby everything moves toward a predestined erotic encounter. The story even becomes a kind of harem fantasy since Diogo enjoys access not only to Paraguaçu but also to her equally beautiful sister, thanks to the Indians' lack of sexual jealousy. But this lack of jealousy benefits only the European man; Indian men in the series have no erotic agency whatsoever. The series is also interesting in terms of class mobility. It presents Diogo as a commoner who becomes the "King of Brazil" while Paraguaçu is an authentic "princess." Diogo also illustrates the perennial tendency to allegorize the Americans as female, as being encapsulated in the moment, whereas the protagonist describes Paraguaçu's body in geographical terms—remember, he is a cartographer—so that her head is Europe, her breasts are North Africa, and so on within a voyage of sexual, anatomical, geographical discovery.

The Documented Indian

In the silent period, a marked tension exists between the Indianist adaptations and the "documentary" record provided by filmmakers such as Major Tomás Luis Reis and Silvino Santos in the 1910s and 1920s and Claude Lévi-Strauss in the 1930s. In these films, white men in suits observe real seminude Indians shooting arrows, grinding corn, breastfeeding, and dancing. Here it is important to underline a historical contrast between the United States and Brazil. The Brazilian government rarely dispatched armies to crush the Indians, sending instead scientists, "pacifiers," and the Indian Protection Service. Furthermore, the discourse, if not the practice, was paternalist, benevolent, and cordial. The 1910–1930 period marks the decades of the Rondon Commission, named after army officer Cândido Rondon, who became famous as the pacifier of the Indians. The army and Rondon were very much influenced by positivism, and their goal as positivists was to catapult the Indians from "barbarism" into the scientific stage. Rondon was famous for his pacification of the Bororo and Nambiquara. Despite his slogan "Die, if need be, but never kill!" Rondon's goal was ultimately to turn Indians into Brazilians so that, of their own free will, they would choose "civilization."

Photography and cinema were important in memorializing these pacification campaigns. Reis headed the photographic division of the Rondon Commission in Mato Grosso, and his films were designed to attract funding for the commission. He even arranged screenings of his films at Carnegie Hall in 1918, presided over by former president Theodore Roosevelt, who had accompanied Rondon on scientific expeditions in the Amazon.[10] In *Rituais e festas bororo* (Bororo Rituals and Feasts, 1916), Reis focuses on funeral rites, always emphasizing the differences between the Indians and Western society. The final intertitle indirectly invokes Cabral: "We had the sensation of witnessing the remote times of the Discovery." In *Os sertões de Mato Grosso* (The Backlands of Mato Grosso, 1916), a record of the installation of the telegraph lines in the interior of Brazil, Reis depicts what he called "the pacification of numerous Indian tribes encountered in a primitive, Stone Age state."[11] *Ao redor do Brasil* (filmed between 1924 and 1930), meanwhile, documents the flora, fauna, and social practices of the region, usually presenting the Indians directly to the camera or in profile, as if Reis were cataloging them.

The Modernist Indian

The 1920s featured another version of the Brazilian Indian, that of the modernist movement in literature and the arts, which unfortunately never linked up with Brazilian cinema. Instead of the *bon sauvage* of the romantics, the modernists preferred the "Bad Indian," the cannibal, the devourer of the white colonizer. The modernists made the trope of cannibalism the basis of an insurgent aesthetic, calling for an "anthropophagic" devouring of the techniques and information of the developed countries to better struggle against domination. Modernism articulated cannibalism as an anticolonialist metaphor in its "Cannibalist Reviews," its "Anthropophagic Manifestos," and its famous slogan "Tupi or not Tupi, that is the question"—whether Brazilian intellectuals should "go native" by symbolically imitating the putatively cannibalist Tupinamba or alienate themselves into European domination. Modernism also took a critical position toward Cabral and the conquest, calling for "de-Cabralization." Radicalizing the Enlightenment valorization of the indigenous Amerindian freedom, modernism highlighted aboriginal matriarchy and communalism as a utopian model for a society free of coercion and hierarchy, without police or capitalism. As it did for the European *philosophes*, philo-indigenism enabled a deep anthropological critique of the political and moral bases of Eurocentric civilization. The movement reached the cinema, as we shall see, only with the Cinema Novo in the 1960s.

The Patriotic Indian

In the late 1930s, Humberto Mauro's film *O Descobrimento do Brasil* (The Discovery of Brazil, 1937) was sponsored by the Cacão Institute, a large landowners organization. *Descobrimento* presents the official version of the encounter between the European and the Indian. First proposed as a project by Roquette Pinto, the film draws on various intertexts. First, Mauro chooses the version of history that sees Cabral's "discovery" as being intentional rather than accidental. Mauro bases his portrayal on the famous letter often called the "birth certificate of Brazil," which Pero Vaz de Caminha, official scribe of the Portuguese fleet, sent to the Portuguese monarch. Caminha is the film's protagonist-narrator, whose description gives birth to the scene. But the staging of the encounter in *Descobrimento* was also inspired by a famous painting by Victor Meirelles, *The First Mass*, painted in Paris in 1860 and itself inspired by a French painting set in North Africa, Horace Vernet's *Premiere Messe en Kabilie*. The Meirelles painting places the Portuguese center frame in a shady grove under a canopy of tall trees. The climactic "First Mass" sequence of the Mauro film clearly picks up on the cues provided by the painting, as seen most notably in the repeated long shot of the Europeans and Indians gathered around the cross.

A discursive palimpsest, the Mauro film embeds multiple discourses drawn from diverse historical periods: the Christianizing mentality of the conquest, the romantic idealizations of nineteenth-century Indianismo, the scientific optimism of positivism, and the populist nationalism of president Getúlio Vargas's Estado Novo (New State). Like the Hollywood films devoted to Columbus, the Mauro film idealizes the European discoverer and sanctifies the conquest. The choral religiosity of Villa-Lobos's music "blesses" the conquest with a sacred aura, while incorporating some indigenous motifs. Unlike the 1949 Hollywood version, where the Indian has no voice whatsoever, the Mauro film has the "Indian" actually speaking Tupi-Guarani, although the absence of subtitles makes the words incomprehensible to the Portuguese characters and to non-Tupi-speaking spectators. The Indians are not depicted as being menacing, as in the Hollywood versions, but rather as being innocent, harmless, and not completely in control of their own bodies. Their scripted behavior mirrors their official legal status as children needing protection. Although they happen to reside on the land, they do not really deserve to dominate it. Despite linguistic self-representation, the film has its native mimic men applaud what must have been an alien ceremony, while the actor playing Caminha gently covers the nakedness of an Indian woman. The Indians abandon their own beliefs and culture to embrace Christianity and the culture of Europe as being irresistibly true. Their genuflections translate into audiovisual representation of the fantasy of the conquistadors: that reading a document in a European language to uncomprehending natives signifies a legitimate transfer of ownership. In short, the Indians are perfectly good candidates for European disciplining, Christianization, and dispossession. This paternalist undercurrent was noted at the time. Novelist Graciliano Ramos, in one of his chronicles, denounced the film for idealizing the "invaders who came to enslave and assassinate indigenous peoples."

Glauber Rocha's *Terra em Transe* (Land in Anguish, 1967), a baroque allegory about Brazilian politics, offers a contrasting "unofficial" representation of Pedro Cabral. While *Descobrimento* is a kind of superproduction, with the proverbial cast of thousands, *Terra em Transe* is a low-budget exemplar of what Rocha himself called the "aesthetics of hunger." While the Mauro film deploys an aesthetic of realistic reconstruction, the Rocha film is transrealist, interested less in reconstruction than in making viewers reflect on historical process. Although in no way a film "about" Indians, it does feature a remarkable sequence that alludes to the "First Mass." In a fantasy sequence dreamed by the narrator-protagonist Paulo Martins, the right-wing figure of the film (named Porfirio Díaz after the Mexican dictator) arrives from the sea in a scene suggesting a myth of origins. As much as Walter Benjamin spoke of "memories flashing up in a moment of danger," whereby repressed aspects of history take on fresh meaning in the light of contemporary crises, here Rocha, in the wake of the traumatic 1964 military coup, conjures up the memory of Cabral. Díaz's ritual raising of the chalice and the outsized cross alludes to Cabral's "first mass" and even to Mauro's filmic version of it, but here the anachronism highlights continuities between the conquest and contemporary oppression. The contemporary *putchiste* is portrayed as the latter-day heir of the conquistadors. Díaz and his religion of violence have replaced the priest and his religion of love. And while the 1937 Mauro film shows the natives in postures of servility and worship, here there is no submission.

Rocha further destabilizes meaning by making Africa a textual presence. The very aesthetic of the sequence, first of all, draws heavily from the Africanized forms of Rio's annual carnival samba pageant, with its zany forms of historicism, polyrhythms, and delight in extravagant *alegorias* and *fantasias*. Indeed, the actor who plays the conquistador is Clovis Bornay, a historian of carnival. Second, the mass is accompanied not by Christian religious music but by Yoruba religious chants, evoking the "transe" of the Portuguese title. Rocha's suggestive referencing of African music, as if Africans had been in Brazil before the arrival of the Europeans, reminds us not only of the continental drift theory, which sees South America and Africa as being once part of a single land mass, but also of the theories of Ivan Van Sertima and others who contend that Africans arrived in the New World "before Columbus."[12] The music suggests that Africans, who shaped and were shaped by the Americas over centuries, are in some uncanny sense also indigenous to the region.

The sequence displays a dazzling aesthetic originality. It exemplifies a "trans-Brechtian" aesthetic through which Rocha manages to tropicalize, Africanize, and carnivalize the theories of Bertold Brecht. While

Brechtianism deploys contradiction and disjunction between image and sound, Rocha goes further by staging historical contradictions between vast cultural complexes existing in relations of subordination and domination where the Chalice—or "Cale-se" (be quiet as Chico Buarque would put it)—of Catholicism is superimposed on music that incarnates precisely the religion historically suppressed by Christianity. Here music represents not merely a factor of disjunction but also the return of the historically repressed. Instead of the austerity and minimalism that characterize a certain Brechtian tradition in the cinema, we find a multilayered saturation of image and sound, a hysterical dream sequence linked to both carnival and Candomblé. The scene's fractured and discontinuous aesthetic stages the drama of life in the colonial "contact zone," defined by Mary Louise Pratt as the space where "subjects previously separated" encounter each other within "conditions of coercion, radical inequality, and intractable conflict." Rocha's neobaroque Afro-avant-gardist aesthetic figures the discontinuous, dissonant, fractured history of the multination through equally dissonant images and sounds.

The Tropicalist Indian

Terra em transe had a strong influence on the films of the "oral-cannibalistic-tropicalist-allegorical" phase of Cinema Novo (1968–1971), where filmmakers turned for inspiration to the modernist writers of the 1920s and especially to Oswald de Andrade's notion of "anthropophagy." While cannibalism was a common trope among European avant-gardists, only in Brazil did anthropophagy become a key trope in a cultural movement that was to last for many decades, ranging from the first "Cannibalistic Review" in the 1920s through Oswald de Andrade's speculations in the 1950s concerning anthropophagy as "the philosophy of the technicized primitive" to the pop recyclings of the metaphor in the tropicalist movements of the late 1960s. As exploited by the Brazilian modernists, the cannibalist metaphor had a positive and a negative pole: the positive pole showed aboriginal matriarchy and communalism as utopian model, while the negative pole made cannibalism a critical instrument for exposing the exploitative social Darwinism implicit in "savage capitalism" and bourgeois civility.

Mario de Andrade's 1928 novel *Macunaima* was the epitome of the modernist movement and the powerful precursor of what became known as "magic realism." The author, himself of mixed racial ancestry, culturally and phenotypically embodied the indigenous, African, and European inheritance, giving him a proleptic sense of what came to be called "nomadic" and "palimpsestic" identity. Of the two poles of the cannibalist metaphor, Joaquim Pedro de Andrade's 1969 adaptation of *Macunaima* clearly emphasizes the negative pole.[13] Fusing what he knew of Oswald's anthropophagical movement with the theme of cannibalism that runs through the de Andrade novel, the director turns cannibalism into the springboard for a critique of repressive military rule and the predatory capitalist model of the short-lived Brazilian "economic miracle." In a preface written to accompany the film at the Venice Film Festival, the director offers a kind of cannibalistic hermeneutic to help spectators decode the Rabelasian allegories of the film:

> Cannibalism is an exemplary mode of consumerism adopted by underdeveloped peoples. In particular, the Brazilian Indians, immediately after having been "discovered" by the first colonizers, had the rare opportunity of selecting their Portuguese-supplied bishop, Dom Pedro Fernandes Sardinha, whom they devoured in a memorable meal.
>
> It is not by accident that the revolutionary artists of the twenties—the Modernists—dated their Cannibal Manifesto "the year Bishop Sardinha was swallowed." Today we can note that nothing has changed. The traditionally dominant, conservative social classes continue their control of the power structure—and we rediscover cannibalism.
>
> Every consumer is reducible, in the last analysis, to cannibalism. The present work relationships, as well as the relationships between people—social, political, and economic—are still basically cannibalistic. Those who can, "eat" others through their consumption of products, or even more directly in sexual relationships. Cannibalism has merely institutionalized itself, cleverly disguised itself. The new heroes, still looking for a collective consciousness, try to devour those who devour us. But still weak, they are themselves transformed into products by the media and consumed.
>
> The Left, while being devoured by the Right, tries to discipline and purify itself by eating itself—a practice that is simply the cannibalism of the weak. The Church celebrates communion by eating Christ. Victims and executioners are one and the same: devouring themselves. Everything, whether it is in the heart or in the jaw, is food to be consumed. Meanwhile, voraciously, nations devour their people. *Macunaíma* is the story of a Brazilian devoured by Brazil.[14]

While *Macunaíma* does not stage the Europe-indigene encounter per se, it does present the results of five hundred years of conquest and miscegenation. The names of the family members—Macunaíma, Jigue, Manaapa—are Indian, but the family is at once black, Indian, and European. The decor and costumes are oxymoronic, syncretic, culturally miscegenated. A sequence of racial transformation in which the black-Indian Macunaíma (Grande Otelo) turns into the white Macunaíma (Paulo José) ironically alludes to the Indianist movement. After Sofara's magic cigarette turns Macunaíma into a handsome prince, we hear an old carnival song ("Ai Ceci, nunca mais beijou Peri") that references the characters from *O Guarani*. As Randal Johnson points out, the sequence is a satirical barb directed at the Brazilian "economic miracle" of the late 1960s.[15] Sofara, the European Ceci of the allegory, is dressed in an "Alliance for Progress" sack. Her magic cigarette, a symbol of American intervention, has turned Macunaima, the Peri of the allegory, into a papier-mâché prince, just as the "economic miracle" touted by the junta supposedly turned Brazil into an apparently prosperous nation.

The tropicalist allegorical phase of Cinema Novo resurrects the Indianist theme expressed not only in *Macunaima* but also in a number of other 1970s films. Nelson Pereira dos Santos's *Como Era Gostoso Meu Francés*, meanwhile, performs an "anthropophagic" critique of European colonialism. The film is set in the sixteenth century, at a time when France was trying to found the colony of France Antartique in Rio de Janeiro. It was in this period that the French brought scores of Tupinamba Indians back to France to perform in a kind of proto–Disney World in Rouen, where the Tupinamba staged their daily practices for French observers, among them the French philosopher Montaigne, who later wrote his famous essay *Des Cannibales*. Although the film cites many writers of the time—Jean de Lery, Nicolas Durand de Villegaignon, José de Anchieta—it is based largely on Hans Staden's travel tale, the title of which bespeaks its sensationalist nature: *Hans Staden: The True History and Description of a Country of Savages, a Naked and Terrible People, Eaters of Men's Flesh, Who Dwell in the New World Called America*. The film concerns a Frenchman captured by the Tupinamba and sentenced to death in response to massacres inflicted upon them by Europeans. Before he is ritually executed and eaten, however, he is given a wife, Sebiopepe (widow of one of the Tupinamba massacred by the Europeans) and is allowed to participate in the tribe's daily activities. As he is taken to his execution, the Frenchman refuses to follow the prepared ritual and instead says in French, "My people will avenge me, and no Indian will remain in the land." The camera then zooms in to Sebiopepe's face as she devours her Frenchman, with no apparent regret despite her close relationship with him, an image that segues to a quotation from a report on genocide committed by Europeans.

In *Como Era Gostoso*, dos Santos attempts to subvert the conventional identification with the European protagonist of the captivity narrative. The title implies an indigenous-anthropophagic perspective that reverses the trope of ownership so that the European is now the slave. But more generally, the film offers a lesson in cultural relativism, indirectly posing Montaigne's question, who are the real barbarians? Ironically inverting the convention in which Europeans perceive only generic Indians (they all look alike), here the Indians are unable to distinguish the French from the Portuguese. Relative nudity (the Indian characters still wear ornaments, body paint, and *tangas*) becomes the cultural norm. The film systematically cuts off the conventional escape routes, maintaining an ironically neutral attitude toward the protagonist's demise. The European protagonist is not the hero, and romantic love is less important than tribal loyalty.

The title of the 1975 film *Iraçema* refers to the José de Alencar classic but turns the novel's Pocahontas-like story of romance between virginal Indian and Portuguese nobleman into a brutal encounter on the Trans-Amazonian Highway between a cynical white trucker and an Indian adolescent forced into prostitution. Here the "virgin with the honey lips" has become a highway whore. The multilevel text is at once specific and general, documenting an allegorical view of the entire process of "conservative modernization." Given the centrality of documentation to the film's project, Jorge Bodansky and Orlando Senna carefully authenticate images and sounds registered on the ground. For example, an interminable tracking shot records a gigantic humanmade forest fire, showing that the fire's dimensions on the screen do not depend on manipulative editing.

In *Iraçema*, ecological disaster and social exploitation configure an institutionalized hell. The highway brings in capital (from the distant south of Brazil and abroad) that organizes an intensified exploitation of the labor force, illegal land seizures, contraband in precious hardwoods, and new circulations of goods and human beings. One scene parallels migrant workers, prostitutes, and cattle as pieces being hauled in trucks and sold to a foreign-owned plantation. Instead of collage or discontinuous editing, Bodansky and Senna deploy incongruous documentary strategies derived from the cinema verité tradition. The male lead plays in and comments on the scenes, serving simultaneously as the character Tiao Brasil Grande and a cinema verité interviewer. Within the asymmetrical couple, Tiao is active agent, initiator, and entrepreneur while Iraçema is passive receiver, prostitute, and commodity. Tiao is associated with the modernizing nationalism that the highway project represents. He speaks in the jingoistic slogans of the period: "Onward Brazil!" "There's no stopping this country!" "Love it or leave it." He embodies the arrogance of the "economic miracle" and the pharaonic ambitions that produced the Third World's largest foreign debt. His grotesquerie forces the "patriotic" spectator to acknowledge his or her complicity in the deplorable invasion of the Amazon. The film develops, then, a structural contrast between two filmic approaches: first, cinema reportage, with handheld cameras registering the ecological devastation and human exploitation in the Amazon; and second, the fictional and allegorical procedures involving the relationship of Tiao and Iraçema. In a total interpenetration of documentary and fiction, the film denounces the human toll of frontier "development." If Iraçema in Jose de Alencar's novel responds to colonization by offering her love to a European knight, her contemporary namesake is clearly the victim of a twentieth-century conquistador, the embodiment of imperializing ambition.

THE INDIAN REVISITED

At the end of the twentieth century, Brazilian cinema hardly forgot Indians and Indianismo. The "anti-American blockbuster" *At Play in the Fields of the Lord* (1991), directed by Hector Babenco, offers disillusioned subtlety, social contradiction, and spectatorial ambivalence instead of Hollywood's usual Manichean resolutions.[16] Despite the film's high production values, star actors (e.g., Daryl Hannah), spectacular scenery, and its source in a best-selling novel by Peter Matthiessen, its hostile portrait of the role of Brazilians and Americans in the Amazon unsettled many First World audiences. Most of the changes from Matthiessen's novel had to do with Babenco's attempt to present indigenous conceptions of the world. In an interview with Neil Okrent, Babenco explains,

> Everything the Indians say or do in the movie . . . was suggested by them. They told me how they would react if a white man dropped from the sky into their village. They did the mise-en-scène. I just took my scissors and shaped it, but the inner concept, the core of everything came from workshops we did with them. They told stories from their families and relatives, including old people who remembered when they were first contacted.[17]

Thus Babenco seeks a collaborative representation based on indigenous participation. In this spirit, he makes a crucial alteration in the plot. In Matthiessen's novel, when Moon kills Aeore, the dying Indian says, "You are Kisu Mu." But Babenco chooses to have the Indian denounce Moon, calling him a "son of a bitch": "You are not one of us. You are a white man." Babenco also criticizes the hippy romanticism that believes that taking hallucinogenic drugs in the jungle magically turns white people into spiritual Indians. On the Indian side, Babenco shows active, diverse indigenous people who debate how to react to the incursions by outsiders. Aeore, as leader of the Nairuma, sees through Moon's constructed identity as a cultural transvestite. The apparently "pacified" Tiro people, meanwhile, use a kind of "sly civility" to outwit the conquerors. They merely pretend to pray, acting out white expectations of them in order to acquire food and presents. They interpret Protestant Christianity through their own cosmological filter and refuse to give up their own practices and beliefs.[18] Ultimately, however, Babenco's vision is elegiac, rooted in the trope of the inevitably vanishing Indian. The natives fight but for a cause that is doomed in advance. Indian arrows cannot compete with the invaders' bombs.

Another film released in the same year, Bruce Beresford's *Black Robe*, also treats the imposition of European religions on native peoples. But unlike *At Play*, *Black Robe* was immensely successful in the North American market.

The different response to the two films has everything to do, one suspects, with the fact that while *Black Robe* was set in the safely distant past (the sixteenth century), Babenco's film is set in the explosive present. While *Black Robe* is mildly critical of Jesuit actions in Quebec, it forgives them because Jesuits "did it all for love." *At Play*, in contrast, portrays the Protestant missionaries specifically, and Europeans and Euro-Americans generally, as being neurotic, arrogant, puritanical, insensitive, and ultimately dangerous to the general well-being. The pilots and the missionaries are symbolically linked in their mission: as they fly over the Amazon, the plane casts its reflection on the water in the form of a cross. Despite the tensions among them, the missionaries, the pilots, and the gold prospectors mutually reinforce one another within a common project of domination.

Silvio Back's compilation film *Yndio do Brasil* (1995) presents a wide spectrum of representations of Brazilian Indians superimposed on his own poems denouncing genocide. The film is prefaced by the phrase "The Only Good Indian Is the Filmed Indian," an intertextual variation on the well-known exterminationist slogan. Sequences from the most diverse sources are laid end to end without apparent rhyme or reason—Brazilian features such as *Iraçema* (1931), *O Caçador do Diamantes* (1933), and *A Lenda de Ubirajara* (1975); German films such as *Eine brasilianische Rapsodiie* (1935); and American films such as *Jungle Head Hunters* (1950). "Alien" music, such as ironic sambas, is superimposed on preexisting image tracks.

In the mid-1990s, Norma Benguel directed a completely uncritical version of Alencar's 1857 Indianist novel *O Guarani*, which featured the "foundational fiction," the gendered myth of the "good Indian" Peri, who prizes his beloved Cecilia above all else. One Portuguese noble in the film describes Peri as having the soul of a Portuguese nobleman wrapped in the body of a savage. The usual colonialist binarism separates the good Peri from the bad Aimores, the enemies of both Peri and the Portuguese. The language of the film is stilted, as is that of the novel, and Ceci and Peri address each other in the third person: "Is Ceci angry with her Peri?" Imbued with contemporary ecological sentiments, Peri dialogues with the jaguars. The film adopts the redface convention of having non-Indians play Indians, even though the new constitution freed Indians from the infantalizing status as "wards of the state." The soundtrack, by Wagner Tiso, spins out electronic variations on Carlos Gomes's *O Guarani* while incorporating some indigenous sounds and instrumentation.

Luiz Alberto Pereira's *Hans Staden* (1999), meanwhile, tells the story of a German artilleryman who was shipwrecked in 1550 off the coast of Santa Catarina. In January 1554, while in search of a slave who had disappeared, Staden was captured by Tupinamba Indians. Brought to their site in Ubatuba, he claimed to have narrowly escaped being devoured in an anthropophagic ritual. The film's point of departure is Staden's 1557 sensationalist account of his two trips to Brazil. While French Protestant writers such as Jean de Lery and Andre Thevet (and later Montaigne) tend to defend ritual cannibalism (while denouncing Spanish Catholics as the real cannibals), Staden sees cannibalism as just one more trial that can strengthen his faith. At the same time, he depicts Tupi cannibalism not as a pure act of revenge but rather as a way of acquiring "beautiful names."

The Pereira film displays scrupulous reconstitution of language, decors, and costumes but not much imagination. Indeed, Pereira seems to be the last person alive who actually believed it possible to show "exactly what Brazil in the sixteenth century was like."[19] According to its author, "the film tells what happened, nothing more," all within a spirit of journalistic objectivity. But such a view assumes that Staden himself told only what happened, without ideological filters, when in fact Staden's writing is an exercise in allegorical homiletics designed to demonstrate the superiority of the Christian religion. Pereira revisits the theme of *Como Era Gostoso* but only to render it more conventional and Eurocentric. While Nelson Pereira dos Santos synthesizes the stories of the German Hans Staden and the Frenchman Jean de Lery, Pereira concentrates solely on the German while explicitly rejecting allegory as a "modernist syndrome which drives away the public."[20] While dos Santos was ironic toward his "hero," Pereira struggles with Staden as hero and encourages the spectator to identify as well. While the Frenchman is ultimately devoured in *Como Era Gostoso*, the German tricks his captors and escapes. While the Frenchman is integrated into the tribe, the German returns to his family.[21] Eduardo Marettin points out that Pereira improves on Staden by portraying him in the film as being more curious and sympathetic than how Staden portrays himself in the book.[22] The film fails to dialogue with a rich multicentury discussion of cannibalism that includes Thevet, Montaigne, Oswald de Andrade, Florestan Fernandes, Caetano Veloso, and many others, dismissing all these analyses in favor of a naive "just the facts" version.

The quincentennial year of 2000 brought us not only *Invenção do Brasil* but also two fiction features. The children's adventure film *Taina: Uma Aventura na Amazonia* (2000) revolves around an eight-year-old Indian girl named Taina, who lives with her grandfather Tige in the Amazon forest. A feminine version of the Indianist *bravo guerreiro*, Taina possesses an ecological consciousness as she confronts the smugglers who steal and sell threatened animals for genetic research abroad. She acts in solidarity with the Indian woman Tikiri, the pilot Rudi, and the Brazilian biologist Isabel and her son Joninho. In a new version of an *Iraçema*-style romance, one clearly inflected by the spirit of Steven Spielberg, Taina loves Joninho and helps him see the wisdom of Indian life and values. Lucia Murad's *Brava Gente Brasileira* (Brave Brazilian People, 2000), meanwhile, is set in the year 1778, when another Diogo (played by Portuguese actor Diogo Infante), a cartographer like Diogo Alvares, is marking borders claimed by both Portugal and Spain. Diogo abuses and then falls in love with Anote (Luciana Rigueria). *Brava Gente Brasileira* tells a kind of anti-*Iraçema* story, where love between the Portuguese man and the indigenous woman is rendered impossible by the violence of the *bandeirantes* in the colonial "contact zone." Even the most sensitive of the colonizers, men such as Diogo, cannot have their dream of peaceful coexistence. Nor are the Indian characters without agency, for in the end they devise an ingenious plan of retaliation, involving seduction followed by massive destruction of the Europeans.

VIDEO IN THE VILLAGE

In the 1980s "ethnographic films" attempted to divest themselves of vestigial colonialist attitudes.[23] Documentary and experimental films discarded the covert elitism of the pedagogical or ethnographic model, calling instead for "dialogical anthropology" and "interactive filmmaking." The most remarkable recent development has been the emergence of "indigenous media"—that is, the use of audiovisual technology (camcorders, videocassette recorders, etc.) for the cultural and political purposes of indigenous peoples. Finally, the Indian is no longer represented, fetishized, idealized, and allegorized by non-Indians. The Centro de Trabalho Indigenista (Center of Indigenista Work) in São Paulo, for example, has been working in collaboration with indigenous groups since 1979, teaching video production and editing and making available technologies and facilities to protect indigenous land and consolidate resistance. The goal of the center's Video in the Villages project is to put Indians "face to face with their own image." Vincent Carelli, a leading figure in Video in the Villages, scrupulously avoids salvationist discourse, that video can "save the Indian."[24] And indeed both Carelli and his critics have called attention to the unequal power relations in this situation, inequalities that make real cultural reciprocity elusive. He stresses the different aesthetic notions of insiders and outsiders. For example, non-Indians frequently express a desire to see the "real" Indian films (films made by Indians for Indians), but they are often bored by the slow pace of such films, since the indigenous filmmakers are intent on respecting the spatial-temporal integrity of the event, even if it takes six hours.

In *O Espíritu da TV* (The Spirit of TV, 1991) Carelli and Dominique Gallois, a collaborator who spoke the language of the indigenous Waiapi tribe, brought videotapes about other Indian groups (the Gaviao and the Nambiquara), television news broadcasts about Indian issues, and basic equipment (generators, videocassette recorders, cameras, blank cassettes) to leave with the Indians. In the film the members of the tribe, newly introduced to television, reflect on the uses of video in defending themselves against the encroachments of federal agencies, gold miners, and loggers. Taking an eminently pragmatic approach, the Waiapi ask the filmmakers to hide their weakness to the outside world: "exaggerate our strength," they say, so "they won't occupy our land ... tell them we're killers." The Waiapi are dynamic, active, in constant movement. The uncensored feeling of the film and the relaxed body language of the Waiapi are striking. The constant laughter suggests that they are completely at ease with the filmmakers. And the anger they express toward the outside becomes a guarantee of the authenticity of the materials, since the videos are obviously not designed to flatter the "well-meaning" Western spectator.

In *Meeting Ancestors* (1993), directed by Carelli and produced by the Centro de Trabalho Indigenista, Chief Wai Wai recounts his trip to meet the Zo'e, a recently contacted group that the Waiapi knew only through having seen videos of them. Both groups speak dialects of Tupi. Since the Waiapi were contacted twenty years before, they warn the Zo'e about some of the dangers they are about to confront. The Zo'e, in this respect, represent a kind of former life or earlier incarnation of the Waiapi. Instead of the anthropological "allochronic" approach, which sees Indians as living in condemned historical time, we see people accustomed to airplanes, incarnations of what Oswald de Andrade called the *indio technizado*. Rather than the generic Indian, we encounter the cultural distinctions between closely related tribes. In *Video Cannibalism* (1995), the Enuaene tribe, inspired by a screening of *Dances with Wolves*, tells a story about some gold prospectors who encroach on Enuaene territory and are killed, much to the delight of the village. The filmmakers use a film-within-a-film technique to create a story for the tribe's own pleasure but also a warning and object lesson to whites.

In the background of these video projects is an implicit refusal of the usual predatory attitudes of journalists and documentarists who simply take their loot (i.e., images) and run, without showing the films to the Indians themselves or in any way "giving back." And indeed, Indians have complained about the opportunism of filmmakers who win awards in festivals and yet never give a copy of the film to the Indians who made it possible. The more serious filmmakers, such as Carelli, respect certain taboos, such as not trying to probe into what the tribe regards as secret knowledge. Carelli also refuses to work with any group where leadership and power are in dispute, to avoid the danger of somehow influencing these disputes. He is also aware of the danger of elitism, whereby those members of the group who control the videos can acquire special power in the community.

Among the most media savvy of the indigenous groups are the Kayapo, a Go-speaking people of central Brazil who live in fourteen communities scattered over an area roughly the size of Great Britain. When a documentary crew from Granada Television went to film them in 1987, the Kayapo demanded video cameras, videocassette recorders, monitors, and videotapes as a quid pro quo for their cooperation. When they received the technology to make their own tapes, they called on three independent filmmakers to train them (Monica Frota, Luis Rios, and Renata Perreira), and together they created the film *Taking Aim: The Kayapo Appropriation of Video Technology*. The three filmmakers formed another indigenous media project, Mekaran Opoi D'Joi (He Who Creates Images). The Kayapo have subsequently used video to record their own traditional ceremonies, demonstrations, and encounters with whites (to have the equivalent of a legal transcript). The Kayapo not only sent a delegation to the Brazilian Constitutional Convention to lobby delegates debating indigenous rights but also videotaped themselves in the process, winning international attention for their cause. Widely disseminated images in *Time* and the *New York Times Magazine* of the Kayapo wielding video cameras derive their power to shock from the premise that "natives" must be quaint and allochronic: "real Indians don't carry camcorders."

Indigenous media films bring up a host of theoretical and political issues. Who gets to hold the camera? Who edits? According to what aesthetic? What conventions or decorum guide the camera movements? If Westerners are training indigenous filmmakers, is there a danger of imposing a Western aesthetic? Although anthropologist Terry Turner, who has trained the Kayapo in filmmaking, claims that he does not teach Western notions of style—only some elementary technical procedures (such as cutaways and the compatibility of adjacent cuts)—perhaps these minimal technical procedures themselves enjoy Western notions, such as the principle of invisible continuity editing. But Turner also stresses the strong aesthetic sense of the Indians, their sensitivity to the beauty of feather design, body decorations, and so forth.[25] Yet other analysts have been critical of these films. Rachel Moore speaks of "marketing alterity" and a redemptionist narrative whose real purpose is to rescue anthropology as a discipline. The pretense is that "they are representing themselves, and we have nothing to do with it." But the act of handing over the camera, Moore argues, comes in the wake of many years of exposure to media and to ethnographers. Thus the emergence of voice becomes linked to a project of containment, which leads to the "self-marketing" of the Kayapo.[26] This critique seems somewhat ungenerous and uninformed, however, because, first, activists such as Carelli are completely aware of these dangers and, second, the objections of faraway outsiders seem somewhat silly when the indigenous people themselves seem satisfied with the process.

The indigenous media films demonstrate a complex interface of the local and the global, what some have coined the "glocal." On the one hand, what could be more "local" than a tiny indigenous village inhabited by a single indigenous group with its language and customs far from the urban areas and the populated coast of Brazil? On the other, these groups have real connections to other spaces and locations, struggling indigenous groups elsewhere, filmmakers such as Carelli, world film festivals, philanthropic foundations, pop-star activists such as Sting, and ecological enterprises such as "Body Shop." While people like James Faris and Rachel Moore stress the manipulation of Indians by outsiders, it seems undeniable that Indians nonetheless exercise some agency.[27] As Oswald de Andrade has suggested, the *indio tecnizado*, the high-tech cannibal, can be selective about what he or she chooses to "devour" from the West.

This chapter has surveyed the various incarnations of the Indian through a century of cinema: the romantic Indian, the ethnographic Indian, the allegorical Indian, the activist Indian. Lamartine Babo once said in a song that Cabral discovered Brazil on April 22, just two months after carnival. It is no accident, therefore, that carnival too has appropriated the figure of the Indian, with *blocos* named the Apaches, the Comanches, and Cacique de Ramos. Popular music too has constantly referenced the Indian in postmodern recombinant ways, often permutating the tropes of romantic Indianist literature. I am thinking, for example, of the Chico Buarque de Holanda song "Iraçema," where the Alencar heroine is reenvisioned as a woman from Ceará who has emigrated to the United States, or the Caetano Veloso song suggesting that "after the last Indian tribe has been exterminated," a new Indian hero will emerge—not only "fearless like Muhammad Ali" and "agile like Bruce Lee" but also "passionate like Peri." Brazilian cinema and popular culture, as we have seen here, have both prolonged and critiqued the myths and fictions inherited from Indianismo.

NOTES

1. For a comprehensive survey and further analysis of individual films, see my *Tropical Multiculturalism: A Comparative History of Race in Brazilian Cinema and Culture* (Durham, N.C.: Duke University Press, 1997).

2. John E. Kicza, *Resilient Cultures: America's Native Peoples Confront European Colonization 1500–1800* (Upper Saddle River, N.J.: Prentice Hall, 2003).

3. My translation.

4. Indeed, Caetano was partially inspired by Sousandrade's poem "Inferno de Wall Street." The jazz overtones of the music remind us of Manhattan's strong connection to African American music and the fact that people of African descent have been living in Manhattan for five centuries.

5. See João Carlos Rodrigues, "O indio brasileiro e o cinema," in *Cinema brasileiro: Estudos* (Rio de Janeiro: Embrafilme/Funarte, 1980).

6. See Doris Sommer, *Foundational Fictions: The National Romances of Latin America* (Berkeley: University of California Press, 1991).

7. For a discussion of transracial male bonding in American literature, see Leslie Fiedler, *Love and Death in the American Novel* (New York: Criterion, 1960).

8. Diogo Alvares arrived in Brazil in a wrecked ship at the beginning of the Portuguese colonization, after which he resided in Bahia for many decades. He learned the languages and customs of the Indian and participated in local wars, thus gaining the respect of Indian chiefs. In the presence of the king, he married Paraguaçu in France on July 30, 1528, and subsequently had children with her (and probably with other indigenous women). According to legend, Alvares reigned over the Tupinamba for fifty years.

9. See Janaina Amado, "Mythic Origins: Caramuru and the Founding of Brazil," *Hispanic American Historical Review* 80, no. 4 (November 2000): 783–811.

10. See Carlos Roberto de Souza, *Nossa aventura na tela* (São Paulo: Cultura Editoras Associadas, 1998).

11. Quoted in Fernão Ramos, *Historia do cinema brasileiro* (São Paulo: Arte Editora, 1987), 74. Excerpts from some of these documentaries form part of Silvio Back's 1995 documentary *O Yndio do Brasil*.

12. See Ivan van Sertima, *They Came before Columbus* (New York: Random House, 1975). The sequence even resonates with the recent discovery of Luzia, a skeleton thought to be over eleven thousand years old and said to have Negroid features.

13. Joaquim Pedro de Andrade is the Brazilian filmmaker with the clearest links to the modernist movement in the sense that he made many films related to it: *O Poeta do Castelo* is a short piece about the modernist poet Manuel Bandeira (with whom Mario de Andrade exchanged letters); his first feature, *O Padre e a Moça*, adapts a poem by another modernist, Carlos Drummond de Andrade; *Macunaima* is taken from Mario de Andrade; and *O Homen do Pau Brasil* is inspired by Osvald de Andrade.

14. Author's collection.

15. See Randal Johnson, "Cinema Novo and Cannibalism: *Macunaima*," in *Brazilian Cinema*, ed. Randal Johnson and Robert Stam (New York: Columbia University Press, 1995), 178–90.

16. See Eugenio Bucci, "Do filme brasileiro que parece americano (E do americano que parece brasileiro," *Revista USP* 19 (September–November 1993). See also Lucia Nagib, "Nota em favor de um filme internacional" in the same issue. Although American financed, the film employed a Brazilian producer (Francisco Ramalho Jr.), a Brazilian director of photography (Lauro Escorel), and well-known Brazilian players (including José Dumont and Nelson Xavier). The Babenco film used hegemonic financing circuits to make what looks at first glance like a Hollywood-style superproduction (costing $3 million, more than the combined budget of scores of Brazilian features put together).

17. Neil Okrent, "*At Play in the Fields of the Lord*: An Interview with Hector Babenco," *Cineaste* 19, no. 1 (1992): 44–47.

18. Ana M. Brigido-Corochan, in an unpublished paper, "Indigenous Resistances: Representations of the Native in Contemporary 'Brazilian' Films," compares the indigenous survival tactics to Gerald Vizenor's notion of survivance as

an "active repudiation of dominance, tragedy and victimry." See Gerald Robert Vizenor, *Fugitive Poses: Native American Indian Scenes of Absence and Presence* (Lincoln: University of Nebraska Press, 1998), 15.

19. Interview with Paulo Santos Lima, "'Hans Staden mostra os dentes nos cinemas,'" *Folha de São Paulo* (March 17, 2000).

20. Santos Lima, "'Hans Staden.'"

21. See Guiomar Ramos, "Como era gostoso o meu Hans Staden," *Sinopse* 5 (2000).

22. Eduardo Morettin, "Hans Staden: O individuo e a historia," *Sinopse* 5 (2000).

23. See David MacDougall, "Beyond Observational Cinema," in *Principles of Visual Anthropology*, ed. Paul Hockings (The Hague: Mouton, 1975).

24. My summaries of Carelli's views are based on my frequent participation in seminars and film screenings held by Carelli and by remarks gathered from others. See Patricia Aufderheide, "Making Videos with Brazilian Indians," in the *Daily Planet: A Critic on the Capitalist Culture Beat* (Minneapolis: University of Minnesota Press, 2000). See also the special dossier on "Os Brasis Indígenas" in *Sinopse* 5 (2000).

25. For Terence Turner's views on indigenous media, see Turner, "Visual Media, Cultural Politics, and Anthropological Practice," *The Independent* (January–February 1991); and Turner, "Defiant Images," *Anthropology Today* 3, no. 6 (1992).

26. See Rachel Moore, "Marketing Alterity," *Visual Anthropology* 8, no. 2 (Fall 1992).

27. James Faris, "Anthropological Transparency: Film, Representation, and Politics," in *Film as Ethnography*, ed. P. Crawford and D. Turton (Manchester: Manchester University Press, 1992).

8

❧

The Emperor and His Pedestal: Pedro I and Disputed Views of the Brazilian Nation, 1860–1900

James N. Green

A large public square lies at the edge of Rio de Janeiro's historic down-town area. At the center of the Largo do Rossio, as this plaza was popularly called in the nineteenth century, stands a monumental statue of emperor Dom Pedro I (1898–1834) dressed in full military regalia and mounted on a warhorse (figure 8.1). Dom Pedro II (1825–1891) inaugurated this statue in 1862, honoring his father in an elaborate public ceremony that also marked the fortieth anniversary of Brazil's independence from Portugal. This equestrian sculpture was the Brazilian imperial capital's first public monument and was thus embedded with particular importance as a symbol of the genesis of a new nation, its founding myths, and its early history.[1]

The political symbolism attached to this square is complex. The Largo do Rossio was intimately intertwined with events related to the nation's independence and first constitution. Thus, the erection of a monument in honor of Dom Pedro I in 1862 provoked a public debate about contending versions of the early national period's history. Political satirists used the equestrian statue of Dom Pedro I to criticize his son, Pedro II. As a symbol of the nation, the statue became a convenient image to represent the ills of the imperial regime. Moreover, the multiple names attached to the square evoke political tensions and contradictions. In 1821, in the aftermath of the Porto revolution that demanded a liberal constitution for Portugal, Dom João VI and his son and heir, Pedro I, swore allegiance to the idea of estab-lishing a constitutional monarchy in Portugal at the Royal Theater right off the square. The next year, the Senate, by direction of the king's minister José Bonifácio de Andrada e Silva, who happened to live in a large residence

181

Figure 8.1.   Statue of emperor Dom Pedro I, Praça Tiradentes, Rio de Janeiro. *Source:* Arquivo Geral da Cidade do Rio de Janeiro. Photographic reproduction by Marco Antonio Belandi. Mat-10/16254-5 SMC.

in front of the square, issued a decree renaming it Praça da Constituição (Constitutional Plaza). Sixty-eight years later, only months after Pedro II was overthrown in 1889, the new republican government renamed the site Praça Tiradentes as a tribute to the late-eighteenth-century republican conspirator Joaquim José da Silva Xavier, popularly known as Tiradentes. Because Dom Pedro I's father, Dom João VI, was ruling Portugal in 1792 when Tiradentes was hung, drawn, and quartered near the square, the new republican government used the renaming of the plaza to consecrate new national heroes and myths while discrediting the monarchy. Contested claims over whether Tiradentes or Dom Pedro I represented the authentic founding hero of Brazilian independence pitted republican partisans against defenders of the monarchy.[2]

At the turn of the twentieth century, fashionable buildings surrounded the newly rechristened Praça Tiradentes. An elegant theater on one side of the park provided diversion for the city's elite. Other theaters in the area featured musical reviews, vaudeville, and cabaret for a wider audience. The municipal government invested in elegantly landscaping the square to create a pleasantly gardened urban oasis for this important public space.[3] The park, however, was located in the midst of bohemian sociability, with nearby cafés, nightclubs, brothels, and street prostitution readily available to bourgeois *bons vivants* as well as the laboring classes. Moreover, as early as the 1870s, the square was a social meeting ground for men seeking homoerotic liaisons, offering an ironic twist on its original significance as a site for public celebrations and civic ceremonies.[4]

The controversies about this space offer us the opportunity to examine how elite politicians and intellectuals projected symbols of the nation, contested versions of history, and competing myths onto this geographic location to consolidate or dispute alternative visions of Brazil's past, present, and, by implication, future. So, in this chapter, I first offer a brief overview of the period's history and its relationship to the plaza, after which I examine the symbolic use of the emperor and his pedestal to discuss how these competing interpretations of early national history play out in civic ceremonies, public discourse, and political satire.

INDEPENDENCE AND A CONSTITUTIONAL MONARCHY

In the late colonial period, the Largo do Rossio was also known as the Campos dos Ciganos, or Gypsies' Field, because Romany, prohibited from living within the colonial capital's walls, pitched their tents in the swampy land on the city's outskirts.[5] In 1808 the square was renamed Campo da Polé when a *pelourinho* (stone pillory) was erected in its center to publicly whip intractable slaves.[6] As mentioned, the field was renamed Praça da Constituição on March 2, 1822, to honor the royal public oath to the new Portuguese constitution. Six months later, on September 7, Dom Pedro I, tarrying along the banks of the Ipiranga, unsheathed his sword and proclaimed "Independência o Morte" (Independence of Death).[7] Numerous artistic renderings consecrate the Grito de Ipiranga as the symbolic founding moment of the Brazilian nation.[8]

Acclaimed emperor Dom Pedro I a month later and crowned six weeks thereafter, the new ruler swore to defend the new constitution still to be written. Subsequently, the emperor disbanded the Constituent Assembly and then had a new draft written that, among other provisions, gave him considerable power over the judicial, legislative, and executive branches of government, with the *poder moderador* (moderating power) that allowed him to dissolve the Chamber of Deputies, select life-long senators from a list of the top three candidates elected in a given province, appoint and remove provincial presidents, and block any and all legislation. On March 25, 1824, Dom Pedro I swore allegiance to the new Magna Carta in a solemn ceremony in the capital's cathedral.

As historian Pierre Nora has pointed out, temporal and topographical memory sites and monuments emerge at those times and in those places where there is a perceived or constructed break with the past.[9] Indeed, within a year, loyal royalists petitioned the emperor to erect a statue in his honor and to consecrate the rupture with Portugal.[10] In 1827, Auguste Henri Gandjean de Montigny of the French Artistic Mission drew up two proposed statues to honor the emperor. Both placed him on horseback. One monument, to be erected in the Praça da Constituição, rested on a simple pedestal. The second, planned for the Campo de Sant'Anna, today the Praça da República, had a more complex design. The statue, however, did not render a likeness of Dom Pedro I in a military uniform. Instead, he stood as a crowned emperor wearing royal robes and carrying a scepter. From the pedestal below, Brazil's nineteen provinces offered him additional crowns.[11] The emperor had not yet been transformed into a leader who ensured national unity through military might. Rather, it was his role as a legitimate monarch that had won his loyal subjects' allegiance.

Rio's municipal government began collecting donations from the citizenry to cover the costs of the proposed monument. According to Haddock Lobo, who sponsored the resolution that finally led to the erection of the statue in 1862, representatives from all social strata contributed to the campaign initiated in 1825.[12] However, the unpopular war in the Río de la Plata region dampened enthusiasm for the emperor and a statue in his honor. Ensuing political turbulence against Dom Pedro I and his renunciation in 1831 further discouraged the construction of a monument.[13]

Subsequent projects and the final 1862 statue, however, consistently suggest an equestrian military theme. Borrowing from a long tradition ranging from classic portrayals of the Roman emperors to French neoclassical renditions of Napoleon, Dom Pedro I became a modern-day conqueror, warrior, and liberator, even though he never personally engaged in a military campaign to defend the new nation, nor did he lead his troops into battle in the conflict over territories in the south. What is most striking about the statue is the posture of the emperor. Rather than bearing an unsheathed sword in his right hand, he is waving an unfurled scroll. Two episodes in the history of independence—namely, the cry for "Independência o Morte" on September 7, 1822, and the oath to the constitution on March 25, 1824—are conflated into a single historical moment. Although the future emperor was traveling on horseback in the province of São Paulo when he uttered the famous cry for independence, his pledge to adhere to a new Brazilian constitution was enacted in a ceremony in a cathedral in Rio. Moreover, the portrayal of the monarch in uniform suggests a military career that obscures his failed war over the Banda Oriental, present-day Uruguay. The statue conflates military prowess with loyalty to the constitution even though he ordered his troops to close down the Constituent

Assembly. Dom Pedro I's sword is replaced with a constitution penned by the monarch's ministers that granted him exceptional powers to overrule the three branches of government. The location of the statue in the Praça da Constituição, the site where both Dom Pedro I and his father had sworn to uphold the not-yet-written Portuguese constitution (not the Brazilian constitution of 1824), adds another awkward layer of confabulation to the mythmaking about the emperor as the nation's founding father.

As embodied in Rio de Janeiro's first statue in a public venue, Dom Pedro I is a hero because he breaks ties with Portugal and yet does not become an absolute monarch. His defense of the nation and his allegiance to the constitution create the image of a liberal monarchy whose legitimacy lies in the consent of the people. One can imagine the celebrating masses cheering the mounted ruler, as depicted in classic portraits of the "Grito de Ipiranga." In François-René Moreaux's 1844 rendition of the event, entitled *The Proclamation of Independence*, Dom Pedro I waves his military cap. In an anonymous lithograph published in 1866, the future emperor of Brazil unsheathes his sword (figure 8.2). Common to all of the artistic representations of the proclamation of independence are highly gendered renderings of a virile monarch exhibiting military and masculine prowess that affirm his supremacy over nation.

Figure 8.2.   Anonymous lithograph. "O Grito de Ipiranga," a representation of Dom Pedro I's call for independence in 1822. *Source*: Miguel Maria Lisbôa, Barão de Japura. *Romances históricos, por um brasileiro*, 2nd ed. (Brussels: n.p., 1886). Fundação Biblioteca Nacional.

During the tumultuous regency (1831–1840) and the first reigning years of young Dom Pedro II, the monarchy continued to confront a string of regional revolts and separatist movements that threatened to shatter national unity. However, by the 1850s, political calm had settled over the country. The end of the slave trade had released capital for internal economic development. Coffee production expanded to meet international demand. The young emperor encouraged the development of the nation's infrastructure, which accelerated the export-driven economy.[14] During this period of civil peace and economic prosperity Rio's politicians resurrected the proposal to honor Brazil's first ruler with a monument.

On September 7, 1854, Independence Day, twenty years after the death of Dom Pedro I, the Municipal Council, in an extraordinary session, unanimously approved a motion to revive the 1825 fund-raising campaign to collect sufficient private donations from "all classes of society, from capitalists and the highest government officials to workers and the lowest public employee" to duly honor Brazil's "philosopher prince."[15] This title, an allusion to his role as the grantor of the nation's constitution, was more apropos of the current emperor, who was a voracious reader, a would-be scientist, and an enthusiastic scholar. The constitution of 1824 had established a constitutional monarchy within an early-nineteenth-century framework that saw its origins in the Enlightenment philosophers. Pedro I was hardly a philosopher himself, but flattery was the order of the day. At a time of economic and social stability, what better way to create and promote symbols of a united and prosperous nation than through homage to its founding ruler? What better way to pay respects to the current emperor than through finally erecting the proposed statue of his father?

The Brazilian constitution had given the emperor the moderating power to keep him at the pinnacle of the nation's political and social pyramid. He made the ultimate selection of anyone aspiring to become a lifelong senator or provisional president. He could dissolve the Chamber of Deputies at will and call on any politician to form a new government. A corrupt electoral system favored the faction tapped by the emperor. Thousands of government posts and positions of power flowed to the election's winners.[16] Thus, an excessive deference to the emperor was the politically expedient order of the day. While his father's 1824 constitution gave him considerable power, Dom Pedro II was not an absolute monarch. He skillfully used this moderating power to pit factions, parties, and interests against each other, making him the final arbiter of government policies, appointments, and political spoils. The constitution introduced by Dom Pedro I had codified an economy of politics that depended on a complex and hierarchical network of patronage relationships. The statue that was designed to honor the emperor's father was a gesture by the beneficiaries of a system that was based on reciprocal obligations of deference and support that by the 1850s had finally ensured relative political, social, and economic stability. For the slave-owning elite, merchants, and coffee barons, the emperor, and by extension his father, embodied the nation's ultimate patriarch, who ruled over a social order that provided a secure and comfortable life to a thin layer of planters, businessmen, politicians, and bureaucrats. A public gesture of gratitude acknowledging and legitimizing the role of the monarch as the guiding light of the nation's successes was, according to the proponents of the statue, long overdue.

HONORING THE EMPEROR

Prosperity due to the expansion of coffee production in the region around Rio framed the economic backdrop to this effort to forge a strong national identity after decades of regional revolts. A temporary truce among the nation's political actors explains the broad-based support for honoring the Imperial House of Bragança. For the first time in the history of the young nation, members of the Liberal and Conservative Parties formed a government of *conciliação* in 1853 that represented the political unity of the ascendant coffee planters in the region between Rio and São Paulo.[17] High coffee prices and an expansion of the railroad infrastructure offered a burst of wealth to these coffee barons. Economic and political optimism brought together previously warring political factions. The national campaign to collect contributions from Brazilians from the high to the humble offered a symbolic gesture of national unity during these heady years of coffee-driven opulence. Conciliation, however, was not to last long. A severe drop in coffee prices in 1857 undercut the political concord. By 1860 a more radical wing of the Liberal Party emerged. It did not question the underlying issue of the nation's reliance on slave labor for its economic prosperity. Rather, it focused on a critique of the concentration of power in the hands of the emperor. And as we shall see, members of the Liberal Party used the inauguration of the statue to the emperor's father to wage a campaign against the emperor himself.

Historian Jeffrey D. Needell has offered an alternative interpretation regarding the support mobilized among the nation's political elite in the 1850s for the erection of a monument to Emperor Pedro I.[18] The chairman of the 1854 committee in charge of raising funds for the statue was Eusébio de Queirós, the leader of the *saquaremas*, the right wing of the Conservative Party that had dominated the state since 1848. As Needell has observed,

It is noteworthy that not only was Eusébio put in charge, but the committee was explicitly set to organize public contributions from the top down of the socio-political order. And not the empire's political order as a whole, but one very specific one: the very heartland of the *saquaremas*, the imperial capital and the Province of Rio de Janeiro. It would be entirely characteristic of Eusébio to use this monument to make a political point clearly, if indirectly . . . that the monarchy's great support was the merchant-planter elites of the empire's greatest port and richest export province and that they supported the monarchy as a *constitutional* monarchy.[19]

In addition to the failed campaigns to erect a statue in 1825, mentioned earlier, devotees of the nation's first emperor launched proposals in 1839, 1844, and 1852, the last leading to the successful 1854 campaign. Needell suggests that these earlier propositions failed because "they were correctly perceived as the attempt by political reactionaries to foist their point of view over the nation when the political world was still badly divided between such reactionaries and radicals."[20] By the 1850s the radicals had been cast aside. The Conservative Party itself was internally divided with the less-conservative Marquês de Paraná serving as prime minister in coalitions with moderate Liberals and implementing a series of reforms that the *saquaremas* saw as undermining the constitutional order. Thus, these reactionary leaders' principal role in the fund-raising drive, Needell argues, served to send a "reminder to the Emperor and the larger political world that the monarch was an institution that they had defended and designed as constrained by law and balanced by parliament. They made clear their loyalty to the regime, but emphasized its *constitutional* quality."[21]

After the Municipal Council had duly initiated a fund-raising campaign to finance the commissioning of the statue, the committee in charge of the monument organized a public competition to choose an appropriate design. Artists from Brazil and abroad entered drawings and plaster models. João Maximiano Mafra, a professor at the Imperial Academy of Fine Arts, won the prize for the best design, but the French statue maker Louis Rochet, a runner-up in the competition, was awarded the task of executing the project.[22] Ironically, a foreign artist residing in Paris created Brazil's first national monument, a fact that mirrors the nineteenth-century Brazilian elites' deference to all things French.[23]

SYMBOLS OF THE NATION

The statue's guiding motif was Pedro I's magnificent dual achievement: securing independence while guaranteeing a constitutional regime. The emperor's pedestal offered an opportunity to represent the symbols of the nation that he benevolently ruled. How did different members of the Brazilian elite (in this case the artist, the judges of the contest, and the emperor himself) think about Brazil? What visions of the country did they project onto the nation's first monument?

One way to answer that question is to examine how intellectual and political figures debated the issue in the august meetings of the Brazilian Historical and Geographical Institute, which was founded by gentlemen scholars and politicians in 1838 in part to encourage the creation of an official national historical narrative. In 1843 the institute sponsored a competition that asked the question "How should Brazilian history be understood?" Karl F. P. von Martius, the winning essayist, argued that any written version of the country's past must take into account its indigenous, European, and African roots.[24] This vision of how to think about Brazilian history was only seriously embraced ninety years later, when Gilberto Freyre published *Casa-grande e senzala* (The Masters and the Slaves), a work that with all of its serious limitations nevertheless acknowledges Indian and especially African contributions to the establishment of a unique Brazilian culture.

Why did the creators of the statue ignore Martius's essay and choose to erase African sweat and blood from the national narrative, as embodied in this monument? One way to answer that question is to consider that in the 1850s slavery still constituted the backbone of economic prosperity enjoyed by the European-descended elites who governed the nation. Planters and slaveholders became defensive about the institution as Britain forced an end to international slave trade in 1850. The Brazilian elites, who judged their own cultural, social, and political progress by European standards, found that the institution of slavery was now an uncomfortable embarrassment, although a necessary fact of life. The planter classes had not yet seriously considered an alternative source of labor for sugar and coffee production. So, they defended slavery by claiming that Africans were an inferior race, suited for hard labor but not for anything else, certainly not for becoming symbolic members of the nation. Moreover, Africans remained a rebellious threat. The 1835 Malé slave revolt in Salvador, Bahia, was a reminder of their potential danger.

Instead, the artist who designed the project that won the seal of approval of the Imperial Academy of Fine Arts and the emperor turned to Brazil's Indians as an allegoric representation of the nation. Indianism had recently come into literary vogue. Novelist José Alencar and poet Gonçalves Dias created a national version of the international romanticist movement by penning idealistic accounts of the initial encounters between Portuguese settlers and the indigenous population. Although violent clashes with the survivors of the nation's once-extensive native population still continued in the country's outlying frontier regions, the mid-nineteenth-century Indianist movement looked to an idyllic preconquest and colonial past. They linked Rousseau's doctrine of the "noble savage" with nationalistic notions of the Indian and indigenous culture as "a symbol of spiritual, political, social and literary independence."[25] The childlike naiveté of Brazilian Indians, as portrayed by these authors, mirrored a notion of a young and innocent nation built in a tropical land of exotic animals, majestic nature, and pure and simple original inhabitants.

The country's narrative obscures the indigenous populations' histories, cultures, and languages, conflating them with the empire's vast territories and natural resources. The composition of the emperor's pedestal captures this fusion of Brazilian nature and its noble population. The four sides of the massive granite dais display romantic and nostalgic images of generic Brazilian Indians. Rather than be represented by their linguistic and cultural differences, Brazil's stylized native sons and daughters are transformed into allegories for the country's four major rivers: the Amazon, Paraná, Madeira, and São Francisco. The exotic tropical animals—capybara, jacare, jiboa, and tatu—that commingle with the Indians at the statue's base evoke the country's tropical "otherness." Reigning over this natural kingdom of noble savages, plants, and animals is the emperor, dominating a vast land that has justifiably granted him such a lofty title.

Among the representations of Brazil's first inhabitants are shapely Indian women. To the gaze of the masculine elite, accustomed to viewing proper women in layers of silk, velvet, and wool, these "noble savages" with their naked bodies evoke innocent licentiousness and available allure. Many Indianists believed that it was the unclothed indigenous woman's body that had captivated the Portuguese male colonizers. According to these authors and artists, as well as the gentlemen scholars crafting the first national narratives, the offspring of Portuguese conquerors and indigenous women are the symbolic founding generation of the new Brazilian nation. Yet, while Alencar and other authors write about the mixed-race children of Portuguese men and Indian women as progenitors of the Brazilian nation, the indigenous figures on the pedestal show no phenotypical indication of racial mixture. There are no mestizos on the pedestal. By the mid-nineteenth century, with rare exceptions, the indigenous population had been exterminated, absorbed into Brazilian society, or pushed into the hinterlands. Those placed on the pedestal were Rousseauean archetypes that did not even reflect an important element in the Indianist trope, namely, the mixed-race offspring of Europe and America.

For anyone who knows nineteenth-century European monuments, statues, or fountains, some of these symbols seem familiar. Bellini's Fontana dei Fiumi in the Piazza Navona in Rome also uses four mighty rivers to represent the four corners of the world. European artists painted generic figures of nude women to represent the four continents. Stylized Indian woman usually represented America. Almost all European artistic representations of Africa included an allegorical likeness of Africans. However, the Brazilian statue did not include a similar image. This choice reveals a clear vision about how to portray Brazilian national identity. Upper-class Brazilians looked toward Europe as a model for how to create art and culture, but they were selective when representing their country. In 1843, essayist Martius offered a counternarrative of how to understand Brazilian history. His idea was available, but it was not appropriated. I suggest that any representation of Afro-Brazilians as legitimate members of the Brazilian nation would have destabilized a hegemonic notion among the elites about the political and social order. Africans were simply not suited to appear on a patriotic monument to imperial rule, especially twenty-five years before abolition.

Romantic portraits of generic Indians symbolize the nation's preconquest and colonial past. The bronze placards bolted to the emperor's pedestal offer a biographical narrative of recent Brazilian history. In addition to naming twenty provinces to express national unity, eight metal plates on the iron fenceposts surrounding the statue commemorate the key moments in the emperor's career as the ultimate leader of the Brazilian people: his birth, two marriages, the declaration of his intentions to remain in Brazil, his acclamation as the nation's perpetual defender, the proclamation of independence, his acclamation as emperor, his coronation, and his oath to uphold the constitution. The historical narrative is pure and simple. A straightforward chronology crafts a direct line from heir to throne to leader of the independence movement and defender of the constitution. Noticeably absent, however, are the messy details about the dissolution of the Constituent Assembly in 1823 and his forced abdication in 1831. The sanitized and purified emperor becomes the founding symbol of the nation.

DEDICATION OF THE STATUE

The statue's inauguration was slated for March 25, 1862, the fortieth anniversary of Dom Pedro I's oath to uphold the Brazilian constitution. However, torrential rains caused the emperor to suspend ceremonies.[26] Five days later the entire imperial government joined the festivities in an elaborate procession that circled the statue. Participants ranged from the highest echelons of the government bureaucracy—politicians, military figures, and religious leaders—to lowly bureaucrats, priests, and government employees. At the center of the plaza stood the sixteen-foot-tall bronze statue high above its thirty-foot-tall pedestal (figure 8.3). For purposes of the inauguration a plaster Arc de Triomphe was installed to one side of the statue, and a Greek temple, serving as the viewing stands for the imperial entourage, was installed on the other side. These symbols suggest imperial lineage

Figure 8.3. Inauguration of the statue of Dom Pedro I, 1862. *Source*: Anonymous lithograph in Miguel Maria Lisbôa, Barão de Japura. *Romances históricos, por um brasileiro,* 2nd ed. (Brussels: n.p., 1886). Fundação Biblioteca Nacional.

reaching back to the Roman Empire and classical Greece. Civilization had come to the tropics.

To complement the festivities, the houses in the area were decorated with bedcovers, and banners were hung from residents' windows. Aromatic flowers and laurel leaves reminiscent of Roman imperial processions covered the streets and the plaza. After the imperial family arrived in coaches, the emperor marched to the covered statue, accompanied by an orchestra and chorus of nine hundred musicians and singers, including several hundred schoolchildren. The emperor removed a green and yellow silk cover to reveal his father's image. Soldiers fired rounds of shots, and the ordinary populace cheered from afar. Dom Pedro II then mounted a steed and paraded around the square in imitation of his father's equestrian talents and his bronzed representation. Finally, the imperial entourage retreated to the Royal Theater to hear speeches by prominent figures and leading politicians.[27]

The accolades to Dom Pedro I by the president of the commission in charge of financing the statue synthesized the elite public discourse regarding the emperor and his pedestal. He equated Dom Pedro I's talents and energy to those of Alexander the Great for having founded, like the Greek warrior, a "grand and free empire." Brazil's constitutional, representative monarchy was held up as being second only to England, the nineteenth century's largest and most powerful empire. Another orator noted that while its neighbors continued what seemed to be incessant internal struggles and when even "the sublime work of Washington was trembling at its foundations" with the ongoing civil war in the United States, Brazil, thanks to the efforts of Dom Pedro I, enjoyed peace and tranquility. The Municipal Council president further reminded his audience that just as William Tell, Gutenberg, Columbus, and Fulton represented progress for humanity, so the name of Pedro I symbolized the progress embedded in independence, the monarchy, and the Brazilian constitution.[28]

Most journalistic accounts of the day's celebration repeat the same story, noting the emperor's august presence, his father's noble deeds, and the inaugural ceremony's pomp and circumstance. There was one noted exception, however. On the day before the rains prevented the first inaugural ceremony, Liberal Party politician Teófilo Ottoni published a pamphlet, *A Estátua Eqüestre* (The Equestrian Statue), that was reprinted throughout the country by the newly revived radical wing of the Liberal Party. Ottoni had built his political career as an opponent of imperial rule. What better way to attack the current emperor than by questioning the official national founding myth linked to his father? Ottoni poses a set of simple questions in his essay about the "Bronze Lie," as he calls the statue: Who was actually responsible for independence? Based on whose authority was the constitution of 1824 written? How should one interpret Pedro I's abdication in 1831?[29]

Ottoni argues that Pedro I only reluctantly took up the cause of independence. What's more, the emperor brutally dissolved the Constituent Assembly, imposed his own constitution on the nation, and was forced to abdicate by a popular revolt. Ottoni's critical version of the official national narrative then looks back to late colonial times to resurrect an alternative figure as the nation's founding father. He points to Joaquim José da Silva Xavier, Tiradentes, as the authentic precursor to Brazilian independence. As a member of the 1789 conspiracy against Portuguese rule that transpired in Ottoni's own home province of Minas Gerais, Tiradentes proved a convenient alternative symbol of national independence, in more ways than one. Not only was he executed under the reign of Pedro I's grandmother Maria I and the regency of his father, Dom João VI, but the sentence had been carried out, according to Ottoni, on the very location where the 1862 statue was erected. Most scholars have since disputed this assertion that the square in question was the actual site where Tiradentes was executed. However, in 1862, Ottoni's claim about the alternative historical significance of this public space gave the Liberal Party opposition a kind of equal access to this newly consecrated site. By questioning the official founding myth and by planting another historical meaning on the same hallowed ground, Ottoni destabilized the statue's inviolability as the pre-eminent public representation of both the nation and the state. Proffering an alternative public memory that could be attributed to the plaza opened the door to new historical narratives that could undermine imperial legitimacy and authority. Indeed, thirty years later, when republicans overthrew the monarchy, they quickly rechristened the plaza Tiradentes Square as they buried the constitution of 1824 and left Brazil's first emperor atop a monument resting on ground consecrated by an earlier and more authentic martyr for Brazilian independence. Modern memory constructs are born not just from the sense of a break with the past but also from an intense awareness of the conflicting representations of the past and the effort of different groups to make their version the basis of a national identity.

CARICATURES AND CRITICISMS OF THE EMPIRE

In the concluding section of this chapter, I illustrate how late-nineteenth-century critics used the images of Dom Pedro I on his pedestal to undermine aspects of imperial rule, by examining a set of political cartoons that attacked slavery and the monarchy as symbols of a decadent regime. In 1876, Angelo Agostini, an Italian immigrant, ardent abolitionist, and republican, founded *Revista Ilustrada,* a weekly publication that systematically criticized slavery and the state. For example, an 1880 lithograph titled "Escravidão ou Morte," a play on the Grito de Ipiranga, lambastes the Liberal Party for its support of slavery (figure 8.4). The Liberal Party leader and planter who rides astride the slave clutches a whip rather than the constitution. Saddened Indians, representing the "authentic" nation, gaze downward as if bearing collective shame. Dom Pedro I, silhouetted in the background, implies a link between the constitution and the whip. Agostini's lampooning of the Liberal Party accents the hypocritical positions regarding slavery of this political mainstay of the imperial regime.[30]

A lithograph published four years earlier pokes fun at official Independence Day festivities (figure 8.5). An Indian—who has perhaps escaped from the statue's pedestal, which looms in the background amid the smoke of official revelry—sadly celebrates the national holiday. Dual balls and chains, representing the church and the state institutions united under the imperial constitution, restrain his dance. The caption reads, "September 7: Brazil officially celebrates its independence." Once again, the political system hampers freedom.

Figure 8.4. "Escravidão ou Morte" (Slavery or Death). *Source*: *Revista Ilustrada* (1880).

Figure 8.5. "September 7: Brazil officially celebrates its independence." *Source*: *Revista Ilustrada* (1876).

Figure 8.6.   Indian and slave held captive in the imperial crown. *Source: Revista Ilustrada* (1881).

Two 1881 cartoons likewise use the Independence Day celebrations to attack the meaninglessness of official government ceremonies. One in Baktianian carnivalesque irony parodies the excessive fireworks associated with the event. An orgy of stray rockets forces Indians, animals, and the emperor himself to flee their trajectories. The caption reads, "The courageous people not having found another way of demonstrating their enthusiasm other than through rockets, the bronzed independence monument and its retinue will end up really getting mad some day." The other 1881 drawing launches a more direct attack against the state (figure 8.6). Here both Indian and slave are imprisoned in the imperial crown. Clouded in smoke are symbols of the nation and the army, as well as the emperor riding in his coach. The caption reads, "The nation that only celebrates the 7th of September by official cannon fire and rockets begins to understand that its independence translates into smoke, a lot of smoke." Once again imperial rule and the celebration of patriotic dates such as September 7, represented by the statue, have become formal and meaningless events, since the regime offers no real freedom for the nation or its chattel slaves.

As Dom Pedro II entered the fourth decade of his reign, the aging emperor received more and more attacks by those who considered that he had grown weary of his role as ruler and had retreated to his vocation for scientific investigation. In an 1882 cartoon, Agostini uses the statue of the emperor's father as a takeoff point to criticize the entire system of government (figure 8.7). Pedro II rides atop a snail gazing off into the sky. Sloths rather than golden dragons slouch up against the imperial crest. Members of parliament perched atop a giant tortoise are all asleep. The inscription on the pedestal reads, "Here rests the Empire's political and social progress. People, pray for them." The cartoon caption declares, "The country's Moral State requires the building of this monument whose project is shown here." By 1882 republican forces had begun to gain political momentum offering a more coherent critique of the imperial regime. One of their arguments against the political status quo was that the concentration of power in the emperor and a centralized state hindered economic progress. As the emperor aged, so it seemed, the machinery of government slowed down. The monarchy that had once represented the youthful nation's vitality had become a symbol of a moribund system of governance.

Figure 8.7. "The moral state of our country." *Source: Revista Ilustrada* (1882).

A cartoon referencing the 1886 independence celebrations captures the political death throes of the old regime. Here Dom Pedro I's own entourage of Indians and animals must rally to pay him homage, as the population is weary of the event. The caption reflects widespread cynicism: "September 7, seeing the indifference of courageous modern people for the great day of independence, the Indians from the pedestal celebrate their own monument themselves, crying out their own cheers. Pedro I had to thank this demonstration." In an aside, the cartoonist comments, "They say that he even ordered them to do it."

The Golden Law of 1888, signed by princess regent Isabel, marked the end of a long and vigorous abolitionist campaign. It also caused a momentary upswing in popularity for the imperial family before military and republican forces overthrew Dom Pedro II fourteen months later. The proclamation of abolition sparked an uninterrupted month-long celebration among Rio's residents. An 1888 cartoon portrays the popular enthusiasm for the imperial decree. An Indian climbs up from the pedestal to ride atop the emperor's steed to celebrate freedom. The Indian's gesture seems more powerful and energetic than that of the emperor. Yet even in this moment of freedom, Afro-Brazilians have been erased from symbols of the nation or its constituent parts.

Political turmoil characterized the first ten years of republican rule, as sectors of the military vied for political control with the powerful coffee interests, radical Jacobins battled Portuguese merchants in Rio, and pro-imperial forces made unsuccessful bids for a return to their former power and influence. An 1899 cartoon reflects how symbols of the empire had faded into the obscure corners of Rio's collective memory. José Bonifácio de Andrada e Silva, one of Dom Pedro I's most powerful early ministers and an important proponent of independence, awakens sleeping Indians with a visit to the emperor. A statue of this senior statesman is located a block away from the square in the Largo de São Francisco, so this visit has a certain comic logic to it. José Bonifácio offers Pedro a stool to get down from his horse since the ungrateful Brazilians, especially the Jacobins, have forgotten to celebrate either patriotic figure, leaving the usually illuminating gas lights unlit as the two linger in the dark.

This cartoon seems to predict the future. Over the next century, the bronze statue of Pedro I would slowly corrode, and the plaza surrounding it would ultimately become a place frequented by the poor and lower classes, who would barely look up to acknowledge the lofty emperor astride his noble stallion. Renaming the plaza Tiradentes Square in 1890 marked a turning point in reshaping the official national narrative. A compromise was struck between those who looked to the emperor as the embodiment of the nation as it moved toward independence and others who chose to reach further back in time to Tiradentes as a pseudorepublican alternative to Brazil's rebellious royalty. In the first half of the nineteenth century, the proponents of the bronze statue as a representation of national identity brought together multiple events surrounding independence and the 1824 constitution and conflated disparate moments to consecrate a national monument that echoed official historical narratives. After the founding of the republic, Pedro I and Tiradentes, who could be considered symbolic political enemies, were woven into a single new narrative. An unsuccessful popular conspiracy led by Tiradentes against royal governance became the wellspring of republican idealism. Space, however, was created inside that same narrative to include the notion that Pedro I's impetuous love for his country inspired him to break the shackles of Portuguese rule, turn his back on filial allegiances, and forge a new nation.

Although the new republican forces allowed Pedro I to remain within the national historical narrative, his monument and the surrounding plaza were pushed to the sidelines. As part of Rio's early-twentieth-century urban redevelopment, inspired by Hausmann's redesigning of Paris, the republican government created Avenida Central, a broad avenue that cut through downtown Rio and established a new civic, entertainment, and political center with new monuments to contemporary republican heroes. Tiradentes Square slowly declined into the crossroads of sin and cheap amusement.

Finally, something else is missing from this storyline that links public spaces to political events and ties geography to national symbols. Two groups have been totally eliminated from this compromised tale between imperial and republican versions of how the nation's past should be commemorated at the Largo do Rossio. No public markers honor the Campo dos Ciganos or the Romany residents who traded horses and slaves in the swampy field on the outskirts of late-eighteenth-century Rio. Naming can both create and eradicate memories. In 1865, three years after the statue's inauguration, the Municipal Council ordered the thoroughfare known as Rua dos Ciganos, which connected Praça da Constituição to the Campo de Sant'Anna Park, to be rechristened Rua da Constituição. Today only a handful of historians interested in the nineteenth century know about this fragment of Rio's Romany past.

Likewise, long ago the imperial statue obliterated any collective recollection of the tall stone obelisk placed in the center of the square to punish rebellious slaves in public spectacles designed to discourage insubordination and insurrection. The massive monument to Pedro I erected over an instrument of slavery offers no space for an even modest memorial to this aspect of Brazil's past.

After all, official patriotic narratives require simplicity, not complexity. Those who molded conflicting and contradictory elements into the monumental homage to Pedro I created a simple symbol of optimism, precisely when Brazil was passing through a decade of confidence and hope. In his 1862 diary, Pedro II recorded his impressions of the inauguration of the bronze statue as night fell and the Royal Theater's lights pierced through the misty rain to magically illuminate the tribute to his father. He was pleased that the nation had paid homage to a man whom he had never really known.[31] As the light seemed to descend from the sky over the statue, Pedro I's raised arm proclaimed constitutional freedom and suggested a glorious future for all. No better national myth than one that has a happy or at least hopeful ending.

NOTES

I would like to thank the University Foundation of California State University, Long Beach; the Fulbright Program; and the National Endowment of the Humanities for funds to support the research for this study. Jeffrey D. Needell, Roderick J. Barman, and Hendrik Kraay carefully read an earlier version of this chapter, presented at the annual meeting of the American Historical Association in January 2002 and offered valuable criticisms and suggestions for which I am extremely grateful. In addition, Hendrik Kraay has been quite generous in sharing images and valuable research material with me.

1. For other analyses of the inauguration and significance of the statue of Dom Pedro I, see Maria Eurydice de Barros Ribeiro, "Memória em bronze: Estátua Eqüestre de D. Pedro I," in *Cidade vaidosa: Imagens urbanas do Rio de Janeiro*, ed. Paulo Knauss (Rio de Janeiro: Sette Letras, 1999), 15–28; Iara Lis Carvalho Souza, "O monumento na praça pública," in *Pátria coroada: O Brasil como corpo político autônomo, 1780–1831* (São Paulo: Editora da UNESP, 1999), 351–65; and Gisele Cunha dos Santos and Fernanda Fonseca Monteiro, "Celebrando a fundação do Brasil: A inauguração da Estátua Eqüestre de D. Pedro I," *Revista Eletrônica de História do Brasil* 4, no. 1 (January–June 2000): 47–61.

2. See José Murilo de Carvalho, "Tiradentes: Um herói para a república," in *A formação das almas: O imaginário da república no Brasil* (São Paulo: Companhia das Letras, 1998), 55–73.

3. James R. Curtis, "Praças, Place, and Public Life in Urban Brazil," *Geographical Review* 90, no. 4 (October 2000): 484–85.

4. See James N. Green, *Beyond Carnival: Male Homosexuality in Twentieth-Century Brazil* (Chicago: University of Chicago Press, 1999), 23–34. Scattered references to the linkage in the public imagination between this public space and sexual and social transgressions continue to surface in my research. For example, the picaresque publication *Rio Nu* posted a satirical news item in 1901 announcing that "the statue of Dom Pedro I is going to ask to be relieved of the position he holds in the Largo do Rossio. The *boys* intend to dissuade him of this attempt and to do so they are going to organize a demonstration headed by the well-known Gregorio." "Noticiário," *Rio Nu* 4, no. 297 (May 12, 1908): 2. One knows that the boys in question are considered to be effeminate homosexuals

by the reference to Gregorio, a contemporaneous slang term for *frescos* (faggots). Francisco José Viveiros de Castro, *Atentados ao pudor: Estudos sobre as aberrações do instincto sexual*, 3rd ed. (Rio de Janeiro: Livraria Editora Freitas Bastos, 1934), 221.

 5. See Vivaldo Coaracy, *Memórias da cidade do Rio de Janeiro*, 3rd ed. (São Paulo: Editora da Universidade de São Paulo, 1988), 78–79; Bill M. Donovan, "Changing Perceptions of Social Deviance: Gypsies in Early Modern Portugal and Brazil," *Journal of Social History* 26, no. 1 (Fall 1992): 43; Brasil Gerson, *História das ruas do Rio (e da sua liderança na história política do Brasil)*, 5th ed. (Rio de Janeiro: Lacerda Editora, 2000), 109, 121, 208; Mello Moraes Filho, *Os ciganos no Brasil e cancioneiro dos ciganos* (São Paulo: Editora Itatiaia and Editora da Universidade de São Paulo, 1981), 30–31.

 6. Gilberto Ferrez, "O que ensinam os antigos mapas e estampas do Rio de Janeiro: O campo da cidade, Largo de São Francisco de Paulo, o Rossio, futura Praça Tiradentes, o campo de Sant'Anna," *Revista do Instituto Histórico e Geográfico Brasileiro*, no. 278 (January/March 1968): 94.

 7. The next year the Constituent Assembly, called to write a constitution for Brazil, decreed the date for a national festival and "the Anniversary of Brazilian Independence." Roderick J. Barman, *Brazil: The Forging of a Nation, 1798–1852* (Stanford, Calif.: Stanford University Press, 1998), 272n1.

 8. See Cecilia Helena de Salles Oliveira and Claudia Valladão de Mattos, eds., *O brado do Ipiranga* (São Paulo: Editora da Universidade de São Paulo; Museu Paulista da Universidade de São Paulo, 1999).

 9. Pierre Nora, "Between Memory and History: *Les Lieux de Memoire*," *Representations*, no. 26 (Spring 1989): 7.

 10. Moreira de Azevedo, *O Rio de Janeiro: Sua história, homens notáveis, uso e curiosidades*, 3rd ed. (Rio de Janeiro: Livraria Brasiliana, 1969), 2:11–14; de Azevedo, "A Estatua Equestre do Senhor D. Pedro I," *Revista Popular* 1, no. 2 (1859): 37–38. See, for example, the Senado da Câmara document calling for a voluntary subscription campaign to collect funds to erect a statue to the imperial monarch. Código 43-1-59, July 11, 1825, Arquivo Geral da Cidade do Rio de Janeiro, Setor de Documentação Escrita e Especial.

 11. Stanislaw Herstal, *Dom Pedro: Estudo iconográfico* (São Paulo: Ministério de Educação e Cultura, 1972), 219; Souza, *Pátria coroada*, 351.

 12. "Estatua." Motion introduced by Haddock Lobo to erect a statue to Dom Pedro I. Câmara Municipal, 30a Sessão Extraordinária (September 7, 1954), Código 43-1-59, Arquivo Geral da Cidade do Rio de Janeiro, Setor de Documentação Escrita e Especial.

 13. For recent scholarship on popular opposition to Dom Pedro I, see Gladys Sabina Ribeiro, "Ás noites das garrafadas: Uma história entre outras de conflitos antilusitanos e raciais na Corte do Rio de Janeiro em 1831," *Luso-Brazilian Review* 37, no. 2 (Winter 2000): 59–74.

 14. Roderick J. Barman, *Citizen Emperor: Pedro II and the Making of Brazil, 1825–91* (Stanford, Calif.: Stanford University Press, 1999), 159–60.

 15. "Estatua," September 7, 1854. See also Câmara Municipal (September 16, 1854), Código 43-1-59, Arquivo Geral da Cidade do Rio de Janeiro, Setor de Documentação Escrita e Especial.

16. See Richard Graham, *Patronage and Politics in Nineteenth-Century Brazil* (Stanford, Calif.: Stanford University Press, 1990).

17. Barman, *Citizen Emperor*, 163–67.

18. Jeffrey D. Needell offered this alternative interpretation for the reason that the statue proposal garnered such widespread support in the 1850s, in his comment on a version of this chapter presented at the 2002 annual meeting of the American Historical Association in a panel titled "From Public Celebration to Political Lampoons: The Monarchy and Shifting Symbols of the Brazilian Nation." I have attempted to summarize his arguments, and I appreciate his meticulous reading of my work.

19. Jeffrey D. Needell, "Comments on the Papers of 'From Public Celebration to Political Lampoons: The Monarchy and Shifting Symbols of the Brazilian Nation'" (session 2 of the Conference on Latin American History in Association with the American Historical Association 2002 annual meeting, San Francisco, California, January 3–6, 2002), 7–8.

20. Needell, "Comments," 7.

21. Needell, "Comments," 8.

22. Azevedo, *O Rio de Janeiro*, 15–20. See the 1856 agreement to execute the statue signed by the Consulate General of the Empire of Brazil in France, "Estatua" (March 6, 1856), Código 43-1-59, p. 29, Arquivo Geral da Cidade do Rio de Janeiro, Setor de Documentação Escrita e Especial.

23. Jeffrey D. Needell, *A Tropical Belle Epoque: Elite Culture and Society in Turn-of-the-Century Rio de Janeiro* (Cambridge: Cambridge University Press), 28.

24. Karl F. P. von Martius, "Como se deve escrever a história do Brazil," *Journal do Instituto Histórico e Geográfico Brasileiro* 24 (January 1845): 389–411.

25. Afrânio Coutinho, *An Introduction to Literature in Brazil*, trans. Gregory Rabassa (New York: Columbia University Press, 1969), 143.

26. "Inauguração da estatua eqüestre," *Jornal do Comércio* (March 26, 1862): 1.

27. *Jornal do Comércio* (March 31, 1862), 1.

28. *Jornal do Comércio* (March 31, 1862), 1.

29. Paulo Pinheiro Chagas, *Teófilo Ottoni: Ministro do povo*, 3rd ed., rev. and exp. (Belo Horizonte: Editora Itatiaia, 1978), 314–15.

30. See Herman Lima, "Angelo Agostini," in *História da caricatura no Brasil* (Rio de Janeiro: Livraria José Olympio, 1963), 2:780–804.

31. Dom Pedro II, "Diário do Imperador D. Pedro II," in *Anuário do Museu Imperial* (Petrópolis: Ministério da Educação e Cultura, 1956), 17:71.

IV

SOUNDS

9

❧

Two Musical Representations of Brazil: Carlos Gomes and Villa-Lobos

Cristina Magaldi

Every weekday at 7:00 P.M., all Brazilian radio stations join in a national broadcast titled *A voz do Brasil* (The Voice of Brazil), a government-sponsored program aimed at publicizing the daily acts of the president and parliament.[1] President Getúlio Vargas initiated this nationwide broadcast in the late 1930s to unite the vast country and its diverse population in a one-hour act of patriotism. But unlike other moments of national unity, *A voz do Brasil* does not feature the expected musical symbol, the national anthem. Instead, Brazilians hear an operatic sinfonia: the Protofonia from the opera *Il Guarany* (1870) by the Brazilian composer Antônio Carlos Gomes (1836–1896). Substituting for Brazil's national anthem, Gomes's Protofonia is thus heard daily, from the bustling cities of the Brazilian coast to the most remote villages in Brazil's northwestern territory.[2]

The use of an operatic sinfonia in such a civic moment might at first be considered inappropriate; there is nothing Brazilian about the music—that is, there are no identifiable musical materials derived from the Amerindian, Afro-Brazilian, or Luso-Brazilian traditions. The identifier of Brasilianness, or *brasilidade*, is nowhere to be found. Rather than through its musical elements, the Protofonia of *Il Guarany* is known to embody the idea of a connected Brazil through the subject matter of the opera's libretto. Written by the Italian Antonio Scalvini and revised by Carlo D'Ormerville, the libretto is based on José de Alencar's Indianist novel *O Guarani* (1857). With a plot that portrays the love of a Guarany Indian for the daughter of a Portuguese nobleman, the opera glorifies the formation of the Brazilian race through the unification of the Amerindian and the European. From this perspective, the choice of Gomes's Protofonia in *A voz do Brasil* has little

205

to do with the music per se but rather reflects the state's recognition of the significance of *Il Guarany*'s plot within the historical process of constructing a Brazilian national identity. Nonetheless, performed daily outside its operatic context and disassociated from Alencar's story, Gomes's music continues to embody the idea of "national."

Ironically, when a Brazilian music student is asked to identify the most important Brazilian composer of art music, one usually recalls the name Heitor Villa-Lobos (1887–1958). The identification of Villa-Lobos as a national icon offers a less-subjective example of how music has portrayed ideals of national identity in Brazil. No matter how interspersed with foreign musical elements, in Villa-Lobos's work *brasilidade* is always expected to emerge. A good example is his Choros no. 10 (1925), a large-scale work for full orchestra and chorus that combines into a musical collage of tunes, instruments, and sounds taken from a variety of sources of the Brazilian ambiance. Unlike Gomes's Protofonia, Villa-Lobos's Choros no. 10 clearly displays the composer's intentions to musically depict Brazil's rich ethnic and cultural heritage combined with the grandeur of its geography.

We are thus led to believe that music of Villa-Lobos is more Brazilian because he, unlike Carlos Gomes, skillfully incorporates a variety of elements of Brazilian traditional and popular music into his compositions.[3] Moreover, these composers have repeatedly been viewed as direct opposites of one another: Gomes as a composer who triumphs by writing in the international musical genre most popular in his time, Italian opera, and thus essentially as a composer of foreign music; and Villa-Lobos as a nationalistic composer whose work exhibits what is musically unique to Brazil. In addition, Villa-Lobos has been credited with being a vanguard composer, of utilizing compositional techniques that broke with the past and revitalized not only the Brazilian musical idiom but also the international musical language of his time.[4] Gomes's merit, on the other hand, lies mostly in his mastery of an established international musical language.[5]

Despite the differences in their music, the works of both Gomes and Villa-Lobos have continually been used as symbols of Brazilianness. The reasons why such disparate reputations and distinct musical languages both end up representing a Brazilian identity have to do with the historical moments in which these composers were active as well as with the history of the reception of their music. In the sections that follow, I discuss the ways in which the music of Gomes and Villa-Lobos have been interpreted and transmitted as symbols of Brazilian national identity. Gomes's *Il Guarany* and Villa-Lobos's Choros no. 10 serve as examples of different instances in which music, reflecting distinct political and intellectual agendas, has embodied ideals of Brazilianness.

MODERNISTS AND THE NATIONAL
MUSICAL LANGUAGE

Our understanding of the music of Gomes and Villa-Lobos owes a great deal to the ideas put forward in 1928 by Mário de Andrade (1893–1945) in his landmark work *Ensaio sobre a música brasileira* (1928). Written when defining *brasilidade* was a central issue for intellectuals and artists, Andrade's *Ensaio* is essentially a prescriptive text: it sets guidelines for art music production and criticism and establishes the future of Brazilian music. Given that Brazilian music, as Andrade defines it, had to reflect the nation's racial and cultural identity, Andrade's essay establishes that before the twentieth century, Brazilian culture and Brazilian music did not exist as such.[6] As a result, Andrade's interpretation of the musical past is vague and problematic as he attempts to assess compositions stemming from different aesthetic ideals through the framework of his nationalistic agenda. Throughout *Ensaio* he speaks strongly against the appropriation of European music by Brazilian composers, deeming "universal [European] music" as being "anti-national" and inadequate for "the phase of construction" of Brazilian national culture.[7] Since the music written in nineteenth-century Brazil was strongly modeled on contemporary European music, Andrade largely dismissed the value of such music for the formation of a national musical production. Nineteenth-century Italo-French opera, so popular in Brazilian cities in the last century, became a special target for Andrade's criticisms.[8] The work of Carlos Gomes did not escape scrutiny, as it was modeled on the Italian operatic idiom. Andrade did not advocate performances of Gomes's work and rejected his music as a model for Brazilian composers, arguing that "one cannot look for inspiration in the music of Gomes.... Our music will be one of a different kind."[9]

Andrade's evaluation of Villa-Lobos's work raises questions of a different nature. As a contemporary of the composer, Andrade respected Villa-Lobos for doing what Andrade thought should be done: using elements from Brazilian traditional and popular music in his compositions. But Andrade was not totally convinced of Villa-Lobos's maturity as a nationalistic composer, a composer who could produce a "truly Brazilian art."[10] According to Andrade's nationalistic project, Brazilian art music should go through several stages of transformation in which the inherited European elements blend with the local traditional music into something uniquely Brazilian. Only through the synthesis of these elements could artists ultimately reach "the essence of Brazilian musicality."[11] In addition, the European musical language had to be used with a refined new technique that reflected the characteristics of the Brazilian nationality, a task that not even Villa-Lobos could fulfill. Andrade had serious concerns about the composer's explicit use of folklore and his lack of skill in transforming it.[12] Although Andrade used Villa-Lobos's work as examples of modernism in music, it was the work of composers Luciano Gallet (1893–1931) and Camargo Guarnieri (1907–1992) that Andrade chose as representatives of a truly "Brazilian national musical language."[13]

Even though the music of Gomes and Villa-Lobos never exactly fit the agenda of Andrade and other nationalists, the two musicians continue to serve as national icons, for their music has been retained in the nationalistic canon for reasons other than *brasilidade* alone. One important factor that contributed to the perception of these composers as national icons is their relatively large degree of success abroad: Gomes in the nineteenth-century operatic scene in Milan, Italy, and Villa-Lobos in the 1920s in Paris. Both composers had their music performed in concert halls and opera houses throughout Europe and North America, and both had the opportunity to have some of their music published abroad. Based on their successful national and international careers, Gomes and Villa-Lobos have repeatedly filled the role of music ambassadors of Brazil.[14] Outside the country, their music might be performed side by side in official occasions to fulfill a dual role: first, as showcases of Brazil's best in terms of artful music, attesting to the Brazilian competence on par with the "civilized" First World; second, as displays of the "exotic" music from the Southern Hemisphere, mostly for European and North American eyes and ears. Because Gomes's and Villa-Lobos's works are able to fulfill these apparently contradictory roles outside the country, they have been repeatedly utilized as national symbols inside Brazil. Therefore, the role that both composers have played as national icons has to be understood as a balance between their national and international images.

Furthermore, reflecting the changing governmental policies and intellectual ideologies since Brazilian audiences first received their works, the images of Gomes and Villa-Lobos (and of their music) have inevitably changed over time. While Gomes was a model in the 1870s but merely a composer of foreign music in the 1920s, in the 1990s he has once again been included among those who ingeniously used music to help create a sense of national identity in Brazil.[15] Similarly, while in the 1920s the eyes and ears of the Brazilian public were attentive to the Brazilian aspect of Villa-Lobos's music, today scholars' interests are focused on the modernist side of his musical language. Villa-Lobos's eccentricity and musical experimentation, once looked upon with suspicion by Brazilian critics, are now what most entice the music student's curiosity toward his music.[16]

In 1996, as part of the commemoration of the centennial of Gomes's death, the Brazilian Ministry of Culture published a pamphlet emphasizing governmental efforts to issue scholarly editions and new recordings of Gomes's entire oeuvre.[17] Similarly, the publication of authoritative editions of Villa-Lobos's work is currently a priority of the Museu Villa-Lobos.[18] Thus, the works of these composers are now being preserved as national monuments. Nonetheless, the understanding of the institutional frameworks in which their music emerged, as well as the history of the reception and diffusion of their music inside Brazil and abroad, continues to take a backseat in the study of their music as symbols of Brazilian national identity.

CARLOS GOMES AND *IL GUARANY*

When Gomes arrived in Rio de Janeiro to study music in June 1859 from his provincial home city of Campinas (state of São Paulo), he had a considerable musical background, acquired through his father, who was the director of the city's band. But it was in Rio de Janeiro that Gomes was first exposed to staged versions of Italian and French operas in vogue, from Rossini, Bellini, Donizetti, and Verdi to Auber and Meyerbeer. Opera soon became central in Gomes's musical studies and in his career as a composer. He deeply absorbed the Brazilian view of music and opera as a single entity and rapidly grasped the prestige locally attached to the imported genre.[19]

Significantly, the period of Gomes's stay in Rio de Janeiro coincided with the most productive years of the Academia Imperial de Música e Opera Nacional (later Opera Lyrica Nacional, 1857–1863), an institution organized by the Spaniard José Amat with the patronage of the imperial government. The goal of the Opera Lyrica Nacional was not to encourage the creation of a uniquely Brazilian musical language but rather to promote the performance of operas in Portuguese—translations of Italian and French operas and Spanish zarzuelas—and to commission operas with librettos on Brazilian subjects. It also offered lessons for local singers, helping them to perform side by side with foreign divas. In short, the Opera Lyrica Nacional equipped Rio de Janeiro's residents with the means to produce homemade European opera. In six years, Amat presented *Cariocas* (residents of Rio de Janeiro) with a long list of operas and zarzuelas translated into Portuguese. The Opera Lyrica Nacional also produced two operas by foreign composers living in Brazil and five operas by Brazilians, including two works by the young Carlos Gomes: *A noite no Castelo* (1861, libretto by José Fernandes Reis), which won him the imperial Ordem da Rosa, and *Joana de Flandres* (1863, libretto by Salvador de Mendonça), which earned him a scholarship to study in Europe.

The subtitle *brasileira* was seldom used in operas in mid-nineteenth-century Brazil. Nevertheless, librettos based on Brazilian subjects were greatly valued by Carioca critics who argued for the native character of such works.[20] A Brazilian opera meant an opera based on a local subject; when the music was concerned, however, that was quite a different matter. For local composers, writing an opera was an exercise in aligning Brazil with Europe. The composer's task was not to display Brazilian unique-ness in terms of musical language but to attempt some kind of equivalence with European composers. The composer's goal was to produce music as good as, understood in this sense to mean as similar as possible to, imported operas brought to Rio de Janeiro by European lyric companies. There seemed to be no contradiction in asserting Brazilianness by stressing a European connection. Contemporary critics never recalled the foreign-ness of Gomes's work as cause for distaste. On the contrary, a comparison with Verdi always came to Gomes's advantage, and his patrons in Brazil were always eager to see a Brazilian follow the path of Verdi. The role of Gomes's music in the construction of a Brazilian national identity had a lot to do with ambiguous nineteenth-century notions of "national" and "foreign" and the blurred boundary between them.[21] These concepts were further jumbled by the prestige locally attached to the notion of "inter-national." As emblematic of European culture, opera embodied the idea of modernity, civilization, and ultimately power. For a composer from the Southern Hemisphere, producing an opera was to follow a path to devel-opment and progress and to eliminate one's peripheral status.[22] Therefore, the more European-like the musical work, the easier it was for the Brazilian composer to gain local recognition. When that recognition reached inter-national proportions, as it did in the case of Gomes, the composer would ultimately become a national icon.

The emphasis on opera did not detract from local composers' interest in native musical materials. Reflecting the trends in European romanticism, local artists regularly improvised on native tunes and rhythms, treating them as exotic elements in fantasies and variations for solo instruments. Following a fashion launched by the North American composer Louis Moreau Gottschalk (1836–1869), Brazilian composers regularly explored Afro-Brazilian themes in short piano pieces.[23] Before he left Campinas for Rio de Janeiro, Gomes had published a collection of dances for piano that included his arrangements of Gottschalk's *Bamboula* and *Le bananier, dance des negres*. To the collection he attached his own *A Cayumba, Dance de nègres* (1856), a piece in a similar vein to those by Gottschalk.[24] Pieces like *A Cayumba*, stylized versions of Afro-Brazilian popular dances, were written for internal consumption, to be performed at local family gath-erings and *saraus*, and for filling in theatrical intermissions. But despite their native appeal, in the nineteenth century they did not register as sig-nificant Brazilian musical contributions. If *A Cayumba* portrayed the local Afro-Brazilian music by excessive use of ostinato rhythmic patterns not prevalent in European music, the work did not afford Gomes the stature of a national composer as did his success in the operatic field. It was *Il Guarany*, an opera in the Italian style, that brought Gomes to the forefront of the Brazilian music scene.

When Gomes left for Milan in 1863, he had a fellowship contract with the imperial government requiring that he send to Brazil at least one large work to be performed by the Opera Lyrica Nacional. During Gomes's early years in Italy he produced a few short intermezzi for comic plays that were quite successful locally, but only with *Il Guarany*, a full-length opera in the dominant musical language, was he able to fulfill the terms of his contract with the Brazilian government. While in Italy, however, Gomes gave away his previous plan for a Rio de Janeiro premiere for *Il Guarany* in favor of a more daring performance at the famous Teatro La Scala in Milan.[25]

Gomes evidently faced expectations of a different nature in Italy than in Rio de Janeiro, and the success in Milan did not come easily. Drawing inspiration from the Italian success of Meyerbeer's *L'Africaine* (1865), premiered in Milan on March 1, 1866, Gomes consciously explored the exotic aspect of *Il Guarany*'s subject matter in order to appeal to the Italian audiences. The Brazilian subject of the libretto, with the added exotic touch, was exactly the kind of operatic plot praised by Italians in midcentury operas. Granted a generous subsidy by Pedro II to cover the high costs of the Italian production, Gomes enhanced the exotic scenery by including specially crafted indigenous instruments made to order for the opera's *bailado*.[26] And it was exactly the Brazilian and exotic aspects of the work that most caught the attention of international critics. The first edition of George Grove's *Dictionary of Music and Musicians* (1879) mentions Gomes's opera as follows: "The best parts of *Il Guarany* (1870), a Brazilian story, are said to be those which are concerned with native subjects."[27] Gomes's Brazilian nationality was in itself a reason for general curiosity in the nineteenth-century Italian press, which blatantly conjectured about a "savage" who could write opera.[28]

After a successful premier at La Scala, *Il Guarany* was performed in Rio de Janeiro on December 2, 1870, a presentation honored by the presence of Emperor Pedro II. Commenting on the opera's opening-night success, a contemporary commentator reported that "commotion and deliriousness invaded the audience.... The public invaded the stage and carried [Gomes] in their arms.... D. Pedro II was moved and called [Gomes] into his box and enthusiastically praised him."[29]

Such a warm reception was hardly an expression of impartial acceptance. *Il Guarany*'s tremendous success in Rio de Janeiro lay above all in its previous validation by the Italian audience at La Scala's premiere. Gomes was the first Brazilian to achieve the status of an international composer, elevating Brazil to the status of "civilized" nation. Henrique Alves de Mesquita (1830–1906), also a recipient of a grant by the Opera Lyrica Nacional a few years earlier, had sent some works from Paris, including an opera, *O Vagabundo*, staged in Rio de Janeiro in 1863. Mesquita's opera had limited resonance in Brazil, probably because the work was not based on a Brazilian subject but, most important, because it did not reach the Parisian stage and therefore had no international status.

Il Guarany's immense success in Rio de Janeiro did not, however, happen without a few glitches. Some Cariocas dared to complain that the work was "boring"; others even speculated about the similarity between the beginning of the *bailado* and Offenbach's *La Belle Helene* and between Cecilia's *ballada* and a local *modinha*.[30] José de Alencar himself commented to a friend that "Gomes made a big mess out of my Guarani, [it is now] full of nonsense.... [Gomes made] Ceci sing duets with the Aimoré cacique, who offers her the throne of his tribe, and convinced Peri to be the lion [king] of our forests."[31] Ironically, it was the subject matter of the opera's libretto that most disturbed the local audience. If Cariocas shared the Italians' appreciation for the exotic in the opera's libretto, it was certainly not without reservation. The portrayal of the native Brazilian as the exotic Other was seen by Brazilians with suspicious eyes. Cariocas were reluctant to accept the image of the savage as being praiseworthy, for the real thing was very near them and threatened their view of themselves as Europeans. While the local elite were reserved about the issue, the local press did not shun the subject and was quick to openly mock the idea of an Indian dressed "in costume," singing in Italian. The periodical *O Mosquito* (November 4, 1876) included caricatures of scenes from the opera, ironically contrasting the "Aimorés (Indians) that sing in the stage" to the "Aimorés that applaud in audience."[32] The idea of a tenor dressed as an Indian singing in Italian struck some Cariocas as a contradiction, as did the threatening situation of a "savage" invading the sanctuary of their opera hall.[33]

If the character of Peri made Cariocas uncomfortable, *Il Guarany's* bel canto melodies sung in Italian made up for the few initial flaws and boosted the opera's general approval in Rio de Janeiro. Gomes's choice for a libretto in Italian rather than one in Portuguese, for *Il Guarany* rather than *O Guarani*, also contributed to the work's local acceptance. If, from today's vantage point, the Italian libretto might be perceived as a major impediment to the opera's Brazilianness, in the 1870s it was quite the opposite. As Góes points out, even if Gomes was interested in a Brazilian story and originally had in mind a Brazilian premiere, since the beginning he envisioned an Italian libretto.[34] There was nothing unpatriotic about this. Every nineteenth-century opera composer aspiring to a successful career preferred librettos in Italian to facilitate presentations in European capitals. Gomes was no exception. Portuguese translations would eventually follow, but the original work had to be conceived in the "natural" operatic idiom that enjoyed a higher status. In fact, Gomes's deliberate choice of *Il Guarany* was part of what made the opera appeal to Carioca elite, whose unequivocal taste for things European let them identify more with the idea of an opera in Italian than with one in Portuguese. Only in 1938, more than sixty years after the Rio de Janeiro's premiere, was a Portuguese translation of *Il Guarany* published. The translation, however, did not gain public acceptance and in fact was cause for much local debate and discontentment.[35]

Even if only a few could understand the language of the libretto and even if most did not identify with *Il Guarany*'s plot, Gomes had succeeded outside Brazil, and that counted for more than anything else: the appeal of the work as an international opera was a strong factor in its reception as a national identity symbol.

The immense success of *Il Guarany* in the Brazilian capital was also greatly due to the political momentum of the opera's presentation. The successful premiere in Milan happened just nineteen days after the Brazilian army defeated Solano Lopez in Paraguay. The news of Solano Lopez's death arrived in Rio de Janeiro not long after the news of *Il Guarany*'s triumph in Milan. Brazilians, already delirious with the victory in the war, were undoubtedly predisposed to accept the achievement of the Brazilian composer as a national glory. Not surprisingly, Gomes was expected in Brazil as a national hero. The composer himself was overwhelmed with the reception and commented in a letter to Carlo D'Ormeville his amazement with "the balls and soirées they offered [me] and the Holy Week they created in my honor."[36] It would not be excessive to compare Gomes's return to the warm welcome received by the Brazilian soccer team upon returning to Brazil after conquering the World Cup.

Furthermore, Gomes premiered his opera in Rio de Janeiro on December 2 as part of the celebrations honoring Pedro II's birthday. At the same time, Cariocas heard *Il Guarany* one day before the publication of the manifesto of the Republican Party, which was signed by no fewer than three enthusiastic devotees and organizers of the Opera Lyrica Nacional: Quintino Bocayuva, Saldanha Marinho, and Salvador de Mendonça—the last of whom had provided lyrics for two of Gomes's operas. As Marcus Góes perceptively points out, while the opera marked the zenith of the Second Empire, it also announced the ascendance of the Republican Party.[37] In the midst of such passionate moments, *Il Guarany* might have been interpreted as being patriotic, particularly when Peri's "savage" character was overlooked and the focus was switched to his heroic acts. To Brazilians, *Il Guarany* recalled Verdi's popular midcentury operas stemming from the Italian *risorgimento*, which were loaded with ideas of unification and moments of patriotic display.

A few months after *Il Guarany*'s premiere, Gomes replaced the original overture with the Protofonia—the music used as opening theme in the radio program *A voz do Brasil*. Looking for an introduction that would have a better effect as an opening to the opera, Gomes carefully chose popular excerpts of the work and pasted them together, following a common practice in nineteenth-century Italian operas. At the time the Protofonia was added, the opera already carried with it a whole set of symbols associated with glory, heroism, and national pride, and the Protofonia was born already embodying those meanings. To enhance that effect, in the Protofonia's very opening Gomes uses a short fanfare-like section that displays all of the musical effects that one has historically learned to associate with civic events. It is thus a conglomeration of factors that have permitted the music of *Il Guarany*'s Protofonia to substitute so well for the national anthem in *A voz do Brasil*, even when its performance is disassociated from the libretto's Indianist plot.

Finally, as part of a genre enjoyed by the elite, *Il Guarany* has been interpreted as a work that represents "the divorce between upper and lower classes."[38] While it is unquestionable that an opera appealed to a minuscule portion of the Brazilian population in the 1870s, the history of *Il Guarany*'s staged performances does not offer a clear picture of the popularity gained by Gomes's opera in late-nineteenth- and early-twentieth-century Brazil. As was common practice in Europe, so in Rio de Janeiro the splendor of the opera house was regularly transplanted to small private circles in arrangements and piano reductions of operatic excerpts. Piano arrangements were also alternatives for those who could not afford a ticket to the theater. In this new *roupage*, operatic music then lost its elitist character and infiltrated all levels of Brazilian society. Excerpts from Gomes's *Il Guarany*, first heard in staged performances, soon emerged as fantasies for the piano and later served as tunes for popular dance music. To give an idea of how fast the music from *Il Guarany* spread, just one year after its premiere in Rio de Janeiro, the catalogue of a major publishing house listed twelve instrumental fantasies based on the opera's most popular tunes.[39] In terms of the number of pieces it spawned, *Il Guarany* lost only to Verdi's *Il Trovatore*, which provided themes for seventeen pieces but which had premiered in Rio de Janeiro sixteen years earlier (1854). Tunes from *Il Guarany* then spread into Brazilian rural areas, and by the 1930s the music was popular enough to make into several carnival marches.[40] Thus, *Il Guarany* and its Protofonia already embodied the idea of a national identity symbol when it was chosen as the opening to *A voz do Brasil* and became a trademark of Brazilianness.

VILLA-LOBOS AND THE CHORO NO. 10

No more than fifty years separate Gomes's presentations at the Opera Lyrica Nacional from Villa-Lobos's first concerts in Rio de Janeiro, and the audiences' expectations of both composers were not much different: in both cases, Brazilians looked for a young artist with exceptional compositional skills comparable to European masters. Although these composers have been portrayed as opposites, their careers are both based on the same prototype: European musical culture. Nonetheless, while Gomes's image as a national icon was shaped by his ability to write Italian opera, Villa-Lobos built his image by highlighting Brazilian musical specificities, even if his musical language unequivocally paralleled that of contemporary European composers.

Like Gomes, Villa-Lobos first experienced European art music at home, from his father. As a lover of opera, Raúl Villa-Lobos frequently took the young Villa-Lobos to the opera house and to concerts, where they heard programs that included orchestral excerpts of Wagner's operas performed alongside Puccini's popular arias. Although less popular, works by German "classics," such as Beethoven, Mozart, and Haydn, and romantics such as Mendelssohn and Schumann were also part of the repertory performed at concerts in Rio de Janeiro during Villa-Lobos's formative years.[41]

Despite the overwhelming prevalence of opera and chamber music from the German canon in local concerts, at the turn of the twentieth century Brazilian composers were already imbued with the idea of musical nationalism. Part of the European romantic musical idiom, nationalism was being reflected in Brazil in works by composers such as Leopoldo Miguez (1850–1902) and Alberto Nepomuceno (1864–1920). Popular urban melodies and characteristic rhythms inherited from the Afro-Brazilian tradition favored by these early nationalist composers were particularly appealing to the local elite, who were greatly attracted to the exotic in native music. Nonetheless, dominated by the idea of modernity and of preserving the view of themselves as Europeans, the elite were still weary of being associated with the savagery and primitivism that they perceived in Brazilian popular traditions. Thus, the native element had to be softened in stylized pieces for the concert hall written in the familiar European romantic language. The assumption that native music diluted in European idioms could serve as a symbol of a connected Brazil, however, was not fully contemplated until late in the 1920s.

Nepomuceno was particularly devoted to building a Brazilian school of composition, but his most notable accomplishment was a commitment to diversify the music repertory and to introduce Brazilians to contemporary theoretical and philosophical issues being discussed in European musical circles.[42] Reflecting the appeal to modernity that dominated Rio de Janeiro's Belle Epoque, he was particularly interested in bringing to Brazil the most "modern" music in vogue in Europe. In his concerts, Nepomuceno frequently included works by contemporary French composers, such as Camille Saint-Saëns (1835–1921), and especially works by composers from the Russian nationalist school, such as Mikhail Glinka (1804–1854). Glinka's music, well known (and perhaps already old-fashioned) in Europe in the second half of the nineteen century, had been a favorite with Brazilian audiences since the 1880s.[43] His use of Russian traditional music as a means for creating new compositional devices, such as unique instrumental colors and harmonic combinations, had a particular impact on the young Villa-Lobos. In 1908, as part of the commemorations celebrating one hundred years of the opening of Brazilian ports to foreign trade, Nepomuceno organized a series of concerts that featured "state of the art" works by French composers such as Claude Debussy (1862–1918) and Paul Dukas (1865–1935).[44] The latter composers' explorations of new harmonic devices were particularly important in Villa-Lobos's formation.

Inculcated with the idea of becoming a "modern composer" from an early age, in 1907 a twenty-one-year-old Villa-Lobos refused the traditional academic music training at the National Institute of Music in Rio de Janeiro, where he had enrolled as a cello and theory student.[45] With a driving personality and a reputation of enfant terrible, Villa-Lobos dismissed the artistic status quo and the European-based music conservatory and embarked on a self-motivated investigation of the musical sounds available to him in Brazil. In a series of trips to Brazil's interior he had the chance to hear and collect traditional music. His experience as a guitar and cello player also allowed him to interact with well-known popular musicians in Rio de Janeiro and to gain knowledge about emerging Brazilian urban popular genres. These new experiences fulfilled Villa-Lobos's urge for new discoveries and ultimately for freedom of expression and provided fuel for the modern sounds that he eagerly sought to create.

Villa-Lobos's first compositions, presented to Carioca audiences on November 13, 1915, reveal his particular interest in the ideas of modernism in music. For the concert Villa-Lobos felt the need to provide program notes explaining the nature of his works. It was not the inclusion of native elements that he emphasized but rather the daring and free character of the compositions. He described his *Sonata Phantastica* no. 2, op. 29, as

> part of the collection of "fantastic sonatas" written for piano and violin.... The collection is characterized by its form, sometimes descriptive, sometimes mystic, sometimes free, always representing the freedom of thought.[46]

This program note shows Villa-Lobos as being more concerned with his cutting ties with the old, romantic school of composition than with his specifically identifying with a nationalistic school. Accordingly, it was the daring and modern composer whom the organizers of the Semana de Arte Moderna (Week of Modern Art) envisioned when they invited Villa-Lobos to participate in the event of February 1922. Left alone in charge of choosing the music repertory for the presentation at the Teatro Municipal in São Paulo, Villa-Lobos included two French contemporary composers, Debussy and Blanchet, and only one Brazilian, himself.[47] Two other French composers, Satie and Poulenc, were performed as illustrations for Graça Aranha's conference, and a fifth one, Vallon, was performed by pianist Guiomar Novaes in a concert outside the weeklong program. Villa-Lobos's predilection for French composers and for Debussy in particular is clearly manifested in the Debussyan sounds that permeate his early works and the nickname *debussysta zangado* (angry Debussy) given to him by modernist Oswald de Andrade.[48] His attention to French contemporary music is also reflected in his contact with French composer Darius Milhaud (1892–1974), who took refuge in Rio de Janeiro during the war years and who was vital in introducing Brazilians to the music of a new generation of French composers, including the controversial Erik Satie. Soon, Brazilian modernists were also condemning the "old-fashioned" Debussy in favor of composers from the French group Les Six, whose commitment to renew French music led to severe criticisms toward European art music of the past.[49]

Not yet fully devoted to the project of nationalism during the week of 1922, Villa-Lobos followed the French modernist trends but kept his own imaginative alternatives. Polytonality, unstable tonal centers, new timbres, unconventional use of instrument combinations, and varied orchestral colors were among the "new" characteristics of the works presented during the week. But it was Villa-Lobos's attentive use of native materials to achieve those results that allowed him to creatively renew the exhausted European tonal system. In his *Danças Africanas*, Villa-Lobos used stylized rhythmic patterns derived from Afro-Brazilian music as a means to explore new harmonies, and thus he achieved the most coveted goals of Brazilian modernists: the conciliation of the local, native tradition with the European model of modernity.

Villa-Lobos's works presented during the week, although previously performed in concerts in Rio de Janeiro, were grounds for both praise and reproach while passionate debates in local newspapers fueled the war between the "old" and the "new" music.[50] Despite his claims that he "was a revolutionary before [the week],"[51] Villa-Lobos's participation in the week was crucial to the development of his career, as the controversies that surrounded his music continued to bring wide attention to his persona. Most important, through his participation in the Modern Art Week, he was able to get a partial grant from the Brazilian government for a one-year stay in Paris, a welcome addition to the subsidy offered by friends for his first trip to France.

As Carlos Gomes had done some sixty years before him, Villa-Lobos left Brazil with a governmental fellowship to pursue a career in Europe. Although always eager to emphasize that he went to Paris to show his music, not to learn, he nonetheless had the chance to experience firsthand the primitivism and neoclassic works of Stravinsky and to meet several important composers and music critics. He had already gained some

international visibility when, at the end of 1924, he was forced to return to
Brazil with financial difficulties. As with Gomes before him, Villa-Lobos's
return was surrounded by glories: after all, his music was presented in
Paris with success and gave international exposure to Brazil. A local critic
pointed out with irony that "it would be curious to see those who booed
[Villa-Lobos's] music during the Week of Modern Art, now applauding the
consecrated conductor returning from Paris."[52]

Villa-Lobos returned from Paris with a trunk full of new ideas. The 1920s
turned out to be a decade of extreme proclivity toward experimentation for
the Brazilian composer, a direct result of his Parisian experiences and, particularly, the contact with the music of Stravinsky. Among the works that
Villa-Lobos wrote at this time was the Choros no. 10, a large-scale composition for full orchestra and choir. The work is part of a series of sixteen *choros*
written for various kinds of instrumentations. These are stylized, imaginative versions of the popular Brazilian *choro*, a serenade-like kind of music
played by popular instrumental groups at the turn of the twentieth century.
Choro no. 10 is particularly important because it displays an eclecticism
that permeates most of Villa-Lobos's later oeuvre. Through the combination of various sounds taken from the Brazilian ambiance—descriptive
sounds from the tropical forest, melodic lines suggesting Indian scales,
Afro-Brazilian percussion, urban popular song, and popular poetry—Villa-
Lobos aimed at forming a "collage" that symbolized Brazil musically.

The piece is divided into two large sections: the first is intended to show
the vastness and richness of the Brazilian land through a series of musical descriptions of the Amazon forest. To obtain that result Villa-Lobos
includes melodic lines imitating birds and percussion instruments creating the atmosphere of a forest. According to Villa-Lobos, some motives in
Choro no. 10 show "the great variety of birds that exist in Brazil—above
all the ones who live in the forests, and the ones who sing at the sun-
rise and sunset in the countryside."[53] While modernists such as Mário de
Andrade were preoccupied with defining Brazil musically, in this section
Villa-Lobos's goal was to present a cinematographic view of Brazil. His idea
of portraying the nation in terms of nature and the grandeur of its geography was not unique but rather reflected a view common among Brazilian
intellectual elite at the beginning of the twentieth century. To shun the
country's cultural and racial diversity, which was perceived as a threat to
the idea of national integration, local intellectuals focused on nature and
on the grandeur of the country's territory. This concept could be seen in
contemporary literature—particularly in *Kosmos*, a magazine destined to
promote the new model of "modern society," which often included long
articles describing remote regions of Brazil.[54]

In the second part of Choro no. 10 Villa-Lobos brings the choir above
a large percussion section. The voices are used to produce onomatopoeic

effects and to re-create the atmosphere of the "language of the aborigines" by the repetition of particular syllables in a rhythmic ostinato. Above the massive choir, the composer adds Anacleto de Madeiros's popular song "Rasga Coração" (text by Catullo da Paixão Cearense), a title that has also been used to designate Choro no. 10. Thus, in Choro no. 10 Villa-Lobos synthesized all modes of Brazilian traditional, indigenous, and popular music and topped these elements with new harmonies and a range of unique instrumental and voice combinations.[55] While the work embodies several elements used by Villa-Lobos to musically show an "apotheotic vision of the Brazilian reality of his day,"[56] it also shows his assimilation of contemporary European composition techniques, particularly that of Stravinsky's primitivism.

Given the massive use of materials taken from the Brazilian musical landscape in a piece designed for the concert hall and aimed at an elite audience, Villa-Lobos felt compelled to include the following explanatory note in the concert program of the 1926 premiere of Choro no. 10 in Rio de Janeiro:

> To understand these new forms of composition (choro and seresta) in its most elevated sense, we Brazilians should think of our authentic serenatas and choros.... One should also remember that Bach, Haydn, Mozart, Rameau, Beethoven, Schubert, Schumann, etc., have their work permeated with themes and popular songs typical from their respective countries. Even the modern composers now utilize popular themes in their universal compositions.[57]

Villa-Lobos's comparison with European "masters," composers widely accepted by the Brazilian elite, served to justify his composition impregnated with native material. By aligning himself with European composers, he made native music acceptable as art by Brazilian elite. The program note also shows that Villa-Lobos's idealized nationalism did not merely attempt to emancipate Brazilian music from Europe but rather to elevate the music of Brazil to international levels through his own music. As with other non-European composers who strove to write concert music in the West European tradition (including Gomes), in Villa-Lobos's music "liberation comes from facing and matching, not from retreating."[58]

Unlike Gomes's *Il Guarany*, Choro no. 10 was premiered first in Rio de Janeiro in November of 1926 and then in Europe in December 1927, during Villa-Lobos's second visit to the French capital. Similarly to *Il Guarany*'s Brazilian premiere, Choro no. 10 was presented in São Paulo's luxurious Teatro Municipal in a concert in homage to president Washington Luis. The program announced Choro no. 10 as "typical Brazilian music" in a dazzling performance of choir and large orchestra with a total of 250 performers. It also included a conspicuous note that the performance was Villa-Lobos's farewell to Rio de Janeiro "because he is now leaving for Europe."[59]

Villa-Lobos was another Brazilian projecting the country internationally and needed to be idolized accordingly.

Villa-Lobos's second visit to Paris meant more than a "showing off" of his music. He now had a mission to characterize himself as a Brazilian nationalist composer, one whose music was distinct from that of Europeans and thus symbolized a uniquely Brazilian cultural identity. Similarly to Gomes's success in Milan some fifty years earlier, it was primarily the exotic side of Villa-Lobos that attracted the Parisian audience, as reflected in the critique published in *Le Monde Musical* of December 31, 1927:

> Mr. Heitor Villa-Lobos is a pure Brazilian composer from Rio de Janeiro. He dedicates himself at present to the composition of an important production on the folklore of his country.... One has to understand that Mr. Villa-Lobos is a racial (ethnic) composer. "The Soul of Brazil" possesses him entirely.... This soul is frequently savage, harsh, tumultuous, sometimes incoherent. It releases itself more through cries and noises rather than through music as we normally conceive it. Thus one should not be surprised if Mr. Villa-Lobos, in his characteristic works, comes up to *"bruitisme"* (systematic exploration of noiselike sounds), witness this startling Noneto or his Choros no. 10, where the percussive battery becomes the essential stock of the orchestra and is resplendent with indigenous instruments of the most unexpected effect.[60]

TWO BRAZILIAN COMPOSERS

Graça Aranha's inaugural speech at the Modern Art Week focused on the celebration of a new future for the arts and a necessary dismantling of the past, two topics that received frantic approval from the audience. Aranha's harsh criticisms did not spare any "master" from the old European school, from Bach and Beethoven to Wagner. But when the modernist touched on the name of Carlos Gomes, the audience immediately halted the bashing in respect to the Brazilian master. The pianist Ernani Braga provides a report of the event:

> When the irreverent Aranha touched his sacrilegious hands on the idol Carlos Gomes... that was enough. That Graça Aranha downgraded the semi-God of the Oratorios, of the Symphonies, and the Tetralogy, was an innocent joke. But to speak against the father of *Il Guarany*, a Paulista (a native of São Paulo state) from Campinas! No, Mr. Aranha, that was too much and deserved punishment. The audience started to boo immediately, in a tremendous noise that transformed the [Teatro Municipal] into hell.[61]

Despite the attempts of Aranha and other modernists to exclude Carlos Gomes from their archetype of a new and unified Brazilian culture, at the time of the week, the composer and his music had already become an emblem of Brazilianness. The way that happened over the years was a process not altogether clear for those intellectuals who were sure to find a signifier of Brazilian culture in the popular music of the streets, never in an elite music such as opera.

Gomes presumably died unaware of the power of his music as a tool for national symbolism. Whatever native elements scholars like to point out in his *Il Guarany*, they were undoubtedly the result of Gomes's attempts to impress Italian audiences rather than a preoccupation with characterizing Brazil musically. Having received financial support from Pedro II throughout his career, Gomes saw himself in great financial difficulty when the imperial patronage came to an end in 1889. Even so, he remained loyal to the imperial regime and refused the invitation to write the anthem for the new republic. Nevertheless, outside his control *Il Guarany* became an anthem anyway, a work that embodies Brazil's early attempts to define itself as a nation, exactly by aligning its culture with that of Europe.

Unlike Gomes, Villa-Lobos was aware of the political moment and the cultural transformations in Brazil during the first decades of the twentieth century and consciously built a work that reflected that moment. Nonetheless, he followed his own imagination rather than wholeheartedly embracing a specific model of Brazilianness. As Béhague eloquently notes, Villa-Lobos "created his own individual symbols of identity and made them acceptable to his country as uniquely national symbols."[62] Villa-Lobos was also conscious of the impact that the exotic material would have upon international audiences in the 1920s. He explored it fully in his compositions, but in the end he made Brazilian music competitive by joining the European musical milieu on an equal footing.[63] Inside Brazil, Villa-Lobos built a magnificent system of music education, teaching millions of children to sing folk songs and national hymns, thus making music an important tool to unify all Brazilians.

While few lines (or any) about Carlos Gomes can be found in international music sources, Villa-Lobos is included in major international music reference works, and his pieces are discussed in all major general histories of music. But his work is mostly praised for its "difference," for its characteristic nationalism, a stigma that candidly separates non-European music from the European canon. Gomes's work, on the other hand, plays a shadowy role in the general European canon: viewed solely from an international vantage point, he is no nationalist and no prominent "universalist."[64]

Within Brazil Gomes and Villa-Lobos are also perceived differently, mostly due to the different meanings ascribed to "nationalness" during their lifetimes. But the historical differences in their embodiment of nationalness are themselves telling of how one might have missed the whole picture of these composers' roles in the process of creating a symbol of national identity through music. While Gomes's international reputation popularized elite Italian opera and made it available to all social classes, thus making it a symbol of Brazilian national identity, Villa-Lobos internationalized and stylized Brazilian traditional and popular music, making it accessible to the elite in concert halls. Thus, to become symbols of Brazilianness, the music of these two Brazilian composers had to travel quite opposite routes.

NOTES

1. Previously called *A hora do Brasil* (The Brazil Hour), the radio program was established in 1934 and first aired in 1935. On January 3, 1938, the government started to transmit *A hora do Brasil* in a national broadcast. In 1962, the program was renamed *A voz do Brasil*, and the Congress passed a law (law no. 4.117 of August 27, 1962) that required an added thirty minutes for a daily report of the acts of the Senate and the House; see report from Radiobrás (Empresa Brasileira de Comunicação) of June 1, 1995. The law that established *A voz do Brasil* has been challenged by the Association of Radio and Television, which argues that the broadcast is undemocratic and against free speech; see www.ajufe.org.br/index.php?ID_MATERIA=624. For arguments to end the broadcast of *A voz do Brasil*, see "A Distante Realidade," *O Estado de São Paulo*, September 15, 2001. See also, Alessandra Dalevi, "The Only Voice," *Brazzil*, April 2001, www.brazzil.com/p07apr01.htm (accessed January 5, 2005); for São Paulo's Eudorado radio station arguments, www.radioeldoradoam.com.br/html/vozbrasil.asp (accessed January 5, 2005); and for an editorial in the *Jornal do Brasil*, see http://clipping.planejamento.gov.br/Noticias.asp?NOTCod=161789 (accessed September 19, 2005).

2. Given that *A voz do Brasil* has been under close scrutiny by the Brazilian population and the local press, the president of the Dainet Multimídia e da Associação de Mídia Interativa, Antonio Rosa Neto, has commented that Carlos Gomes is doomed because his *Il Guarany* is now "a prelude to a national rage"; see http://ultimosegundo.ig.com.br/useg/cidadebiz/artigo/0,,663089,00.html (accessed January 5, 2005).

3. The treatment of these composers as opposites became clear during the 1920s, when modernist Oswald de Andrade defined Gomes's music as "inexpressive, artificial, and disgraceful" while Ronald de Carvalho referred to Villa-Lobos's music as "the most perfect expression of our culture"; see José Miguel Wisnik, *O Coro dos Contrários: a música em torno da semana de 22*, 2nd ed. (São Paulo: Livraria Duas Cidades, 1983), 81–82.

4. Gerard Béhague notes that "Villa-Lobos was among the first twentieth-century composers to devise cluster aggregates as an integral part of his harmonic vocabulary"; see Béhague, *Heitor Villa-Lobos: The Search for Brazil's Musical Soul* (Austin: University of Texas at Austin, Institute of Latin American Studies, 1994), 63.

5. With Gomes's *Il Guarany*, says Vasco Mariz, "Brazil was born into the [international] musical world." Mariz, *História da música no Brazil*, 5th ed. (Rio de Janeiro: Nova Fronteira, 2000), 79.

6. For the analysis of Andrade's ideas in *Ensaio*, see Christopher Dunn, "The Relics of Brazil: Modernity and Nationality in the Tropicalia Movement" (PhD diss., Brown University, 1996), 56–58.

7. Mario de Andrade, *Ensaio sobre a música brasileira* (São Paulo: Libraria Martins Editora, 1962), 17–18. See also Dunn, "Relics of Brazil," 57.

8. Andrade dismisses the nineteenth-century Italian bel canto as being "exterior" and as a "gigantic banality"; see his *Pequena história da música*, 9th ed. (Belo Horizonte: Editora Itatiaia Limitada, 1987 [1942]), 134–35.

9. Andrade, *Pequena história da música*, 166.

10. Andrade, *Ensaio*, 19.

11. Suzel Ana Reily, "Macunaíma's Music: National Identity and Ethnomusicological Research in Brazil," in *Ethnicity, Identity, and Music: The Musical Construction of Place*, ed. Martin Strokes (Providence, R.I.: Berg, 1994), 81.

12. Reily, "Macunaíma's Music," 84.

13. For Mario de Andrade's view of Villa-Lobos's work, see Béhague's *Heitor Villa-Lobos*, 151–54.

14. The 1996 production of Gomes's *Il Guarany* in Washington, D.C., at the Kennedy Center, for example, was a gala night under the auspices of the Organization of the American States. The Brazilian musicologist Vasco Mariz makes a comparative analysis of Gomes and Villa-Lobos and notes that they are "Two geniuses . . . with distinct musical productions, but both endowed with that creative vitality that crosses [international] borders." See Mariz, *História da música no Brasil*, 75.

15. Mariz notes that Gomes "should serve as a model for all our [Brazilian] composers. . . . Certainly he deserves the title of the best Brazilian and American composers of the 19th century"; see Mariz, *História da música no Brasil*, 95.

16. A case in point is the Brazilian composer Gilberto Mendes's opinion of Villa-Lobos as a liberator, as a composer who used new techniques such as polytonal and polyrhythmic compositional procedures "before [he] came into contact with European music"; quoted in Béhague, *Heitor Villa-Lobos*, 152.

17. Mariz mentions a few publications and performances of Gomes's operas in commemoration of the one-hundred-year anniversary of the composer's death; see Mariz, *História da música no Brasil*, 95. The most important project aiming at the revival of Gomes's work is being undertaken by the São Paulo private company ImagemData. The company has produced three versions of *Il Guarany* in Italy, Manaus (Brazil), and Lisbon, along with videos and CDs for the Brazilian and the international markets. According to the company's website, "Brazil (and Brazilians) has now regained the possession of its own cultural patrimony, by stimulating the performance of a national talent of great historical relevance." See www2.uol.com.br/spimagem (accessed January 5, 2005). The efforts to bring back Gomes's *Il Guarany* as a historical monument also include a revised edition of the opera's score by the conductor Roberto Duarte to be published by FUNARTE. The same movement toward reviving Gomes's music can be observed in the acquisition of the manuscript of Gomes's early opera *A noite do castelo* (1861) by the FAPESP

(Fundação de Amparo a Pesquisa do Estado de São Paulo [Foundation for Research of São Paulo]), along with the music department of the Universidade de São Paulo (USP); see "O resgate de 'A noite do castelo'" in *Notícias FAPESP*, 42.

18. See the website of the Museu Villa-Lobos, in particular, the section "Informatização" that describes the project "A Identidade Nacional na Obra de Villa-Lobos." The project aims at the retrieval, study, and electronic publication of manuscripts, among other goals. See www.museuvillalobos.org.br/mvl5.htm (accessed January 5, 2005).

19. For the prevalence of operatic music in Rio de Janeiro's theater and concert programs, see Cristina Magaldi, "Concert Life in Rio de Janeiro, 1837–1900" (PhD diss., University of California, Los Angeles, 1994).

20. For a discussion of the use of local topics and the Portuguese language in nineteenth-century theatrical works, see Cristina Magaldi, "Alguns Dados sobre o Canto em Português no Século XIX," in annals of the 1995 annual meeting of the ANPPOM (Associação Nacional de Pesquisa e Pós-Graduação em Música; Universidade Federal de Minas Gerais).

21. Benjamin Orlove and Arnold Bauer, "Giving Importance to Imports," in *The Allure of the Foreign: Imported Goods in Postcolonial Latin America* (Ann Arbor: University of Michigan Press, 1997), 13.

22. Orlove and Bauer, "Giving Importance to Imports," 13.

23. For discussion and examples of these pieces see Magaldi, "Concert Life in Rio de Janeiro," 240–93.

24. Gomes's *A Cayumba* was for sale in Rio de Janeiro as early as 1856, according to an advertisement in the *Jornal do Comércio*, October 8, 1856.

25. According to Gomes's biographer Marcus Góes, the composer's choice for setting to music Alencar's *O Guarani* was made before Gomes left for Italy. Given the novel's popularity in Brazil, the vogue for nationalism through romantic Indianism, and Alencar's association with the Opera Lírica Nacional, that was hardly an unusual choice. When Gomes started to seriously work on the project while in Milan, he looked for an Italian translation of Alencar's novel *Guarani, storia dei selvaggi del brasile* and for an Italian librettist, even if he originally had in mind a Brazilian premiere. In 1869 the director of La Scala in Milan accepted the work to be presented there. See Góes, *Carlos Gomes, a força indômita* (Belém: SECULT, 1996), 91–92.

26. Góes, *Carlos Gomes*, 91.

27. George Grove, ed., *A Dictionary of Music and Musicians (A.D. 1450–1889)* (New York: Macmillan, 1879–1890).

28. See Góes, *Carlos Gomes*, 99. Gomes's Italian friend and librettist Ghislanzoni referred to Gomes as "a savage, walking along through cold Italian streets," in Gaspare Nello Vetro's "Correspondências Italianas recolhidas e comentadas," in *Antônio Carlos Gomes* (Rio de Janeiro: Instituto Nacional do Livro, 1982), 317. The Italian newspaper *Gazzeta Musicale* commented on Gomes's temperament, much evident during the *Il Guarany*'s rehearsals: "he puts his hands on his vast hair and starts to run in the stage as if he is possessed, and he screams like a savage very similar to the Guarany [Indians]"; quoted in Mariz, *História da música no Brasil*, 80–81. The parallel of Gomes's persona with his "savage" operatic character was

explored in the recent novel by Rubem Fonseca, *O selvagem da ópera* (São Paulo: Companhia das Letras, 1994).

29. Report by Luís de Guimarães Jr. in *Diário do Rio de Janeiro* (December 4, 1870), quoted in João Roberto Faria, *José de Alencar e o teatro* (São Paulo: Editora Perspectiva, 1987), 138.

30. A. de C., Theatrical Chronicle in *A Vida Fluminense*, December 17, 1870.

31. Quoted in Faria, *José de Alencar e o teatro*, 138.

32. *O Mosquito* (November 4, 1876) included in the section "Coisas que eu Gosto" (Things that I like) caricatures by Rafael Bordalo Pinheiro of several scenes from *Il Guarany*; see Herman Lima, *História da Caricatura no Brasil* (Rio de Janeiro: José Olympio, 1963), 2:564–66.

33. Plácido Domingo's role as Pery in the 1996 production of *Il Guarany* at the Kennedy Center evoked similar contempt from local press. Citing highlights of the performance, a *Washington Post* reviewer writes, "There may be sillier operas in the repertory, but I can't think of any.... Domingo in a bizarre, flame-colored, feathered headdress that makes him look like an acidhead's idea of an Indian-head penny from the front and a plastic sunflower from the back... I've never seen so many people in tuxedos giggling helplessly in the aisles." *Washington Post*, November 11, 1996, C4.

34. Gomes found an Italian translation of Alencar's novel while in Milan and started to work with an Italian librettist to set music to *Guarani, storia dei selvaggi del brasile*; see Góes, *Carlos Gomes*, 91–92.

35. More than sixty years after the Rio de Janeiro premiere, a Portuguese translation of *Il Guarany* by Carlos Marinho de Paula Barros (Rio de Janeiro: Imprensa Nacional, 1937) came out, much to the discontent of Gomes's daughter, who expected the opera to continue to be performed as her father conceived it. See Itala Gomes Vaz de Carvalho, *A vida de Carlos Gomes*, 3rd ed. (Rio de Janeiro: A Noite, 1946).

36. Góes, *Carlos Gomes*, 137.

37. Góes, *Carlos Gomes*, 136.

38. Emilia Viotti da Costa, *The Brazilian Empire: Myths and Histories* (Chicago: Chicago University Press, 1985), 154.

39. Magaldi, "Concert Life in Rio de Janeiro," 37.

40. Vicente Salles has outlined several influences of Gomes's music—in particular, that of *Il Guarany*—in the Brazilian folklore, in the repertory of bands in Brazil's rural areas, as well as in *marchas ranchos* during carnival; see Salles, "Carlos Gomes: passagem e influência em várias regiões brasileiras," in *Carlos Gomes: Uma obra em foco* (Rio de Janeiro: FUNARTE, 1987), 7–11. In 1934, the famous popular singer Lamartine Babo launched a carnival march titled "The History of Brazil" (Victor 33 740-b), in which the opera characters are mixed in topics familiar to the daily life of Cariocas. Another carnival march, "Defendendo a Raça," written by Manoel Dias e Floriano Correa and sung by Januário de Oliveira in the carnival of 1939, includes the introduction of *Il Guarany*'s Protofonia in its beginning. For a study of *Il Guarany*'s tunes in carnival marches, see Hélio Damante "O Guarani, o folclore e o carnaval," *Revista Brasileira de Folclore* 11 (May–August 1971): 171–78.

41. For the repertory of concerts in Rio de Janeiro during the last decades of the nineteenth century, see Magaldi, "Concert Music in Rio de Janeiro," 39–117. See also Magaldi, "Music for the Elite: Musical Societies in Imperial Rio de Janeiro," *Latin American Music Review* 16, no. 1 (Spring–Summer 1995): 1–41.

42. In 1916, Nepomuceno started a Portuguese translation of Heinrich Schenker's *Harmonielehre* (Leipzig, 1911), an influential publication that discusses tonality and analyzes the implications of moving beyond the established tonal system. Nepomuceno attempted to adopt Schenker's treatise at the Instituto Nacional de Música in Rio de Janeiro, but he encountered strong opposition by his peers. See Sérgio Nepomuceno Alvim Corrêa, *Alberto Nepomuceno: Catálogo geral* (Rio de Janeiro: Fundação Nacional de Arte, 1985), 11.

43. Magaldi, "Concert Music in Rio de Janeiro," 39–117.

44. Nepomucenos's program for the 1908 exposition is described and discussed in *Jornal do Comércio*, for the dates of August 14, 15, 16, 19, 21, 1908.

45. For a summary of Villa-Lobos's biography, see Béhague, *Heitor Villa-Lobos*, 1–42.

46. The programs for this and other Villa-Lobos concerts are housed at the Biblioteca Nacional in Rio de Janeiro and in the Museu Villa-Lobos.

47. Wisnik, *O Coro dos Contrários*, 67–71.

48. Wisnik, *O Coro dos Contrários*, 67.

49. Wisnik, *O Coro dos Contrários*, 71.

50. Wisnik, *O Coro dos Contrários*, 80.

51. Béhague, *Heitor Villa-Lobos*, 16.

52. Sérgio Milliet, "Cartas de Paris," *Ariel* 6 (March 1924), quoted in Wisnik, *O Coro dos Contrários*, 164.

53. In *Villa-Lobos: Sua obra*, 2nd ed. (Rio de Janeiro: Museu Villa-Lobos, 1972).

54. See Antônio Dimas, *Tempos eufóricos: análise da revista Kosmos, 1904–1909* (São Paulo: Editora Ática, 1983).

55. The most conspicuous example is in the second section, where Villa-Lobos uses specific syllables in insistent repetition to replicate the idea of a "language of the aborigines"; for a musical analysis of Choros no. 10, see José Maria Neves, *Villa-Lobos, o choro e os choros* (São Paulo: Ricordi, 1977), and Béhague, *Heitor Villa-Lobos*, 87–99.

56. Béhague, *Heitor Villa-Lobos*, 156.

57. Concert program retrieved from the music division of the Biblioteca Nacional, Rio de Janeiro.

58. The idea is articulated by Richard Taruskin while referring to Glinka's music in the broad context of Russian music and the international (Western European) musical scene; see Richard Taruskin, *Defining Russia Musically: Historical and Hermeneutical Essays* (Princeton, N.J.: Princeton University Press, 1997), 42–43.

59. Concert program retrieved from the Biblioteca Nacional, Rio de Janeiro.

60. Luiz Guimarães et al., *Villa-Lobos, visto da platéia e na intimidade (1912/1935)* (Rio de Janeiro: Gráfica Arte Moderna, 1972), 142; and Béhague, *Heitor Villa-Lobos*, 19–20.

61. Ernâni Braga, "O que foi a Semana de Arte Moderna em São Paulo," *Presença de Villa-Lobos*, 2:68–69; quoted in Wisnik, *O Coro dos Contrários*, 81–82.

62. Béhague, *Heitor Villa-Lobos*, 154.

63. As with Gomes in Milan, the Parisian press was quick to highlight Villa-Lobos's "experience with Amerindian life" where he supposedly could "observe extensively his music colleagues [Brazilian natives] with sacrificial clubs, and attend witchcraft festivities"; biography on the composer published in the *Revue Musicale*, no. 10 (1929); the full text is quoted in Béhague, *Heitor Villa-Lobos*, 6.

64. Another parallel taken from Taruskin's interpretation of Glinka's music in Russia; see Taruskin, *Defining Russia Musically*, 49. A reviewer of a 1994 production of Gomes's *Colombo* in Maryland refers to him as an "African Brazilian composer" (*Washington Post*, June 21, 1994); the highlight on his ethnicity (regardless of the accuracy) brings yet another angle from which the composer might be viewed from abroad.

Timeline of Brazilian History

COLONY, 1500–1822

1500	Pedro Alvares Cabral en route to India discovers and claims Brazil for Portugal
1500–1550s	Brazil wood trade
1532	First Portuguese colony established at Sao Vicente
1530s–1600s	Sugar production and trade
1538	First known importation of African slaves arrives to Brazil's northeast (three million to four million slaves were imported until 1850)
1549	São Salvador da Bahia established as colonial capital; Jesuits begin Christianization of the Indians
1565	Founding of Rio de Janeiro
1624–1654	Dutch occupation of northeastern Brazil
1695	Discovery of gold in Minas Gerais opens century-long mining era
1727	Coffee introduced
1756	Jesuits expelled
1763	Colonial capital moved from Bahia to Rio de Janeiro
1789	First attempt to establish a republic with Minas conspiracy led by Tiradentes
1808	Royal court of Portugal under João VI transferred from Lisbon to Rio de Janeiro in the face of Napoleon's invasion of Portugal; Rio de Janeiro becomes capital of the Portuguese empire; Brazil's ports opened to world trade; first printing press

EMPIRE, 1822–1889

1822   Following the return of João VI to Portugal the previous year, his son proclaims the independent empire of Brazil with himself as Emperor Pedro I

1831   Pedro I abdicates and returns to Portugal; a regency governs until his son reaches majority

1840   Pedro II assumes the throne; coffee frontier and economic centers shift from north to south

1850   Slave trade is made illegal

1888   The Golden Law, signed by princess regent Isabel I, abolishes slavery

FIRST REPUBLIC, 1889–1930

1889   Army coup dethrones the emperor and establishes a republic; the first two presidents are General Deodoro Fonseca and General Floriano Peixoto

1891   A new federal constitution is promulgated with separation of church and state

1894   Civilian leadership established with president Prudente de Morais

1896–1897   Rebellion at Canudos inspires Euclide Da Cunha's account *Os Sertões*

1897   Founding of the Brazilian Academy of Letters with Machado de Assis as the first president

1917   Brazil declares war on Germany and joins the Allied powers

1922   Centennial of Brazilian independence; Modern Art Week in São Paulo emphasizes national themes in literature, music, and the arts

SECOND REPUBLIC, 1930–1964

1930   Rebellion brings Getúlio Vargas to power; he serves as constitutional president and then dictator until 1945 and again as elected president from 1951 to 1954

1933   Gilberto Freyre publishes the *Masters and the Slaves,* a landmark of national interpretation

1937   Vargas closes Congress and declares Estado Novo

1942   Brazil declares war on the Axis powers

1944   Brazilian Expeditionary Force sent to Italy; first steel mill opens reflecting Brazil's push for industrialization

1945   The military deposes Vargas

1960   National capital is moved to Brasília, symbolic of the integration of national territory and thrust toward urbanization

MILITARY ERA, 1964–1985

1964   Military coup deposes president João Goulart and establishes a military dictatorship

1965   Second Institutional Act bans political parties

1979   Easing of dictatorial power, granting political amnesty

RESTORED DEMOCRACY, 1985–

1985   The military relinquishes political power to civilian politicians

1989   First direct presidential election since 1960

2000   Brazil celebrates five-hundredth anniversary of discovery of Cabral

Sources: E. Bradford Burns *A History of Brazil*, 3rd ed. (New York: Columbia University Press, 1993); Thomas E. Skidmore, *Brazil: Five Centuries of Change* (New York: Oxford University Press, 1999); Rex A. Hudson, ed., *Brazil: A County Study*, 5th ed. (Washington, D.C.: Library of Congress Federal Research Division, 1998); Rollie E. Poppino, *Brazil: The Land and People* (New York: Oxford University Press, 1968).

Index

About the Contributors

Cristina Antunes, chief librarian of José Mindlin Library in São Paulo, graduated in education at Pontifícia Universidade Católica at São Paulo and in paleography at the Instituto de Estudos Brasileiros da Universidade de São Paulo. She has published "Uma livraria do outro lado do Atlântico: Biblioteca José Mindlin," in *Revista do Livro* (1999) and the paleographic transcription and translation of *São Paulo de Edmond Pink* (2000) and *As Excelências do Governador: O panegírico fúnebre a D. Afonso Furtado, de Juan Lopes Sierra (Bahia, 1676)* (2002).

Dain Borges is associate professor of history at the University of Chicago. He has written *The Family in Bahia, Brazil, 1870–1945* (1992) and edited a new translation of Machado de Assis, *Esau and Jacob* (2000). He has published several articles on Brazilian social thinkers around the turn of the century, focusing on their use of racial sciences to understand political and religious change.

Valéria Costa e Silva (MA, Museu Nacional/Universidade Federal do Rio de Janeiro) is a Brazilian anthropologist who has been working on nationalism and national identity as a sociocultural process. Her master's thesis, defended in 1999, focuses on the Academia Brasileira de Letras as a privileged agent on this process. She is now a doctoral student in the Department of Spanish and Portuguese at University of California, Berkeley. Her studies and research are sponsored by CAPES Foundation, supported by the Brazilian Ministry of Education

James N. Green is associate professor of history at Brown University and director of the Center for Latin American Studies. He is past president of the Brazilian Studies Association (BRASA) and the chair of the Committee on the Future of Brazilian Studies in the United States. The chapter in this volume is part of an ongoing research project entitled "The Crossroads of Sin and the Collision of Cultures: Pleasure and Popular Entertainment in Rio de Janeiro, 1860–1920," which has received support for the National Endowment for the Humanities.

Efraín Kristal is professor of Spanish and comparative literature at the University of California, Los Angeles. He has published numerous articles and books on Latin American literature. He is currently finishing a book on Jorge Luis Borges.

Ludwig Lauerhass, Jr. has served on the history faculty and in the University Library at the University of California, Los Angeles, since 1968. He was assistant director and director of the UCLA Latin American Center (1975–1984) and the founding chair of the program on Brazil (1989–1993). His research on Brazilian and Latin American studies has been sponsored by the Ford, Mellon, and Bank of America foundations as well as by the Fulbright Program and the National Endowment for the Humanities. He has written extensively on Latin America, including the book *Getúlio Vargas: O Triunfo de Nacionalismo Brasileiro* (1986), among other works. He also served as director of the University of California Education Abroad Program in Brazil and most recently on the faculty of UCLA's Center for American Politics and Public Policy in Washington, D.C.

Cristina Magaldi is associate professor in the Musicology Department of Towson University. She holds degrees from the University of Brasilia, Brazil (BS), Reading University, England (MMus), and the University of California, Los Angeles (PhD). She is a fellow of the Guggenheim Foundation and the author of *Music in Imperial Rio de Janeiro: European Culture in a Tropical Milieu* (2004).

Elizabeth A. Marchant is associate professor of Spanish and Portuguese at the University of California, Los Angeles, where she teaches Latin American literature and cultural studies. She is the author of *Critical Acts: Latin American Women and Cultural Criticism* and is currently at work on a book about Brazil and the black Atlantic.

José Mindlin, industrialist, intellectual, patron of the arts, public figure, and bibliophile, was longtime president and chairman of the board of Metal Leve. He also served as minister of culture for the state of São Paulo and on boards ranging from the Escola da Administração de Impresas (Fundação Getúlio Vargas) to the National Library. Abroad, he is on the board of the John Carter Brown Library, as well as a member of the Grolier Club, the International Society of Bibliophiles, and honorary member of the International Council of Museum of Modern Art of New York. He is a graduate of the University of São Paulo School of Law and holds an honorary doctorate from Brown University and several Brazilian universities. His library of *Brasiliana* has long been recognized as the finest still in private hands. He has written widely on public and business affairs and on the cultural history of Brazil.

Carmen Nava (PhD, University of California, Los Angeles, 1995) is associate professor of history at California State University, San Marcos. Her research on Brazilian history explores how the state defined and redefined nationalism and national identity in the twentieth century. She was program coordinator of the UCLA Latin American Center's Program on Brazil (1990–1995). She has published in the *Luso-Brazilian Review* and is currently writing a book on women and gender in Latin America.

José Luiz Passos (PhD, University of California, Los Angeles, 1998) is associate professor of Luso-Brazilian literatures and cultures at the University of California, Berkeley. He is the author of *Ruínas de linhas puras: Quatro ensaios em torno a Macunma* (São Paulo: Annablume Editora, 1998), a study of Mario de Andrade's modernist novel *Macunama* (1928), and has recently completed a book on moral imagination and the novels of Machado de Assis. His contributions on modern Brazilian literature and social thought have appeared in *Estudos de Sociologia*, *Luso-Brazilian Review*, *Espelho: Revista Machadiana*, *Brasil/Brazil*, *Chasqui*, and *Revista de crítica literaria latinoamericana*.

Robert Stam is professor of cinema studies at New York University. He is the author of fifteen books on cinema and culture, including (with Randal Johnson) *Brazilian Cinema* (expanded edition, 1995) and *Tropical Multiculturalism: A Comparative History of Race in Brazilian Cinema and Culture* (1997). His *Unthinking Eurocentrism: Multiculturalism and the Media* won Best Film Book Award in 1994. Recently, he authored *Literature through Film: Realism, Magic and the Art of Adaptation* (2005) and *Francois Truffaut: Modernism, Sexuality and Adaptation* (2006). His work has been translated into Portuguese, Spanish, Italian, Farsi, Chinese, Korean, Arabic, and Japanese.

LATIN AMERICAN SILHOUETTES

Editors: William H. Beezley and Judith Ewell